Markets and Governments

Markets and Governments

edited by

Kaushik Basu
Pulin B. Nayak
Ranjan Ray

OXFORD
UNIVERSITY PRESS

OXFORD
UNIVERSITY PRESS

YMCA Library Building, Jai Singh Road, New Delhi 110001

Oxford University Press is a department of the University of Oxford. It furthers the University's objective of excellence in research, scholarship, and education by publishing worldwide in

Oxford   New York

Auckland   Bangkok   Buenos Aires   Cape Town   Chennai
Dar es Salaam   Delhi   Hong Kong   Istanbul   Karachi   Kolkata
Kuala Lumpur   Madrid   Melbourne   Mexico City   Mumbai   Nairobi
São Paulo   Shanghai Taipei   Tokyo   Toronto

Oxford is a registered trade mark of Oxford University Press
in the UK and in certain other countries

Published in India
By Oxford University Press, New Delhi

© Oxford University Press 2003

ISBN 019 5657888

Typeset in Times New Roman 10 on 12
By Innovative Processors, New Delhi 110 002
Printed at Rashtriya Printers, New Delhi 110 032
Published by Manzar Khan, Oxford University Press
YMCA Library Building, Jai Singh Road, New Delhi 110 001

Mrinal Datta-Chaudhuri
In appreciation

Mrinal Datta-Chaudhuri

Mrinal Datta-Chaudhuri

This is a volume in honour of Mrinal Datta-Chaudhuri. Most of the contributors have known him as a friend of long standing. Some have been his colleagues and some have also been his students.

Mrinal Datta-Chaudhuri was Professor of Economics at the Delhi School of Economics during 1968–99. The Delhi School was enriched by his charismatic and elegant presence during this period of more than three decades. Mrinal was an inspiring teacher, a wonderful colleague, an academic leader, and a person who encouraged ideas and generated debates. He shone brilliantly in seminars, posing questions, offering interpretations, and formulating solutions as will be readily acknowledged by many a seminar presentor, always enhancing the value of the presentation. He dominated discussions in small groups, presenting his point of view with a nat_____ ir a l a degree of cogency that always seemed compelling.

Mrinal was born on 4 Ja_ ary 1934 in a village called Srigauri in eastern India. Srigauri used t be in the district of Sylhet, now part of Bangladesh, but after Independence and partition in 1947 it became a part of Cachar district in Assam. Mrinal came from a land owning rural family. His grandfather Sanat Kumar Datta-Chaudhuri in the early years of the twentieth century burnt all his English clothes and went to jail. Thereafter he attained a measure of local fame as a vocal, albeit eccentric leader of the Independence movement. He was well read in contemporary social theories and was a great admirer of John Stuart Mill. Mill is also one of Mrinal's heroes, though, as he confesses, this must be a coincidence, for he cannot imagine how admiring John Stuart Mill could possibly be a genetic proclivity.

Mrinal started his education in Srigauri High School in his village. From there he moved to Shantiniketan, and then to Presidency College, Calcutta. He graduated in 1953 with an Honours in Statistics. While doing his Master's in Statistics, he dropped out of college and earned his living for a few years doing odd jobs in the formal as well as informal sectors. In 1959 he moved to New Delhi as a research assistant to Pitambar Pant who was an associate of P.C. Mahalanobis and a private secretary to Pandit Jawaharlal Nehru. He managed a research unit on economic planning as a collaborative effort between the Indian Statistical Institute and the Planning Commission. A large number of distinguished economists from all over the world used to visit the research unit to provide advice and assistance in Pant's efforts at formulating the Third Five year Plan. Mrinal's interest in economics grew out of his work in that unit. He went in 1962 to MIT to study economics and returned to India in 1966 with a Ph.D.

In the early 1960s the most exciting area of research at MIT was capital theory and optimal growth. Mrinal's early work was in this area. He also got interested in the area of resource allocation in geographical space under the influence of his teacher and friend Louis Lefeber. After joining the Delhi School, Mrinal's interests varied a great deal within the area of development economics, but he also pursued certain aspects of international trade and labour economics. However the principal focus of his inquiries throughout the period remained in the problems associated with the relative roles of the state and the market in a modern economy. His research in this field has been extremely influential and provides the common thread that binds this collection of papers edited and written by us.

KB, PN, and RR

Contents

Contributors

GEORGE A. AKERLOF University of California, Berkeley

PRANAB BARDHAN University of California, Berkeley

KAUSHIK BASU Cornell University

BHASKAR DUTTA University of Warwick and Centre for Development Economics, Delhi School of Economics

DAVID FAIRRIS University of California, Riverside

GARANCE GENICOT University of California at Irvine

RACHEL E. KRANTON University of Maryland, College Park

LUIS FELIPE LÓPEZ-CALVA Centro de Estudios Economicos, El Colegio de Mexico

DILIP MOOKHERJEE Boston University

PULIN B. NAYAK Delhi School of Economics

KIRIT S. PARIKH Indira Gandhi Institute of Development Research, Mumbai

PRASANTA K. PATTANAIK University of California, Riverside

RANJAN RAY University of Tasmania

AMARTYA SEN Trinity College, Cambridge

EYTAN SHESHINSKI Hebrew University of Jerusalem

JOSEPH E. STIGLITZ Columbia University

Tables

Figures

Markets and Governments

Introduction

Kaushik Basu • *Pulin Nayak* • *Ranjan Ray*

The early debate was nicely uncomplicated. Should we have big government or small? Should we have free markets with no government intervention or should the state run the economy? The battle-lines were clearly drawn and economists, policy-makers and social commentators took sides according to their beliefs, intellectual orientation and, hopefully not too often, convenience. But through a series of compelling papers, essays and books the debate got more nuanced and, some would say, muddled. We believe that, muddled or not, this is a fortunate trend since reality does not allow for the neat categorization that earlier writers had thought existed. Markets, left to themselves, can and often do fail. On the other hand, from the fact of market failure we cannot jump to hand over its functions to government, since governments also fail, as we were so eloquently reminded by Mrinal Datta-Chaudhuri in his well-known paper, 'Market Failure and Government Failure'.[1] We may have to reconcile to a second-best world, crafting a fine balance between markets and government. It is now clear that a modern market economy cannot run efficiently unless there is appropriate government regulation and a proper system of governance. But exactly what constitutes 'appropriate regulation' and what is 'good governance' are very hard questions to answer and will be the subject of research for some time to come.

The present collection of essays takes the above line of inquiry further, by, on the one hand, examining the role of the state and markets in terms of certain foundational questions concerning what constitutes individual freedom and what right government or any other agency has to place curbs on the economic activities of individual citizens, and, on

---

[1] (1990), *Journal of Economic Perspectives*, vol. 4, no. 3, pp. 25–39.

the other hand, by taking a look at specific sectors, such as labour, electricity, and education. The papers also investigate matters of institutional economies, concerning discrimination in markets and the scope for collective action.

This book is dedicated to Mrinal Datta-Chaudhuri, who not only contributed to this important debate but has been a major figure in modern economic research and education in India. We, the editors, have been his colleagues at the Delhi School of Economics, and some of us (Pulin Nayak and Ranjan Ray) were also his students. But apart from that, we have known him as an intellectual of amazing breadth and one always willing to engage in conversation and debate. We consider ourselves lucky for having had this long association with him and look forward to many more years of the same.

Once we break away from the simplistic debate of whether the economy should be left to the invisible hand of the free market or be put under the diktat of the state, we are able to address a host or real world questions concerning policy, the role of the market, and the nature and role of government. Consider, for instance, the question of labour market policy with which Mrinal Datta-Chaudhuri had been so concerned. It is not just naive but harmful to think of this as something that should be left completely to the vagaries of the free market. Equally erroneous and dangerous is the view that worker rights and well-being are entirely matters of government responsibility and the law. There is reason to believe that to legislate too many provisions of worker rights and welfare could run the risk of the workers not being employed at all by the potential employers and so be unable to enjoy those rights.

But unless one recognizes the folly of the two extremes, it is difficult to draft a policy that will be of advantage to not just the economy but the workers themselves. The important discipline of law and development economics is predicated on this understanding.

Another foundation matter on which much of our economic policy is ultimately based concerns human freedom. Government intervention is often viewed as an encroachment on human freedom. That is of course correct, but freedom is a complex notion. The enhancement of one person's freedom can mean the diminution of another's. Moreover, freedom can take many different forms and there may be tradeoffs between different kinds of freedom. In the opening chapter of this volume, Amartya Sen, who has written some seminal papers in economics and philosophy on the subject of rights and freedom, revisits the topic of individual freedom. He draws a distinction between freedom interpreted in terms of the opportunities that a person faces and freedom understood in terms of unfettered processes and procedures. With characteristic analytical lucidity, Sen observes that these two concepts do not describe two mutually exclusive domains. For one, it is wrong to always think of outcomes in terms of 'culmination' characteristics. We may in some circumstances rightly think of the process by which an outcome is reached as part of the description of the outcome. Nevertheless, one can draw a distinction between the 'process aspect' and the 'opportunity aspect' of freedom.

Having developed this distinction, Sen goes on to use it to evaluate market and command economies, arguing that, in evaluating the two systems, it may not be enough to compare outcomes alone, as economists tend to do. By extension, the goodness or badness of government intervention must not be judged solely on the basis of the outcome of the intervention, with no consideration of the procedure.

The remainder of this book is concerned with more applied questions, pertaining to government interventions and markets. George Akerlof and Rachel Kranton, for instance, study the phenomenon of discrimination that is so widespread in markets, be it against the Blacks in the United States or against the backward castes in India. Though they do not actually comment on policy, they make the case for policy intervention, by showing how, left to itself, a market can breed a sense of marginalization in non-dominant groups that then seek psychological fulfilment in counterculture. Their paper produces a new argument in support of affirmative action in favour of groups that have historically faced discrimination.

Affirmative action is also a part of the story told in the paper by Kaushik Basu, Garance Genicot and Joseph Stigltiz, though their analysis is founded on very different considerations. They show that if the choice between whether or not a particular person will seek employment is made by some sort of collective decision-making by the person's household, then an individual's labour supply may depend on macroeconomic characteristics of the labour market. If, for instance, there is a lot of unemployment in the economy, a household will worry that its main breadwinner may lose his job and thus be prompted to send other members out to seek employment, as a kind of insurance. In other words, a greater aggregate unemployment may result in higher labour supply, thereby further exacerbating the aggregate unemployment problem. This problem can be particularly serious in developing countries, such as India, where children and teenagers are often considered potential labourers, who are ready to step in whenever the adults find their wages or jobs threatened.

It is shown that this can lead to multiple equilibria in the labour market. The model is then used to explain why different ethnic or caste groups may have different levels of unemployment and to show how employment benefits may, in certain situations enhance the efficiency of labour markets, by discouraging precautionary over-supply of labour.

Pranab Bardhan's essay moves on to a larger topic—a comparison of India and China based on the differing political–economic structures of the two nations. This paper also moves away much more from the subject of markets to governance. Over the last two decades the Chinese economy has, by most measures, out-performed India. It is standard wisdom that China has shown a greater capacity for large-scale policy changes than India. Whether we talk of the Cultural Revolution, the massive de-collectivization of agriculture or, more recently, the opening up of the economy and the downsizing of firms, China shows a policy flexibility that is quite alien to India. Bardhan argues that this is caused by the Chinese government's greater ability to take hard collective actions, which has turned out to be infeasible for India with its conflict-ridden polity. And these differences are in turn traced to social and political causes that go back some distance into history.

If this is a kind of government failure, we may wish to investigate the microeconomics of government failures. The essay by Bhaskar Dutta moves on to precisely such an enquiry. Employing a political economy perspective, it shows how political factors may cause governments to choose inefficient policies. This is illustrated by using two simple models. In the first model, the rent seeking behaviour of single party and coalition models is contrasted and it is shown that the latter is more predatory. The second model compares the proportional and the first-past-the-post systems in terms of their impact on economic development. It is shown that the latter system would tend to lead to unbalanced development. This would come about because in this regime the incumbent would have an incentive to increase spending in a majority of regions by slashing expenditure in a minority of regions. This would have the effect of increasing the incumbent's probability of winning a majority in the legislature but at the cost of sharpening regional inequalities.

Once it is accepted that government failure is prone to occur in a variety of settings, one may wish to ask what exactly ought to be the role of the state in a market-based economy. This issue is investigated by David Fairris and Prasanta Pattanaik. The authors emphasize that in order to address this, one needs to have a clear understanding of the general principle of efficiency, and a special version of it that economists are most familiar with, viz., the notion of Pareto optimality. The latter seems unexceptionable once one accepts the specification of the options, the definition of feasible options, the specification criteria for assessing the options, and the orderings of the options in terms of these criteria. The authors make a case for widening the concept of social states which would allow for a consideration of institutional features such as rights, freedom of choice, and procedural fairness. Finally, the authors distinguish between two types of feasibility of a social state: feasibility (Type I) refers to purely the 'physical' aspect whereas feasibility (Type II) refers to the achievability of the physically feasible outcome through an institutional set up. It is argued that the latter approach offers richer rewards for it would lead us to delve into an analysis of the alternative institutions.

The essay by Dilip Mookherjee returns us to the central theme of the volume. Is the market versus state issue a sterile controversy? This issue has been addressed by virtually each major political economist from the earliest times. Mookherjee provides a succinct review of the recent literature on this subject, with the point of departure being the piece by Mrinal Datta-Chaudhuri (1990) that was referred to earlier. Starting with the traditional market failure paradigm, Mookherjee's paper goes on to consider the questions of technological externalities, economies of scale and asymmetric information that have been emphasized in the modern literature. The broad conclusion seems to be that only in a few areas can an overarching case for direct state intervention be made. There is however plenty of scope for governments to utilize the benefits of a private sector that is more cost conscious. The author seems to be arguing that the case for privatisation in several sectors is theoretically sound, and quotes some recent empirical surveys that seem to suggest that private enterprise is more effective than public enterprise across a wide swath of products. There is however a qualification, and it arises due to the need to ensure that extreme inequality be avoided, or else it would seriously hinder development. The market mechanism clearly cannot be expected to make the adequate corrections on this front.

Moving on now to some practical matters that are of substantial contemporary interest, Kirit Parikh raises the important question of how to reform the power sector. One cannot overemphasize the fact that this is the key infrastructure that is crucial for economic development. The investment required in this sector is huge and there are important questions pertaining to its pricing and distribution that need to be carefully worked out. All the State Electricity Boards (SEBs) in India that are in charge of generation, transmission, and distribution of electricity have been perennially financially sick, and therefore have had to be subsidized routinely. The author makes a case for opening up power distribution to a number of private bodies, with the proviso of having an effective regulatory commission that sets prices for consumers for a number of years.

Continuing further on a similar theme, the contribution by Eytan Sheshinski and Luis Felipe Lopez-Calva addresses the question of privatization and its benefits from the point of view of theory as well as evidence. The aim of such a programme is to achieve higher microeconomic efficiency and promote economic growth, as well as reduce public sector borrowing requirement through elimination of unnecessary subsidies. The authors show that the distributive effects of privatization are sensitive to the market structure. They argue that from the macroeconomic perspective no conclusive evidence can be drawn, but the trends are favourable in terms of public sector deficit, attraction of foreign direct investment and stock market capitalization. They also emphasize that for privatization to succeed one needs to streamline corporate governance issues as well as introduce legal changes for investor protection.

Moving on from this cluster of papers that assess the role of privatization, let us turn to Ranjan Ray's essay that examines the problem of child labour. This is one area where it is clear that the market, left to itself, is unlikely to arrive at an optimal solution that maximizes the child's welfare. There is need for careful government intervention. The paper analyses the child's participation in the labour market and in schooling paying special attention to the interaction between the two. The study then simultaneously estimates child labour hours and years of schooling recognizing their endogeneity, with data from Peru, Pakistan, Nepal and China. A number of policy conclusions are drawn. For example it is shown that compulsory schooling or free school meal programmes provide effective means of reducing child labour hours.

The last piece by Pulin Nayak returns once again to the principal theme of the volume by examining the notion of Schumpeter's 'tax state' which deals with, among other issues, the relative spheres of activity between the state and the market. Schumpeter feared that with the process of capitalist development the aspirations for ever larger public expenditure will continue to grow while there would be a limit to the amount that may be garnered by way of taxes and other imposts. This might well lead to a collapse of the capitalist system. Whether one is in agreement with Schumpeter or not on this, it is important, as emphasized by him, to examine the economic effects of the tax state.

1

Freedom: Procedures and Opportunities

Amartya Sen

INTRODUCTION

Mrinal Datta-Chaudhuri's deep interest in human freedom is not only clear from his academic work (including his investigation of the respective roles of the market and the state eg. Datta-Chaudhuri (1990)), it has also been a major influence on his life and priorities. His basic commitments were well exemplified in the active part Mrinal played in defending rights and freedoms in India in the so-called 'Emergency period' in the mid-1970s, when Indira Gandhi's government suspended various elementary liberties through the legal device of declaring an 'emergency'. Civil and political rights—vital for Indian democracy—came under severe threat in that trying and critically significant period, which ended only when the ruling government was soundly defeated in the general elections ostensibly called to sanctify the attempted restrictions.

For my contribution to the festschrift for Mrinal, I begin with the question: why is freedom important? Also, if it is important, how should we characterize freedom? These have been the subject matter of many inquiries and a great many debates in the past, and there is little hope of saying something on this general subject that would be uncontroversial. There are, however, connections and interlinkages between different— indeed contrasting—approaches to freedom that can be, I believe, usefully examined and scrutinized. In a small way, this is exactly what I shall try to do in this essay.

Drawing on the diverse literature on this subject, I start from the general recognition that freedom can be taken to be important in at least two distinct ways: (a) freedom can be seen in terms of the substantive *opportunities* that a person enjoys (taking everything into account); and (b) it can be understood in terms of unfettered and unregimented *processes and procedures* (to which we may also attach importance whether or not they extend the substantive opportunities to achieve what we value, or have reason to value).[1]

At the risk of some oversimplification, it can be said that the priorities of economists and those of political philosophers have often tended to diverge on the pre-eminent role that the two groups have tended to give, respectively, to substantive opportunities and to appropriate procedures. Economists have, by and large, been very involved in opportunities and results, but typically taken only instrumental interest in the processes involved, seeing freedom as part of 'ways and means' rather than as something that is intrinsically important. For example, Milton Friedman's championing of the importance of being 'free to choose' is almost entirely based on the presumed efficiency consequences of freedom of choice, rather than on its procedural correctness (I shall return to this issue later on in this essay). In contrast, many political theorists—libertarians, for example—have tended to take strongly 'procedural' views and have been particularly interested in the processes involved, rather than in the actual results that follow from these procedures.

This contrast is, of course, no more than a rough generalization, and one can easily find counter-examples to this categorization. For example, T.H. Green (1881), the political philosopher, strongly emphasized substantial opportunities rather than procedures only, whereas Friedrich Hayek (1960), who was primarily an economist, focused particularly on the importance of right procedures. The contrast between economists and political philosophers is really quite approximate, but there is an important attitudinal dichotomy between those—not necessarily economists—who focus on actual opportunities and those—not necessarily political philosophers—who tend to concentrate on procedures in interpreting and understanding freedom. That can be a big divide.

But how deep is the contrast between the two perspectives? I would argue that the two ways of seeing freedom, distinct as they are also firmly interlinked. In particular, we can see outcomes not merely in terms of their 'culmination' characteristics, but also more broadly, including the

---

[1] This distinction is not exactly the same as that between 'positive' and 'negative' freedoms, even though there are some overlaps. This perspective was more fully discussed in my 1991 Kenneth Arrow Lectures ('Social Choice and Freedom'), included in my forthcoming collection of papers, *Rationality and Freedom*, to be published by Harvard University Press. See also Sen (1985a, 1999), Foster (1993), Arrow (1995), and Suzumura (1999).

processes involved (for example, 'x was achieved through procedure y'). These may be called 'comprehensive outcomes'.[2] The outcomes defined in these broader terms—including the processes used—can be part of what we actually value (and have reason to value). The opportunity to achieve these inclusively defined outcomes can include process considerations, among others. To illustrate, if a person wants to achieve something (say x) *through* her own free choice (and not through x being delivered to her by someone else), or wishes to get to the culmination outcome through a fair process (for example, wanting to 'win an election fairly', rather than just achieving a 'win', no matter how), then having a free process or a fair procedure will 'count' as a part of substantive opportunities as well. In distinguishing between the 'process aspect' and the 'opportunity aspect' of freedom, there need be no presumption that they must always be disjoint concerns, with no interdependence.

The violation of freedom in the Emergency period in India involved infringement of both the process aspect and the opportunity aspect of freedom, and the two often went together. For example, the suspension of the right of free speech (or free assembly) was, it can be argued, both (i) an intolerable intrusion on its own (no matter what else resulted from these infringements), and (ii) also often led to imposed and dictated outcomes that went against what the respective persons wanted. Mrinal Datta-Chaudhuri was both insightful and courageous in resisting the political programme of undermining civil and political rights in the Emergency period. Indeed, the steadfast opposition of people with commitment to freedom greatly helped in ultimately ending the 'Emergency' by the electoral defeat of the aspiring authoritarians.[3]

In the next section, I consider a substantive example to illustrate how standard economic analysis have tended to miss something of importance by focusing too narrowly on culmination results and narrowly defined opportunities, without adequate note being taken of processes and procedures. The example to be discussed concerns the interpretation of competitive markets and freedom of choice. In the third section, I discuss why the assessment of opportunity must go well beyond identifying it with the 'best' culmination outcome, and how processes

---

[2] The idea and reach of 'comprehensive outcomes' are discussed in Sen (1997, 2000).

[3] Indira Gandhi, the deluded architect of the so-called Emergency, did in fact re-win her office as prime minister some years later, but by then she had abandoned the previous programme and had evidently learned something from the citizenry of India (that is to her credit, of course).

may enter into the evaluation of opportunities and consequences. The fourth section considers whether the neglect of the intrinsic importance of processes in much of economics can be remedied through the introduction of uncertainty to vindicate the importance of freedom in the form of 'flexibility' (as proposed by Koopmans (1964), Kreps (1979, 1988) and, Arrow (1995)). It is argued that something substantial is gained by taking note of uncertainty of preferences, but not nearly enough to meet the large neglect of process considerations. In particular, it is argued that autonomy has importance that cannot be subsumed by seeing it (as is sometime proposed) as a kind of uncertainty—real or imagined.

INADEQUACY OF INSTRUMENTAL VIEW OF MARKETS

The early part of the twentieth century witnessed a peculiar debate in which defenders of the market economy, led by Ludwig von Mises and others, argued that no centralized planning can be successful since no central authority can marshall as much information as would be needed for an efficient economic allocation. That work, it was argued, can be done only by the market economy through its peculiarly effective use of information whereby no individual agent need know more than what concerns him or her directly. While von Mises presented a general argument, his own work did not go much beyond being merely declaratory, rather than being conclusively reasoned. That task was pursued dialectically by a number of economists, in particular Oscar Lange (1936–7) and Abba Lerner (1944), who were socialists, on the one hand, and market enthusiasts, on the other. They envisaged a socialist market economy in which the job of resource allocation would be spread among different agents, coordinated by a central agency that would act much like an idealized market and follow simple rules (such as raising the proposed prices if demand exceeded supply, and so on). The resulting system would also avoid, it was argued, the inequalities associated with unequal ownership of external means of production, since non-human resources would be publicly owned. Walras's auctioneer was now back with an invisible hand, but with imperceptibly crimson fingers.

In terms of understanding the working of the market mechanism, the literature on market socialism was, in fact, crucially important. When the allocational structure of the competitive market economy was definitively resolved by Arrow (1951) and Debreu (1959), they were conceptualizing a private enterprise economy in a way that had much similarity with the working of market socialism as outlined by Lange

(1936–7) and Lerner (1944). The so-called 'fundamental theorem of welfare economics' established a remarkable two-way relationship between perfectly competitive equilibria and Pareto efficient culmination outcomes (given certain well specified assumptions, such as no externalities and no economies of large scale—the latter needed for one part of the two-way relationship). These results on the basic features of market allocation constituted a landmark in modern economic theory.

Three different types of limitations of this way of proceeding have become clear with decades of critical economic investigation. I do not intend to dwell on any of them in this essay, but briefly note them here as issues of general importance.[4] First, even though every Pareto efficient outcome with any particular distributional pattern can be 'realized' as a perfectly competitive equilibrium, provided the 'initial' distribution of resources is chosen in an 'appropriate' way, there is a big political problem involved in getting that initial distribution right. The needed initial redistribution may well be radical enough to require a major revolution. That may be just fine, but the practical correlates of the often-repeated claim that one can get any efficient outcome (no matter how egalitarian) *through* the competitive market mechanism have to be seen in political as well as economic light.

Second, the need to assume away significant increasing returns to scale make the modelling of the market economy both unrealistic and, oddly enough, far removed from the original defence of the competitive market system presented by Adam Smith (1776) who had built the case for markets precisely on the importance of economy of scale and the corresponding role of division of labour. It turns out, however, that this gap can be, to a great extent, met through a different approach to understanding how the markets can work effectively, despite increasing returns.[5]

A third line of critique is more subversive, and goes foundationally against the informational assumption underlying the original move of von Mises. Can the agents in fact know enough even about the small—indeed trivial sounding—things that they are meant to know for the markets to work well? Can the buyers know what the sellers do of a not altogether transparent commodity (such as a used car)? Do the sellers know what the buyers do in the market for insurance (such as particular health hazards that the buyers face)? The recognition of asymmetric information tends to undermine the presumption that one can know what

[4] I have tried to discuss these issues elsewhere, particularly in Sen (1987).
[5] See, for example, Krugman (1979) and Romer (1986).

is immediately relevant to one's decision—something that the original champions of market-based efficiency had taken to be obvious. To this problem of asymmetric information, we have to add other types of informational limitations, and the overall effects of imperfect information of diverse kinds make the efficiency promises of the market mechanism vastly more doubtful than had been thought earlier.[6]

These are all extraordinarily important concerns, but let me now move away from them. I want to concentrate on issues that remain even when none of these worries bite. Suppose there is no informational asymmetry and imperfection. Suppose also that the scale economy issue is fully resolved. Suppose further that the initial distribution of resources happens to be just right. Can we now say that the market based allocation is justified on the grounds that it achieves Pareto efficiency of culmination outcomes (with right distributional characteristics) and that this is all that is involved in being 'free to choose'? I would argue that this is still a very limited way of seeing what the market does, since the process of choice can be intrinsically important.

To understand the relevance of processes and freedoms, consider counterfactually that there is some way for the centralized state to know everything that needs to be known to identify the precise Pareto efficient outcome that would emerge through a perfectly competitive equilibrium. We assume, for the sake of this argument, that centralized information is not restricted in the way that Lange and Lerner presumed. The state can, then, proceed to order everyone what they must produce and what they will consume. Obeying these orders will yield a 'culmination outcome' that is exactly isomorphic to what would have emerged through the competitive process. The only difference is that in one case each person *decides* what he or she wants to do, and in the other case, each is *ordered* to do something and not anything else.[7] Is there not a difference here?

---

[6] The recent Nobel award to George Akerlof, Michael Spence, and Joseph Stiglitz was in recognition of their pioneering contribution in identifying and exploring the far reaching implications of informational limitations, in general, and asymmetry, in particular. See Akerlof (1970, 1986), Spence (1973), and Stiglitz (1973, 1985). Two of them (Akerlof and Stiglitz) were former class mates of Mrinal Datta-Chaudhuri at MIT (just as I had the same privilege earlier on at the Santiniketan school and at Presidency College, Calcutta).

[7] It is not suggested, of course, that such a well informed command economy is actually feasible. The exercise is quintessentially counterfactual: had such a well informed command economy been possible, would there be no case, then, for freedom of choice? The central issue here is valuational and normative, not one of empirical feasibility.

In terms of the explicit variables and characterizations in the Arrow–Debreu model, involving commodity transactions, production vectors, etc., the two culmination outcomes are exactly congruent. The Arrow–Debreu model—and indeed much of the standard literature on resource allocation—are concerned entirely with these 'culmination outcomes'. The freedom to choose is not taken to be important in itself: it does not figure even in the utility function of any one involved: for example, in the Arrow–Debreu formulation, the utilities depend only on consumption baskets (including leisure) and are quite independent of the way work and consumption are chosen. There is, thus, no discernible difference, in this perspective, between what happens in this command economy with dictated behaviour and what occurs in the decentralized economy with behavioural choice.

If, however, being ordered about is in itself a violation of one's liberty (and perhaps even of one's happiness), then the two are not exactly the same. In the space of 'culmination outcomes' they may be just the same (given the postulated utility functions defined over consumption vectors), but they are not, in general, the same in terms of 'comprehensive outcomes'. In one case, a person chooses—given her resources, preferences, and prices—what to do, and in the other case she has to follow what she is commanded to do. There are, thus, two neglects in the standard allocational model: (i) the fact that being ordered and compelled can affect one's utility (it does not depend only on the consumption vector), and (ii) whether or not they figure in the scale of utilities (and this may depend on how 'adaptable' the utility functions are), they can be important for the normative acceptability of social arrangements (because of the importance of the process of choice).

One would have thought that the need to recognize the importance of freedom of choice as a process would have figured in the pro-market literature that is so standard in modern economics. But there is not much evidence of that. In fact, the basic defence of freedom of choice, seen as a valued part of human life, has tended to come from philosophical investigations that have often been very critical of the practical correlates of the market economy. It is, oddly enough, to Karl Marx, rather than to the great defenders of the 'free market', to whom we have to turn to see powerful presentation of the importance of the process of free choice. Marx's (1845–6) celebration of the liberated future society asks powerfully for social arrangements such that they would:

make it possible for me to do one thing to-day and another tomorrow, to hunt in the morning, fish in the afternoon, rear cattle in the evening, *criticize* after dinner, just as I have in mind, without ever becoming hunter, fisherman, shepherd or critic. (p. 22)

The issue of importance here is not so much the realism of Marx's idealized vision of a good society (nor the incorrigible 'urbanism' that allowed Marx to think of 'rearing cattle in the evening' (he was clearly more at home with 'criticizing after dinner'), but what it reflects about the valuational importance that Marx attached to the process of free choice (being able to choose 'just as I have in mind').

The commitment to the intrinsic role of free choice is oddly missing in much of the pro-market literature in modern economics. For example, even though Friedman and Friedman (1980) call their book *Free to Choose*, no basic importance is attached at all in that analysis to the freedom of choice. The importance of being 'free to choose' is seen in entirely instrumental terms—only for the help it provides to get us to an efficient culmination outcome. Indeed, the justification of the market economy in standard neo-classical analysis proceeds almost entirely on the basis of its instrumental role, so that there would be no reason to prefer a free-choice arrangement to a command arrangement if the all-powerful commander knew it all and could command people accordingly. (What good luck, we might say, that the informational limitation of putative dictators prevents an inescapable coalition between authoritarianism, on the one hand, and standard textbook economics, on the other!) The neo-classical defence of being 'free to choose' seems oddly uninterested in the actual freedom to choose: the baby is chucked with the bath water.

BEST CHOICE, CULMINATION OUTCOMES, AND THE VALUE OF PROCESSES

Much of standard economics tends to judge the opportunities that a person has by the value of the best option that the person can choose. The overall opportunity represented by an available set S (such as the 'budget set') would be assessed exactly at the value of the *chosen*—presumed to be 'the best' (or 'a best')—element x of that set. Nothing would be lost in this line of assessment of opportunity if the menu S were to be reduced by eliminating other elements of that set so long as x, the 'best choice', remains available to be chosen. In fact, even if *all* other elements are made non-available, except x, there would still be no loss of valuable opportunity, in this approach, since the chosen x represents the most valued opportunity in S.

This 'best choice' view of opportunity, which greatly simplifies the assessment of opportunity, does indeed have considerable plausibility if: (i) the person has, with certainty, a given preference ordering; (ii) she has no basic interest in the process of choice; (iii) her utility function depends only on the chosen option, not on the options that existed but were not chosen; (iv) her preference ordering is complete; and (v) she attaches no significance to any other preference ordering she could have had. However, if any of these conditions are relaxed and the corresponding additional concerns are introduced, the simple 'best choice' view of opportunity would need substantial modification. I leave the issue of uncertainty regarding one's preference until the next section, but briefly discuss the other concerns right now.[8]

CHOICE ACTS AND THE RANGE OF OPTIONS

First, importance may well be attached to the choice process itself. Choosing as an activity can certainly be a valued part of human life and no theory of opportunity or of freedom can ignore this possibility *a priori*. The importance of the choice process may reflect at least two different concerns, which we may respectively call 'choice act valuation' and 'option appreciation'. The former relates to the value that may be attached to the *act* of choice itself, whereas the latter may reflect the importance of the *range* of significant options that one has in the choice set. The freedom to choose oneself can be a valued opportunity, and this has to be distinguished from the opportunity reflected by the presence of a variety of valuable options.

It must also be noted that the opportunity to choose is not always an unmitigated advantage. If, for example, two persons are both strongly influenced by the convention that one must not choose, say, the last of any fruit in a fruit basket, encouraging the other to choose first can be strategically very useful (on this and related issues, see Sen 1997). The opportunity of being the chooser can, in some circumstances, militate against the opportunity of being a successful achiever. And yet there are many cases in which the achievement one values includes choosing freely, or getting one's culmination achievement through one's own choice (cf. 'I know you can say better what I have in mind, but please let me have my say'). In such cases, the relevance of the act of choice is not merely instrumental, but also intrinsic.

---

[8] Each of these considerations are investigated in some detail in my book (2003), *Rationality and Freedom*, Oxford University Press, New Delhi.

Similarly, an enormous variety of options can, in some circumstances, have a somewhat befuddling effect on a chooser, so that a person may actually prefer to have a smaller range of minor options from which he is free to choose (indeed, from which he is *obliged* to choose).[9] These considerations do not suggest, as is sometimes presumed, that freedom of choice may be quite a bad thing, or that we do not in general have reason to want more choice, but rather that we have to decide carefully in what 'space' we seek choice (and what compulsions to avoid). Freedom comes in many different forms, and as Quine (1987) has noted, sometimes we seek 'a freedom of second order: freedom from decision' (p. 68). To recognize the presence of conflicting considerations is not, of course, an argument against freedom of choice in general, but it is reason enough to scrutinize in what way to seek more freedom, and in what area to want more choice. Freedom from the *compulsion* to take a whole lot of minor decisions can be an important freedom—a significant choice of space in which more choice is to be sought.

In fact, the device of thinking of options in 'comprehensive' terms (involving, for example, 'comprehensive outcomes' as opposed to only 'culmination outcomes') makes it possible, at least formally, to incorporate the relevant considerations within the description of the options themselves. We can even consider a 'comprehensive preference ordering' that is defined over all the comprehensive outcomes, incorporating such considerations as (i) the set from which the choice is made (for example, seeing an option not just as the chosen x, but as x chosen from the set S, denoted x/S), (ii) the various features of choice act incorporated in the description of the comprehensive options (for example, the actual process of choice as well as the range of options can be incorporated into the characteristics of x/S), and (iii) the other consequences that follow from the respective choices.

INCOMPLETE PREFERENCE RANKINGS

The process of choice assumes further relevance when the preference ranking of a person is incomplete. Given incomplete preference rankings, a best choice may not in fact exist, and this clearly would undermine the 'best choice' approach. Given this possibility, a person's choices cannot

---

[9] It is, of course, possible for a person's well-being in particular to be adversely affected by having more freedom, and there are various complex relations here that need to be separated out; on this, see Sen (1985a).

be interpreted as reflecting the 'best' for her, even if she sticks to maximizing behaviour, which would only require that the chosen alternative be 'maximal'—one that is not worse than any other option.[10] The *options foregone* cannot, then, be interpreted as being 'at *most* as good' as what is chosen.

There is no great merit in insisting that the ranking of opportunity must be complete in all cases. The importance of evaluating freedom or opportunity does not lie in any possible hope of being able to rank every option against every other, and still less in being able to compare every set of options against every other set. The value of the maximizing approach lies in the relevance and reach of the many comparisons that we can sensibly make. The recognition of the unfreedom of people in many situations (from Nazi concentration camps to the targeting of minority groups in adversarial politics) does not have to await the emergence of a complete ordering of freedom. Nor is there any need to postpone addressing the unfreedom induced by extreme poverty (or unrestrained vulnerability to epidemics) until a complete ordering of freedom or of opportunity emerges over all possible social states. The reach of articulation should not be made into an enemy of significant action.

MULTIPLE PREFERENCES AND METARANKINGS

Process considerations become even more relevant, and also much more complex, when we admit the possibility of multiple preferences. This may be particularly important to invoke in understanding the role of freedom since part of the freedom an individual enjoys can be the liberty to entertain different preference rankings. We have to take note of the foundational idea that 'the freedoms' that an individual has reason to value can go beyond the actual preferences used in her choice acts into the possibility of considering the preferences she could have chosen to have.

I have tried to explore elsewhere (Sen 1977) the idea of 'metaranking' (preferences over preference rankings), which can be invoked to discuss the role of critical scrutiny in choice theory. This can be particularly relevant in the analysis of social interaction and of individual rationality in a social context. That scrutiny is also important for the assessment of opportunity, since the person can recognize the relevance of assessing opportunities not merely in terms of her actual preference, but also through taking note of other preferences that she is free to have.

---

[10] The analytical demands of maximization and their interrelation with the very different concept of optimization are extensively scrutinized in Sen (1997).

There are different possibilities of multiple preferences to consider, each of which has a bearing—often, quite a distinct bearing—on the assessment of opportunity. At one extreme, a person may be herself uncertain about her preferences, particularly related to a future date. She may value having different options because of this uncertainty (more on this in the next section). Another possibility is that a person may have a distinct preference and fully know that fact, and yet would have preferred to have had a different preference ranking (cf. 'I wish I did not prefer to have red meat', or 'I wish I disliked smoking'). The metaranking may point in a different direction, and a person may entertain the hope of changing her preferences, and may particularly resent its being assumed (by some 'opportunity accounting officer') that she is 'stuck' with that preference. Having preferences over preferences can be the reflective basis of the self-exercise of preference reform.

There can also be some incompleteness in the metaranking, so that there may be no 'most preferred' preference ranking. If a person, then, has to make choices over alternative actions on the basis of one of the preference rankings that are no worse than others (even though not shown to be at least as reliable as all other preferences), then the need to consider other preference rankings in assessing a person's opportunity can be particularly strong.

EVALUATION OF OPPORTUNITY AND AUTONOMY

In fact, plurality of possible preferences can relate closely to the autonomy of a person. Autonomy can have various implications in forcing greater attention and respect to the possibility of alternative preference rankings that a person may consider having. Indeed, a person's autonomy may be relevant to the evaluation of opportunity in several distinct ways. First, it can be argued that a person must have a voice on the *status* of her own preferences (for example, to decide whether, as in the case of many addicted smokers, these are 'regrettable' preferences in need of reform). It is for her to decide what importance to attach to the preference that she happens to have, rather than some other preference which she might have preferred to have. The fact that a person has a particular preference ordering does not indicate that she has no further voice in deciding on the importance to attach to that preference, rather than to another. Second, the person must also retain the freedom to revise her preferences as and when she likes (and as and when she is able to achieve this). Like choices between actions, there is the possibility of choosing and revising the preferences she has. Third, whether or not a person is actually able to revise her preferences, she may have reason enough to resent if *others* take her preferences as 'given'—as a full reflection of her subjective attitudes on what she should 'choose to have'. Ultimately, autonomy is concerned not only with what a person can do, but also with what others must not take for granted. A person is more than her preference ordering.

In this context, it is relevant also to take note of the role of preference revision and reform as a part of the strategy—and freedom—of living. The relevance and reach of this consideration for the study of consumer satisfaction have been powerfully discussed by Scitovsky (1976). He distinguishes between a person's actual desires and what would be her 'scrutinized' desires. The volitional possibility of changing one's preference gives Scitovsky's concerns a particularly practical relevance in the analysis of cultural freedom and the role of cultivation in being able to enjoy music and the fine arts. This is a subject that was addressed also by John Stuart Mill in his championing of 'higher' over 'lower' pleasures.[11] The scrutiny and cultivation of preferences, and the freedom to be able to do that (whether or not one actually does it), can be quite relevant to the assessment of a person's overall opportunities.

UNCERTAINTY CONTRASTED WITH AUTONOMY

I turn now to the issue of uncertainty regarding one's own preferences (particularly in the future). The presence of uncertainty calls for the recognition of the importance of 'flexibility'. Koopmans (1964) and Kreps (1979, 1988) have definitively explored this concern, while sticking, in general, to the 'best choice' approach to the assessment of opportunity. Foster (1993) and Arrow (1995) have further explored this line of investigation, and Arrow in particular has also linked the importance of autonomy to some kind of uncertainty about one's preference.

In the solution developed by Koopmans and Kreps, if a person's future preferences are unknown to her now, she tries to select 'opportunity sets' for the future in a way that maximizes her expected utility from the respective maximal elements under different utility functions, weighted

---

[11] On the reach of Mill's ideas on this and related subjects, see McPherson (1982). The analytical implications of these considerations severely compromise the classic approach of 'revealed preference' in economic theory, on which see Basu (1980) and Ben-Ner and Putterman (1998).

by their respective probabilities. This adaptation of the 'best choice' view of opportunity is important in itself, and may well be adequate as a broadening of the 'best choice' approach if no complication other than uncertainty regarding future tastes compromises its applicability.

It does not, however, subsume or displace the other concerns discussed in the last section, such as the importance of the choice act, the range of options, incompleteness of preference rankings, and multiplicity of preference orderings. But what about autonomy? Can we approach the idea of autonomy through the route of uncertainty regarding one's own preferences? That suggestion has been powerfully made by Arrow (1995). I believe that claim is hard to sustain.

There is indeed some similarity between the relevance of multiple preferences related to a person's autonomy and the preference for flexibility with uncertainty of future tastes. Both involve the absence of a canonical complete ordering of preference in terms of which opportunity sets can be valued. However, in the case of choice under uncertainty, *which* alternative will ultimately materialize will depend not on volition or choice of the person, but on an event that is outside the chooser's control (that is precisely why it is taken to be a case of uncertainty). This is the model that Kreps (1979, 1988) pursues, and that approach is entirely cogent for solving the problem that Kreps definitively does solve (to wit, taking note of genuine uncertainty about what one may actually end up preferring in the future). A person, in this model, tries to maximize utility over time and faces the fact that she does not know for sure what her preference orderings and utility functions will be in the future. In this utility maximization exercise, it makes sense to adapt the standard expected-utility formulation of rational choice under uncertainty (assuming that one is persuaded, otherwise, by the case for that expected-utility framework).[12] While this would seem to be the right way of solving the problem that Kreps considers, his problem is not that of measuring opportunity-freedom where the multiple preferences relate ultimately to the person's own choice.

Autonomy is a very different problem from uncertainty, since it concerns the role of the person herself in deciding on the issue at hand (in this case, the set of preferences to be considered and also choosing a member of that set), whereas uncertainty is something that is beyond the control of the person (in this case, the set of preferences that the person

---

[12] Kreps, in fact, derives that formulation on the basis of more primitive, but quite standard, conditions of rational choice.

might conceivably end up having and also the eventuality of one of them turning out to be the correct one). Uncertainty minimizes the role of the person herself, whereas autonomy celebrates it.

CONCLUDING REMARKS

In this essay, I have tried to examine the interconnections between the opportunity aspect and the process aspect of freedom. While they are certainly separate concerns, they are not independent of each other. By using a broader notion of 'outcomes' as 'comprehensive outcomes' that take note, *inter alia*, of the processes involved in what happens, it is possible to broaden the notion of opportunity to include the weight we may have reason to attach to the use or non-use of particular processes and procedures. This does not make the distinction between the process aspect and the opportunity aspect of freedom disappear, but it does make it necessary to consider each with adequate note being taken of the other.

Process considerations include the importance we may attach to the choice act as well as the relevance of the range of options from which choice is made. The influence of process considerations in the assessment of opportunity, broadly defined, has to take note also of the possibility of (i) incomplete preferences, (ii) uncertainty regarding one's own future preference, and (iii) plurality of preferences, which may or may not be themselves completely ranked (or metaranked). These are complex issues, but by no means intractable, and they are critically important for an adequate understanding of the reach and relevance of freedom.

The direct—as opposed to instrumental—importance of process considerations as a part of the assessment of opportunity has been strangely neglected in the championing of 'freedom to choose' in the standard economic literature, and it is perhaps remarkable that we get more recognition of the significance of freedom of choice in the writings of Karl Marx than in those of Milton Friedman. But economics would have been a less exciting subject had it been free of conundrums. This particular conundrum offers important insights into the discipline of assessing the requirements of a good society in which we can be proud to live.

REFERENCES

Akerlof, George A. (1970), 'The Market for "Lemons": Quality Uncertainty and the Market Mechanism', *Quarterly Journal of Economics*, vol. 84, no. 3, pp. 488–500.

Akerlof, George A. (1984), *An Economic Theorist's Book of Tales* (Cambridge: Cambridge University Press).

Arrow, Kenneth J. (1951), 'An Extension of the Basic Theorems of Classical Welfare Economics', in J. Neyman, ed., *Proceedings of the Second Berkeley Symposium of Mathematical Statistics* (Berkeley: University of California Press).

_____ (1995), 'A Note on Freedom and Flexibility', in K. Basu, P.K. Pattanaik and K.P. Suzumura, eds, *Choice, Welfare and Development: A Festschrift in Honour of Amartya K. Sen* (Oxford and New York: Oxford University Press, Clarendon Press).

Basu, Kaushik (1980), *Revealed Preference of Government* (Cambridge: Cambridge University Press).

Ben-Ner, Avner, and Louis Putterman, eds (1998), *Economics, Values and Organization* (Cambridge: Cambridge University Press).

Datta-Choudhari, M. (1990), 'Market Failure and Government Failure', (in Symposia: The State and Economic Development), *The Journal of Economic Perspectives*, vol. 4, no. 3, pp. 25–39.

Debreu, Gerard (1959), *Theory of Value* (New York: Wiley).

Foster, James (1993), 'Notes on Effective Freedom', mimeographed, Vanderbilt University, Nashville, Tennessee.

Friedman, Milton, and Rose Friedman (1980), *Free to Choose: A Personal Statement* (London: Secker & Warburg).

Green, T.H. (1881), *Liberal Legislation and Freedom of Contract* (Oxford: Slatter & Rose, London).

Hayek, Friedrich A. von (1960), *The Constitution of Liberty* (Chicago: University of Chicago Press).

Koopmans, Tjalling C. (1964), 'On Flexibility of Future Preference', in M.W. Shelley (ed.), *Human Judgments and Optimality* (New York: Wiley).

Kreps, David M. (1979), 'A Representation Theorem for "Preference for Flexibility"', *Econometrica*, vol. 47, no. 3, pp. 565–78.

_____ (1988), *Notes on the Theory of Choice* (Boulder, Col: Westview Press).

Krugman, Paul (1980), 'Scale Economies, Product Differentiation and the Pattern of Trade', *American Economic Review*, vol. 70, no. 5, pp. 950–59.

Lange, Oscar (1936–7), 'On the Economic Theory of Socialism', *Review of Economic Studies*, vol. 4, no. 1, pp. 53–71 and vol. 4, no. 2, pp. 123–42; reprinted in O. Lange and F.M. Taylor (1952), *On the Economic Theory of Socialism* (Minneapolis: University of Minnesota Press).

Lerner, Abba (1944), *The Economics of Control* (London: Macmillan).

Marx, Karl (with F. Engels) (1845–6), *The German Ideology*; English translation (New York: International Publishers, 1947).

McPherson, Michael S. (1982), 'Mill's Moral Theory and the Problem of Preference Change', *Ethics*, vol. 92, no. 2, pp. 252–73.

Quine, W.V.O. (1987), *Quiddities* (Cambridge, Mass.: Harvard University Press).

Romer, Paul M. (1986), 'Increasing Returns and Long-run Growth', *Journal of Political Economy*, vol. 94, no. 5, pp. 1002–37.

Scitovsky, Tibor (1976), *The Joyless Economy* (Oxford: Oxford University Press).

Sen, Amartya (1977), 'Rational Fools: A Critique of Behavioral Foundations of Economic Theory', *Philosophy and Public Affairs*, vol. 6, no. 4, pp. 317–44.

———— (1985a), 'Well-being, Agency and Freedom: The Dewey Lectures 1984', *Journal of Philosophy*, vol. 82, no. 4, pp. 169–221.

———— (1985b), *Commodities and Capabilities* (Amsterdam: North-Holland; republished, and New Delhi: Oxford University Press, 1999).

———— (1987), *On Ethics and Economics* (Oxford: Blackwell).

———— (1997), 'Maximization and the Act of Choice', *Econometrica*, vol. 65, no. 4, pp. 745–80.

———— (1999), *Development as Freedom* (New York: Knopf, and Oxford and Delhi: Oxford University Press).

Sen, Amartya (2000), 'Consequential Evaluation and Practical Reason', *Journal of Philosophy*, vol. 97, no. 9, pp. 477–502.

Smith, Adam (1776), *An Inquiry into the Nature and Causes of Wealth of Nations* (London: printed for W. Strahan and T. Cadell; republished Oxford: Clarendon Press, 1976).

Spence, Michael (1973), 'Job Market Signalling', *Quarterly Journal of Economics*, vol. 87, no. 3, pp. 355–74.

Stiglitz, Joseph E. (1973), 'Approaches to the Economics of Discrimination', *American Economic Review*, vol. 63, no. 2, pp. 287–95.

———— (1985), 'Information and Economic Analysis: A Perspective', *Economic Journal*, vol. 95, Supplement: Conference papers, pp. 21–41.

Suzumura, Kotaro (1999), 'Consequences, Opportunities and Procedures', *Social Choice and Welfare*, vol. 16, no. 1, pp. 17–40.

2

A Model of Poverty and Oppositional Culture

George A. Akerlof and Rachel E. Kranton

The problem that we shall discuss in this paper concerns the relation between White and Black in the United States. The relation between Black and White in the US continues to be the American dilemma. A country founded with the highest ideals allowed 13 per cent of its population to be enslaved until almost the beginning of the last third of the nineteenth century.[1] The legal rights given to the former slaves after their emancipation were quickly and arbitrarily rescinded in the Jim Crow legislation in the Southern United States.[2] *De facto* segregation in the North was better, but not by all that much. The rights that were taken away were not restored until very recently, in the 1960s. That restoration of legal rights has led to the growth of a burgeoning Black middle class, but at the same time many African-Americans remain in poverty and misery (see Jencks, 1992). As two symptoms of that poverty, in the

It is wonderful to have an opportunity to participate in this *Festschrift* celebration of Mrinal Datta-Chaudhuri. He has been one of the most important influences on George Akerlof, who spent a year in India under his judicious tutelage in 1967–68. Rachel Kranton spent two years in Egypt some twenty years later, after having studied Middle Eastern Studies at the University of Pennsylvania. This paper results from the confluence of the broader understanding of economics that each of us has garnered from our respective sojourns in the Third World, and for the first author especially from the unique perspective of Mrinal Datta-Chaudhuri. We are very grateful not only for his intellectual guidance and wisdom for so many years, but also for his longstanding friendship.

[1]   According to the 1860 Census, 12.7 per cent of the US population was 'slave' and 1.5 per cent was 'free coloured'. Calculated from data on website: United States Historical Census Data Browser: *http://geography.about.com/gi/dynamic/offsite.htm?site=http%3A%2F%2Ficg.fas.harvard.edu%2F%7Ecensus%2F*

[2]   An account is given in Lewis (1993).

early 1990s imprisonment rates were so high that one out of every three Black males would spend a part of his life in prison.[3] And two-thirds of Black children are born out of wedlock.[4]

We shall present and analyse an economic model that adapts the standard sociological analysis of the modern Black–White disparity.[5] This is a model of alienation and rejection, in which the White society rejects the Black culture. The Whites consider the Blacks to be different—as apparent *ipso facto* in discussion and statistical classification of such differences, of which this paper itself is one example. In reaction to this exclusion, the Blacks adopt a culture that is symbolically in opposition to the White culture. The adoption of this oppositional culture removes them psychologically from a society that conceives a large gap between Black and White. But since the Whites dominate the management of capital in the United States, this symbolic rejection is achieved only at great economic cost.

We shall construct a model of this phenomenon and analyse its different equilibrium regimes. The model follows our earlier paper, Akerlof and Kranton (2000); here, we shall spell out in more detail the nature of that model and its solution. We shall describe some of the important externalities involved in psychologically affirming an alternate culture. We motivate the model, as we have said, on the basis of Black and White in the United States, but the same type of modelling can be applied to many oppositional cultures, be they across or within national or institutional borders. Examples range from the serious to the mundane—from military–civilian and ethnic divisions to the play of boys and girls on the playground. In deference to Mrinal Datta-Chaudhuri, some of the serious questions of division in India for which he has shown the most concern should come under the analytic purview of such models.

THE MODEL

We present here a very simple abstract model that captures the idea central to ethnic studies in the United States that those who are rejected for

[3] Authors' calculations from rates of first imprisonment by age.

[4] The out-of-wedlock birth rate in 1999 for Black children was 68.9 per cent. Source: *Births Final Data for 1999*, National Vital Statistics Report, volume 49, no. 1, 17 April 2001, Table 19.

[5] See, for example, Anderson (1990), Baldwin (1962), Clark (1965), Du Bois (1965), Frazier (1957), Hannerz (1969), Rainwater (1970), Wilson (1987, 1996).

their ethnicity by the dominant White middle class culture of the United States have an alternative: they may choose a different culture which is symbolically very different. The model proceeds as follows.

There are two activities, One and Two. Activity One can be thought of as 'working' and Activity Two as 'not working'. There is a large disadvantaged community, normalized to size one, of individuals. The economic return to Activity One for individual i is v_i, which we assume is uniformly distributed between zero and one, to reflect the heterogeneity in the population and to yield the possibility of interior solutions. The economic return to Activity Two is normalized to zero.

Individuals also have identity utility. They gain or lose such utility depending upon their choice of social category, their choice of activity, and also the nature of their associates. There are two social categories, Green and Red. A Green accepts the dominant culture; a Red rejects it. A Green suffers a loss in identity r, representing the extent to which someone from this community is not accepted by the dominant group in society. The most important parameter of the model is r: it represents the extent to which the dominant culture fails to let members of the minority pass, and thus denies selfhood to those who aspire to belong. Those with the less adaptive Red identity have rejected the dominant culture and thus they do not suffer this loss. Behavioural prescriptions state that the Greens should engage in Activity One, and that the Reds should engage in Activity Two, which is symbolically in opposition to the prescription of Greens for Activity One. Thus, a Green loses identity from Activity Two in the amount I_s^G, and a Red symmetrically loses activity from Activity One in the amount I_s^R. Because the Reds reject the dominant Green culture, they are also likely to have lower economic returns to Activity One than the Greens. A Red individual i will only earn $v_i - a$ from Activity One, as well as suffer the loss I_s^R. The loss in productivity a occurs because there are economic advantages to adopting the style of those in the dominant culture. The dominant culture underlies the style and language of most commercial transactions. In the model, each member of the population meets another random member in each period. When Reds and Greens meet there are identity externalities. The Greens distress the Reds, as the Reds also distress the Greens. For example, Green parents are distressed by Red children, just as Red children have difficulty interacting with Green parents. Thus, a Green suffers a loss I_o^G from meeting a Red, and a Red symmetrically suffers a loss I_o^R from meeting a Green. In addition, Reds who have chosen Activity Two randomly meet and then impose a pecuniary externality, k, on those who have chosen Activity One.

Each person i chooses an identity and an activity, given the choices of everyone else in the community. We assume that people cannot modify their identity or activity for each individual encounter. Rather, individuals choose an identity and activity to maximize expected payoffs, given the probabilities of encounters with those Greens who choose Activity One, Greens who choose Activity Two, Reds who choose Activity One, and Reds who choose Activity Two.

SOLUTION TO THE MODEL

The solution to the model involves specifying the proportions of the population who are Green/One, Green/Two, Red/One, and Red/Two. Let γ denote the proportion of the population who are Green and p denote the fraction of Reds who choose Activity One. We shall assume parameter values so that none of the Greens choose Activity Two (Greens always work).

The solution to the model can be derived from the expected payoffs for the four types of people—Green/One, Green/Two, Red/One, and Red/Two. These expected payoffs are presented in Table 2.1. In the analysis, we assume that all parameter values are non-negative.

Table 2.1: Expected Payoffs to Different Identity/Activity Choices in Opposition Culture Model

Identity/Activity	Expected payoffs
Green/One	$v_i - r - (1-\gamma)(I_o^G + (1-p)k)$
Green/Two	$-I_s^G - r - (1-\gamma)I_o^G$
Red/One	$v_i - I_s^R - a - (1-\gamma)(1-p)k - \gamma I_o^R$
Red/Two	$-\gamma I_o^R$

We assume that $I_s^G \geq k$ so that anyone who chooses a Green identity also chooses Activity One. There are never any Green/Twos in equilibrium. With this assumption, Table 2.2 presents all the possible combinations of γ and p that can arise in an equilibrium.

Table 2.2: Types of Equilibria

Value of γ	p	Interpretation
$\gamma = 1$	na	Everyone is Green/One
$0 < \gamma < 1$	$p = 1$	Mixed Green/One and Red/One
$0 < \gamma < 1$	$0 < p < 1$	Mixed Green/One, Red/One, Red/Two
$0 < \gamma < 1$	$p = 0$	Mixed Green/One and Red/Two
$\gamma = 0$	$p = 1$	Everyone is Red/One
$\gamma = 0$	$0 < p < 1$	Everyone is Red/One or Red/Two
$\gamma = 0$	$p = 0$	Everyone is Red/Two

We examine the conditions for each of the seven types of equilibrium in turn.

EVERYONE IS A GREEN/ONE: $\gamma = 1$

In this happy integrationist equilibrium, everyone chooses to be Green and, as a result there are no negative externalities because Greens meet either a Red/One or a Red/Two. The absence of externalities makes this an equilibrium if barriers to passing, r, are sufficiently small. The marginal worker considers the gain and the loss from being a Red/Two rather than a Green/One. As a Red/Two with productivity zero, he gains r because he can maintain his sense of self without having to pass according to the prescriptions of the dominant culture. But he loses I_o^R in this activity since he will meet a Green/One with probability one. As a result if $r < I_o^R$, the marginal worker will reject being a Red/Two and this will be an equilibrium.

We should emphasize that with these same parameter values there may also be other equilibria with positive values of Reds, in which the externalities from Reds including Red/Two's have tipped the marginal worker into being a Red rather than a Green.

Formally, for $\gamma = 1$ to be an equilibrium, no individual can have an incentive to deviate and choose Red/One or Red/Two, given that everyone else is Green/One. Substituting $\gamma = 1$ into the payoffs for Green/One $\geq$ Red/One, we have:

$$r \leq I_s^R + a + I_o^R \tag{2.1}$$

Consider next Green/One > Red/Two. For $\gamma = 1$, this condition is $v_i - r > -I_o^R$ for all v_i. Since the lowest possible value of v_i is zero, we need

$r \leq I_o^R$. If this inequality is satisfied, (equation 2.1) is also satisfied. Hence, a necessary and sufficient condition for $\gamma = 1$ equilibrium is $r \leq I_o^R$.

THERE ARE SOME GREENS AND SOME REDS; ALL REDS ARE IN ACTIVITY ONE: $0 < \gamma < 1; p = 1$

This equilibrium hardly ever occurs. The lower bound of the marginal product of Red/Ones is $-a$. In addition the marginal worker with such an output will lose identity utility of I_s^R since Reds think they should be doing Activity Two rather than Activity One. A Red/Two has zero productivity. Thus, this equilibrium with no Red/Two's can only occur if both a and I_s^R are zero.

Formally, for this equilibrium we need to find γ such that (the payoff to) Green/One = (the payoff to) Red/One and find the conditions under which Red/One $\geq$ Red/Two for all i. Setting Green/One = Red/One and solving for γ yields:

$$\gamma^* = \frac{r + I_o^G - I_s^R - a}{I_o^G + I_o^R}. \tag{2.2}$$

Note that this value is independent of p. For $0 < \gamma^* < 1$, we need:

$$I_s^R + a - I_o^G < r < I_s^R + a + I_o^R. \tag{2.3}$$

Now we check the conditions under which the payoffs from Red/One dominate those from Red/Two. Setting $p = 1$ and simplifying we have $v_i - I_s^R - a \geq 0$ for all i. Since the lowest value of v_i is zero, and also I_s^R and a are both greater than zero, we must have $I_s^R + a = 0$. Combining this condition with (equation 2.3), we see that the necessary and sufficient condition for this equilibrium is $I_s^R + a = 0$ and $r < I_o^R$. In equilibrium $\gamma^* = (r + I_o^G)/(I_o^R + I_o^G)$. This equilibrium does not exist if either I_s^R or a is strictly positive.

THERE ARE SOME GREENS AND SOME REDS; THE REDS ARE DIVIDED BETWEEN ACTIVITY ONE AND ACTIVITY TWO: $0 < \gamma < 1; 0 < p < 1$

This is an unstable knife-edge equilibrium. In this equilibrium, the returns to being a Red/One are just the same as the returns to being a Green/One. Otherwise there would be only Green/Ones or only Red/Ones. The equalization occurs because the negative externalities from being a Green One in terms of losses from meeting Red/Ones and Red/

Twos, which are I_o^R and k, just balance the positive gains in terms of greater economic reward, a and greater identity returns, I_s^R, net of the costs of passing, r. If there were any more Greens, a Red/One would have greater externalities from meeting Greens and it would pay all of the Red/Ones to switch to become Greens. Similarly, if there were any more Red/Ones, it would pay all the Greens to become Red Ones. Thus, this is only a knife-edge unstable equilibrium.

Note that such a mixed equilibrium would not necessarily be a knife-edge if there were a distribution of the *passing* parameter, r. In that case a few more Greens would only result in the switching of Red/Ones whose passing parameter placed them just at the margin between their choice of Green and Red.

Formally, for this equilibrium, we need Green/One = Red/One, as in the previous equilibrium. Then we solve for the p such that individuals are indifferent between Red/One and Red/Two. We noted above that the condition for Green/One = Red/One is independent of p. We then have here, as above:

$$\gamma^* = \frac{r + I_o^G - I_s^R - a}{I_o^G + I_o^R}, \tag{2.4}$$

and for $0 < \gamma^* < 1$, we need:

$$I_s^R + a - I_o^G < r < I_s^R + a + I_o^R. \tag{2.5}$$

Now we solve for the p such that the payoffs from Red/One equal the payoffs from Red/Two. Solving for the critical value of v_i, we have:

$$v^{\text{crit}} = (1 - \gamma)(1 - p)k + I_s^R + a \tag{2.6}$$

Note here that for $v^{\text{crit}} < 1$, we must have $(I_s^R + a) < 1$. Setting $v^{\text{crit}} = (1 - p)$, solving for p^* yields:

$$p^* = 1 - \frac{I_s^R + a}{1 - k + \gamma^* k}. \tag{2.7}$$

Substituting for γ^* yields p^*:

$$p^* = 1 - \frac{(I_s^R + a)(I_o^G + I_o^R)}{(1 - k) I_o^R + I_o^G - k I_s^R - ka + kr}. \tag{2.8}$$

For $p^* < 1$, both the bracketed terms in the numerator of the second term must be strictly positive.

For $p^* > 0$, the second term should be strictly less than one. This latter condition is:

$$r > I_o^R + I_s^R + a - \frac{(I_o^R + I_o^G)(1 - I_s^R - a)}{k} \tag{2.9}$$

Comparing this condition (2.5), we determine which lower bound on r is binding. For $(I_s^R + a + k) > 1$ (equation 2.9) gives the lower bound on r.

THERE ARE SOME GREENS AND SOME REDS; ALL REDS ARE DOING ACTIVITY TWO: $0 < \gamma < 1; p^* = 0$

This is not a knife-edge equilibrium. Workers who are more productive than a given critical level choose to be Green. Those who are less productive choose to be Red/Twos. The comparative statics of this case is what might be expected. If it is harder to pass, if r is greater, the proportion of Red/Twos will rise. If the externality of Twos against Ones should rise, the fraction of Twos will rise. If the externality to a Green of meeting a Red should rise, again the number of Red/Twos will rise. And if the externality to a Red of meeting a Green should rise, the fraction of Greens will rise. This shows the importance of the externalities in determining the equilibrium level of poverty. The most impoverished people in our model are, of course, the Red/Twos.

Formally, for this equilibrium we need to find the value of γ such that Green/One = Red/Two, then find the conditions under which the payoffs from Green/One dominate Red/One. Assuming $p = 0$, we have $v_i - r - (1 - \gamma)(I_o^G + k) > -\gamma I_o^R$. This gives us:

$$v^{crit} = r + (1 - \gamma)(I_o^G + k) - \gamma I_o^R. \tag{2.10}$$

Setting $(1 - \gamma) = v^{crit}$ and solving for the equilibrium number of Greens, γ^*, we have:

$$\gamma^* = \frac{1 - I_o^G - k - r}{1 - I_o^G - k - I_o^R}. \tag{2.11}$$

Notice that a necessary condition for $\gamma^* < 1$ is $r > I_o^R$.

We now check the condition under which Green/One dominates Red/One. We have:

$$r + (1 - \gamma^*) I_o^G < I_s^R + a + \gamma^* I_o^R. \tag{2.12}$$

Substituting γ^* into (eqn 2.12) gives us the condition:

$$r < (I_s^R + a) \left(\frac{1 - k - I_o^G - I_o^R}{1 - k} \right) + I_o^R \qquad (2.13)$$

The right-hand side of (equation 2.13) is less than $(I_s^R + a) + I_o^R$. Assuming $k + I_o^R + I_o^R < 1$, the right-hand side is no smaller than I_o^R. Putting the condition $r > I_o^R$ together with (equation 2.13), we then have the following necessary and sufficient condition for this equilibrium:

$$I_o^R < r < (I_s^R + a) \left(\frac{1 - k - I_o^G - I_o^R}{1 - k} \right) + I_o^R \qquad (2.14)$$

THERE ARE ONLY RED/ONES: $\gamma = 0$; $p = 1$

This equilibrium may occur if the negative externalities from being a Green and the losses from failure to pass are so great that they dominate the costs of being a Red. Those costs come from the loss in identity, the externalities from interactions with Greens, and also the reduced economic output. At the same time the returns to working may be sufficiently great that it pays Reds to do Activity One rather than Activity Two. The conditions to hold for this equilibrium in this model, however, are quite stringent, since the output of the marginal worker in the model is zero. If either I_s^R or a is greater than zero, that marginal worker would rather be a Red/Two than a Red/One.

Formally, for this equilibrium, we need Red/One to dominate both Green/One and Red/Two. Let us first look at the condition under which Red/One dominates Red/Two. Substituting $\gamma = 0$ and $p = 1$ into the payoffs for these types, we have: $v_i - I_s^R - a > 0$ for all i. This requires that $I_s^R + a = 0$. For strictly positive I_s^R or a (given neither are negative), therefore, this is never an equilibrium.

THERE ARE NO GREENS; REDS ARE DIVIDED BETWEEN
ACTIVITY ONE AND ACTIVITY TWO: $\gamma = 0$; $0 < p < 1$

In this equilibrium the externalities and also the difficulty of passing cause everyone to be a Red. Reds then divide themselves according to ability between Red/Ones and Red/Twos. Higher values of k and I_o^G and lower values of I_o^R increase the range of values of r that permit this equilibrium. Increase in the values of a, k, and I_s^R in this equilibrium will increase the number of Twos.

Formally, for this equilibrium, we find the value of p such that Red/One = Red/Two. We then find the condition under which no one would wish to deviate to Green/One.

Setting Red/One = Red/Two and setting $\gamma = 0$, we have the critical value of v_i such that all those with higher values choose Red/One and all those with lower values choose Red/Two:

$$v^{\text{crit}} = I_s^R + a + (1 - p)k. \tag{2.15}$$

Setting $v^{\text{crit}} = (1 - p)$, we solve for the equilibrium number of Red/Ones, p^*:

$$p^* = 1 - \left[\frac{I_s^R + a}{1 - k} \right]. \tag{2.16}$$

For $0 < p^* < 1$, we need $(I_s^R + a) > 0$ and $(I_s^R + a + k) < 1$.

Now we find the conditions under which no-one wants to be a Green. We compare Red/One to Green/One given $\gamma = 0$. Simplifying, we have: $r > I_s^R + a - I_o^G$.

In summary, if and only if $r > I_s^R + a - I_o^G$, $(I_s^R + a) > 0$, and $(R_s^R + a + k) < 1$ is $\gamma = 0$, $0 < p^* < 1$ an equilibrium outcome.

EVERYONE IS A RED/TWO: $\gamma = 0$; $p = 0$

There may be equilibria in which it is so difficult to pass (i.e. r is so high) and also the externalities are so very great, that no worker will choose to be a Green. Furthermore, if the returns to working as a One are very low, because either I_s^R or a or k are so high then everyone may choose to be a Red/Two.

Formally, in this equilibrium, the payoffs from Red/Two dominate the payoffs from Red/One and Green/One. For $\gamma = 0$, the payoffs to Red/Two are simply zero. For $\gamma = 0$, $p = 0$, the condition that Red/One ≤ Red/Two is $v_i - I_s^R - a - k \leq 0$ for all i. This implies a necessary condition for this equilibrium of $(I_s^R + a + k) \geq 1$. For $\gamma = 0$, $p = 0$, the condition that Green/One < Red/Two is $v_i - r - I_o^G - k \leq 0$ for all i. This implies a necessary condition for this equilibrium of $(r + I_o^G + k) \geq 1$. With the two conditions together, we have the necessary and sufficient conditions for this equilibrium: $(r + I_o^G + k) \geq 1$ and $(I_s^R + a + k) \geq 1$.

Table 2.3 summarizes the necessary and sufficient conditions for each equilibrium as well as the equilibrium values of γ and p:

Table 2.3: Necessary and Sufficient Conditions for Equilibria of Different Types

γ	p	Necessary and Sufficient Conditions	Equilibrium Values of γ and p
$\gamma = 1$	na	$r \leq I_o^R$	$\gamma^* = 1$
$0 < \gamma < 1$	$p = 1$	$I_s^R + a = 0$ and $r < I_o^R$	$\gamma^* = (r + I_o^G)/(I_o^R + I_o^G)$ $p^* = 1$
$0 < \gamma < 1$	$0 < p < 1$	For $(I_s^R + a + k) < 1$, the condition is: $I_s^R + a - I_o^G < r < I_s^R + a + I_o^R$ For $(I_s^R + a + k) > 1$ we have a different lower bound on r	$\gamma^* = (r + I_o^G - I_s^R - a)/$ $(I_o^R + I_o^G).$ $p^* = 1 - [(I_s^R + a)/(1 - k + \gamma^* k)]$
$0 < \gamma < 1$	$p = 0$	$k + I_o^R + I_o^G < 1$, and $I_o^R < r < [(I_s^R + a)(1 - k - I_o^R - I_o^G)/(1 - k)] + I_o^R$	$\gamma^* = (1 - k - I_o^G - r)/$ $(1 - k - I_o^G - I_o^R)$ $p^* = 0$
$\gamma = 0$	$p = 1$	$I_s^R + a = 0$ (necessary condition only)	$\gamma^* = 0, p^* = 1$
$\gamma = 0$	$0 < p < 1$	$(I_s^R + a) > 0$, $(I_s^R + a + k) < 1$ and $r > I_s^R + a - I_o^G$	$\gamma^* = 0$ $p^* = 1 - [(I_s^R + a)/1 - k]$
$\gamma = 0$	$p = 0$	$(I_s^R + a + k) \geq 1$ and $(r + I_o^G + k) \geq 1$	$\gamma^* = 0$ $p^* = 0$

COMMENTS ON THE MODEL AND ITS SOLUTION

The model and its solution show that considerations of identity can potentially have a major effect on poverty. The extent to which non-dominant groups in a society feel *marginalized* and therefore seek psychological fulfilment in opposition to the dominant culture can affect the level of poverty. The parameter r can have a very large effect. Within each of the non-knife-edge equilibria, an increase in r will increase the number of those who are in the counter-culture. A multiplier effect occurs from increases in r, because there will also be increases in the negative externalities from being Green, as they are more likely to associate with Reds.

But the models tell us something more shocking. A high historic value of r may, even after its disappearance, leave a bad residue. The presence of a high value of r is likely to lead the economy into a lower level equilibrium. And this equilibrium is likely to be a trap, even after the reasons for a high value or r have disappeared. The equilibrium becomes a trap because of the negative externalities when Greens meet Reds, and Ones meet Twos. Indeed this is the problem with the logic of the Thernstroms (1997), who have claimed that there is no need for affirmative action. They cite a battery of statistics which show a low level of r: the Whites in the United States believe at least in equal treatment of the Blacks. The model suggests that whether or not this claim is true, it still does not have the negative implications for affirmative action asserted by the Thernstroms. As we have seen, in the model the reduction in r is not the sole issue. The historical question also concerns the extent to which a past high value of r has resulted in a lower level equilibrium trap that is maintained by continuing negative externalities. In such a continuing trap, affirmative action is still needed to offset those externalities and lead to a better equilibrium.

The behaviour of those considered to be in the 'underclass' suggests the existence of such externalities in everyday life in the United States. The underclass relative to our model would be considered Red/Twos. In addition, there are also Red/Ones who pursue Activity One; they 'work', but they also practise separation. The lives of both the Red/Ones and Red/Twos could be much more effective if instead they were fully integrated. Our model suggests that affirmative action is needed not just passively to reduce the value of r; affirmative action is also needed actively to reduce the negative interactions between Green and Red; it is also needed to reduce the externalities between Red/Ones and Red/Twos. We need positive policy to move out of a lower level equilibrium trap.

REFERENCES

Akerlof, George A. and Rachel E. Kranton (2000), 'Economics and Identity', *Quarterly Journal of Economics*, 115: 3, August, pp. 715–53.

Anderson, Elijah (1990), *StreetWise: Race, Class, and Change in an Urban Community* (Chicago: University of Chicago Press).

Baldwin, James (1962), *The Fire Next Time* (New York: The Dial Press).

Clark, Kenneth (1965), *Dark Ghetto* (New York: Harper & Row).

Du Bois, William E.B. (1965), *The Souls of Black Folk* (Greenwich, Conn.: Fawcett Publications).

Frazier, Franklin (1957), *The Black Bourgeoisie: The Rise of the New Middle Class in the United States* (New York: The Free Press).

Hannerz, Ulf (1969), *Soulside: Inquiries into Ghetto Culture and Community* (New York: Columbia University Press).

Jencks, Christopher (1992), *Rethinking Social Policy: Race, Poverty, and the Underclass* (Cambridge, Mass. Harvard University Press).

Lewis, David L. (1993), *W.E.B. Du Bois: Biography of a Race, 1868–1919* (New York: Henry Holt).

Rainwater, Lee (1970), *Behind Ghetto Walls: Black Families in a Federal Slum* (Chicago: Aldine).

Thernstrom, Stephan and Abigail Thernstrom (1997), *America in Black and White: One Nation Indivisible* (New York: Simon and Schuster).

Wilson, William J. (1987), *The Truly Disadvantaged* (Chicago: University of Chicago Press).

_____ (1996), *When Work Disappears: The World of the New Urban Poor* (New York: Knopf).

3

Minimum Wage Laws and Unemployment Benefits, when Labour Supply is a Household Decision

Kaushik Basu, Garance Genicot, and Joseph E. Stiglitz

INTRODUCTION

In economics textbooks one learns to derive supply curves and demand curves in separate chapters. Such compartmentalization, however, renders the textbook model of markets unusable in many domains of real life in which demand and supply turn out to be interdependent. As early as 1950, Harvey Leibenstein, motivated by Thorstein Veblen's classic *The Theory of the Leisure Class*, had noted that, for many goods, a fall in supply may boost demand because there is 'snob value' in being able to have what others cannot.

Nowhere is this interdependence more important than in the labour markets. This happens because in the labour markets each household takes decisions for several individuals, and within each household there occurs a certain amount of cooperation and consumption sharing. Suppose aggregate demand for labour falls, it is then quite natural to expect that a household which had thus far kept its women and children out of the labour force may now send them out in search of work to provide 'insurance' against the risk of the adult male members becoming unemployed. On the other hand, a lower likelihood of finding a job may

The authors are grateful to Pranab Bardhan, Gary Becker, Francois Bourguignon, David Easley, Aaron Edlin, James Foster, Gus Ranis, Arijit Sen, Kunal Sengupta, E. Somanathan, and T.N. Srinivasan for their comments. The paper has also benefited from seminar presentations at Yale University, the Indian Statistical Institute, the University of California-Berkeley, Johns Hopkins University, and the University of Southern California.

discourage some potential workers from searching for work. The aim of this paper is to demonstrate how, in the presence of these effects, standard labour market policies may give rise to paradoxical market response.

It is easy for labour market policy debates to get polarized between those who argue for leaving it all to the market and those who see little role for the market. In the spirit of Mrinal Datta-Chaudhuri's important paper (1990), we show how market incentives need to be blended with government action and put forward the unusual argument that it is possible to justify unemployment benefits purely on grounds of efficiency, that is, even without having to go into issues of equity.

The fact that an increase in unemployment can cause an increase in labour supply, thereby exacerbating the unemployment problem, has long been known: it is called the 'added worker effect'. From the 1940s till recent times, numerous empirical studies have investigated the effect of unemployment on labour supply. However, the theoretical foundations of these works have not been spelled out adequately. As a consequence some very natural implications of the added worker effect seem to have gone unnoticed in the literature. Assume, as seems natural, that a greater likelihood of unemployment (for instance, among adult males) prompts women and children to join the labour force. Now start from a full-employment situation, with wage at some level, say w. It is shown in the paper that, if a legal minimum wage is announced at some wage rate w, which is below w, then market wage can fall from w to w and this can give rise to unemployment. Conversely, the abolition of a legal minimum wage can cause the market wage to rise. Moreover, a rise in the legal minimum wage can actually lead to a fall in unemployment despite the model being that of competition.

At first sight such results may seem academic, for we may wonder why governments would ever impose a legal minimum wage below the prevailing market wage. In reality labour markets are often segmented, with different wages prevailing in different markets—for instance, agricultural wages may be lower than the wages that prevail in the manufacturing sector. Suppose that in some fringe sector the wage happens to be low. Now, minimum wage laws are typically used to boost wages in such 'depressed' sectors. Hence, a legal minimum wage below the wage that prevails in the main labour market but above the wage in the fringe market is not at all uncommon. This is obviously true for countries, such as the United States, where there is a unique minimum wage that applies to all sectors. But even when that is not the case and the minimum wage is made sector or region specific it is arguable that there is so much variation in any real economy that even within a single sector or region there will be sub-segments of the labour market where the free market wage exceeds the legal minimum wage, as is in fact the case in India. In addition, our analysis also applies to models where the wage rigidity comes from an endogenous efficiency wage argument, instead of a legal minimum wage. For this reason, we believe that the effect we are writing about is likely to be important in reality.

The plan of the paper is as follows. The second section recapitulates some of the related literature and empirical findings. The third section presents the model and establishes the paradoxical result concerning the effects of minimum wage legislation. In the fourth section, we investigate other extensions and policy implications of our main result, such as how giving unemployment benefits can increase *efficiency*.

THE BACKGROUND

The effect of one person's employment status on the decision of other members of the household to look or not look for employment was recognized and attempted to be measured by Woytinsky (1940a, see also 1940b). In the words of Humphrey (1940, p. 412), what Woytinsky was getting at was 'the familiar story of the head of the family losing his job whereupon his wife and children also start looking for work so that two or more persons appear to be unemployed and are reported to be unemployed by most censuses'.

Starting with this exchange in the 1940s, this topic became a subject of considerable empirical investigation and debate (see, for instance, Mincer 1966a, b; Belton and Rhodes 1976; Ashenfelter 1980; Layard, Barton and Zabalza 1980; Bardhan 1984; Lundberg 1985; Maloney 1987, 1991; and Tano 1993). This effect, of one person's (the 'primary' worker's) unemployment, or potential unemployment, prompting other family members (the 'secondary' workers) to seek work, came to be known as the 'added worker effect'. Economists subsequently went on to argue about an opposing force, which has come to be called the 'discouragement effect'. This is the response of potential workers losing hope and ceasing to search for jobs, when they see a lot of unemployment around them. The strength of these two effects is a matter of debate.

The empirical results are mixed. There seems to be some consensus, or at least a majority opinion among those involved in empirical research in this area, that the discouragement effect is very strong and frequently offsets entirely the added worker effect. Tano (1993) for instance finds that both effects are significant and coexist (see also Humphrey 1940; Layard et al. 1980; and Maloney 1991). However, there is reason to believe that the empirical literature has tended to underestimate the added worker effect. Cullen and Gruber (2000) point out that the previous studies have ignored the potentially important role of the unemployment insurance programmes. Looking explicitly at this issue, they find that unemployment insurance significantly reduces the labour supply of family members during the unemployment spell. Moreover, most studies investigate the effect of actual unemployment of husbands on the actual employment of women. First, it is important to realize that a more meaningful approach is to investigate the *desired* hours of work of the wife, since the wife's actual employment may also be affected by the increase in unemployment (that is, she may not be able to actually find work). Once this is done, the results can already look different. Maloney (1987), for instance, using reported data on underemployment, finds a significant added worker effect. Second, the added worker effect does not arise solely because of *actual* unemployment of the primary worker, but might be a response to the worsening job *prospects* of the primary worker. It is on the former that most empirical studies have been in effect focusing. A major conceptual difference between our model and the standard literature is that we emphasize the households' and their secondary workers' response to the worsening job *prospects* of the primary worker.[1]

One way to empirically differentiate between the two would be to take two points of time where macro unemployment rates are significantly different. Then by focusing on households for which the primary worker's status is unchanged between these two time periods, we can check if there is a systematic change in the labour supply of the secondary workers of these households. Note that it is in this spirit that Lundberg (1985) studies the effect of employment uncertainty and credit constraint in creating short-run participation and employment patterns. The

[1] In addition, an added worker effect would also arise if household members are substitutes in home production. An increase in the primary worker's non-market time would reduce the relative value of the secondary workers' non-market time, thereby inducing them to join the labour force. Note that this effect would be a response to the *actual* loss of employment of the primary worker. However, we will abstract from this matter here.

estimates are based on employment transition probabilities rather than static measures of labour supply and the results show a small but significant added worker effect.

Finally, we shall show below that once a theoretical model of household supply response is constructed, we could add plausible features to it which can explain why the added worker effect can create an empirical illusion of there being a discouragement effect. In reality we would expect both effects (added worker and discouragement) to be present, but our analysis explains why the discouragement effect may appear larger than it actually is.

Surprisingly little has been written on this specific topic theoretically. An early attempt is Ashenfelter (1980) that analysed the comparative static effect of one person's labour supply being constrained on another household member's supply. This paper fits into the growing literature emphasizing the interdependence of decisions within households. For instance, in Basu and Van (1998) and Basu (1999), the effect of adult labour market conditions on the incidence of child labour is analysed, using a model of household-based decision making.

This paper builds on the results in the work-in-progress by Basu, Genicot and Stiglitz (2002), which tries to explicitly model the added-worker and discouraged-worker effects, and show why the discouragement effect may be, in part, illusory. The present paper highlights some paradoxical results that arise in the presence of this effect, and relates these ideas to other areas of research such as efficiency wage and inflation, unemployment benefits, and race and gender issues.

MINIMUM WAGE AND UNEMPLOYMENT

Let the aggregate demand for labour be the usual downward-sloping function of wage, w, denoted by $D(w)$. What we want to focus on is the 'supply curve'. Let us consider an economy with h households, each household i consisting of m potential workers. When we want to be explicit about the sex and age of the workers we will think of person 1 in each household as the adult male, person 2 as the adult female, and the rest as the children. In case this is a society where young children never work, we may think of a household's members 3, 4, . . ., m as the children who are above 16 years of age.

Recall how the textbook supply curve of labour is derived. We take the market wage, w, to be arbitrarily given and make the household do a maximization exercise and work out the household's labour supply. There is an implicit assumption in such an exercise. The assumption is that a person who supplies his or her labour gets to work. This assumption becomes unrealistic if there is unemployment in the economy. It is for this reason that some economists have worked out the household's supply, taking as given the fact that some members may be supply-constrained.

We shall proceed in the same spirit but conceive of a different model. We shall assume that the level of unemployment in the economy is public knowledge. If the unemployment rate (expressed as a fraction) is u, then we shall take $1 - u = p$ to be the probability of each worker finding a job. Let us assume that this is the same for those who are currently employed and those who are currently unemployed. This assumption is used in the well-known Harris–Todaro model (Harris and Todaro 1970) and corresponds to a search model with random matching and short-term employment. If we think of this as a casual labour market with large turnover, then this is not an unrealistic assumption. If a fraction p of all those supplying their labour currently find jobs, it seems reasonable to suppose that each worker treats p as the probability of being employed in the next period. We shall assume that just as each household is a wage-taker, each household is a p-taker (that is, it ignores the effect of its own decision on the aggregate unemployment rate in the economy). This being so, it is quite reasonable to suppose that the individual labour supply decision will depend on w and p (and not only on w). This is especially so when decision making occurs at the level of the household. For ease of thinking, let us suppose each person sees w and p and then has to decide (even if this is a household-based decision) whether to supply his or her labour or not.

It seems reasonable to suppose that if p is low, the household faces a genuine risk of the primary worker not finding a job. It is then reasonable for some of the other members of the household to supply their labour as well (so as to minimize the risk of the household being left with no one employed).

In this economy each worker is endowed with one unit of labour and has a disutility of labour equal to c. If the total income of the household is Y and the total effort expended by the household is C, then the household's utility, we will assume, is given by $V(Y) - C$, where $V' > 0$, and $V'' < 0$. Hence, if e household members are employed and earn a wage w, and c is per worker cost of work, the household derives a welfare $V(ew) - ec$ from this employment. In addition there is a sunk cost of θ per person associated with searching for work, and we assume that to find work search is a necessary prerequisite. This cost θ can originate from neglected housework, the costs of registering at an agency and subscribing to newspapers and employment gazettes, or acquiring some basic skills such as word processing. These are sunk costs because if one does not find the job one is looking for, the costs cannot be recovered. Assume that turning down an offer (after registering with the employment exchange) is possible but entails a cost of d (≥ 0) units to the household. Let $W(n, p, w)$ denote a household's expected welfare where n is the number of persons who supply labour (that is, search for jobs), p is the probability of each person finding employment, and w is the market wage. With this in mind, and using $p(k|n, p)$ to denote the probability of k persons finding work (when n go out searching) and p the probability of each person finding work, we have:

$$W(n, p, w) = \sum_{k=0}^{n} \pi(k|n, p) \max_{t \leq k} [V(tw) - tc - (k - t)d] - n\theta, \qquad (3.1)$$

where $\pi(k|n, p)$ is the probability of receiving k offers,[2] and $t \leq k$ is the number of these offers that are accepted. The household's problem is to choose $n \in \{0, 1, \ldots, m\}$ so as to maximize (equation 3.1). Let the household's choice be denoted by $s(w, p)$. That is,

$$s(w, p) = \arg \max_{n} W(n, p, w). \qquad (3.2)$$

Hence, the aggregate supply of labour is given by $S(w, p) = hs(w, p)$.

In Basu et al. (2002), we identify a class of models where the added worker effect is invariably present. Whenever $d \geq c$, such that a worker who applies for work never turns down an offer, then:

$$S(w, p) \leq S(w, p') \text{ for all } 0 < p' < p \leq 1 \qquad (3.3)$$

[Theorem 1 in Basu, et al. (2002)]. Assuming that the aggregate supply is continuously differentiable, it means that:

$$\frac{\partial S}{\partial p}(w, p) \leq 0 \qquad (3.4)$$

---

[2] The probability of receiving k offers if supply is n and probability of getting a job is p is simply $\pi(k|n, p) = \dfrac{n!}{k!(n-k)!} p^k (1 - p)^{n-k}$.

We also show that once transactions or sunk costs are allowed, $\dfrac{\partial S}{\partial p}$ can be positive, thereby creating a general model which can explain both the added worker effect and the discouragement effect.

The textbook supply curve of labour is the relation between w and S when $p = 1$. Figure 3.1 shows this curve as OA. We do not insist on any particular shape for this. If we want to think of this as perfectly inelastic (with only adult males working) it will be a vertical straight line. If we believe supply curves bend backwards at high wages, we could build that into our model.

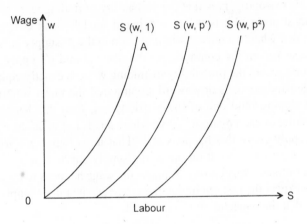

Fig. 3.1: Quasi-Supply Curves of Labour.

Next note that, for each $p \in [0,1]$, we can draw a supply curve $S = S(w, p)$. We shall call each such curve a 'quasi-supply curve' or 'p-supply curve'. Figure 3.1 illustrates a family of p-supply curves. If we wanted to model the discouragement effect of unemployment, we would take $\dfrac{\partial S}{\partial p} > 0$ and so, as p fell, the p-supply curves would move left. If we believed that for low wages the added worker effect is dominant and for high wages the discouragement effect dominates, we would have the p-supply curves intersecting one another. Let us, however, for now, go along with the assumption $\dfrac{\partial S}{\partial p} \leq 0$.

Our aim now is to construct the 'actual (aggregate) supply curve' from the p-supply curves. This will, interestingly, depend on the nature of the demand curve, thereby illustrating our initial ob̶ ̶vation regarding the interdependence of demand and supply.

Let the demand curve, $D(w)$, be as shown in Figure 3.2. Now, given any point on any p-supply curve, we can easily work out the rate of employment that will actually come to prevail. Suppose for instance, we are at point b. Then labour supply is wb and (given the wage implicit at b) labour demand is wk. Hence the rate of employment or probability of finding a job is given by $\dfrac{wk}{wb}$. Note that b is a point on the p'-supply curve. Hence, if $\dfrac{wk}{wb}$ is not equal to p', labour supply can never occur at b.

By this reasoning, note that the probability of finding work at point a is 1 and at point C it is 0 (since demand for labour at C is zero). It follows that when we move from a to c along the p'-supply curve there must occur (given the continuity of the demand and p'-supply curves) some point where the probability of finding work is exactly equal to p'. If the demand curve is downward sloping and the quasi-supply curve upward sloping (and one of these strictly so), then this happens at a unique point of each p-supply curve where $p < 1$. Let us assume that for the p'-supply curve this happens at b. That is, $wk/wb = p'$. We could then think of b as a point on the actual supply curve. It is a point that satisfies rational expectations. Suppose the wage happens to be w. If all workers expect the rate of employment to be p', then their supply would be such that the expectation is confirmed.

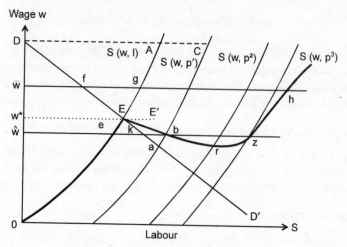

Fig. 3.2: The Aggregate Supply Curve of Labour.

If on each quasi-supply curve we pick the point that satisfies rational expectation and join up such points what we get is the actual aggregate supply curve of labour. Let the thick line going through 0 and b be such a curve.

It may be worthwhile explaining why the aggregate supply curve co-incides with the 1-supply curve (that is the p-supply curve correspond-ing to full employment) to the left of the demand curve. This is because at any such point, for example, e, demand for labour exceeds supply and so the rate of employment is 1.

Let us now demonstrate some of the paradoxical results that this model gives rise to. Suppose DD' in Figure 3.2 represents the demand for labour. If wages are fully flexible, then E represents the only point of equilib-rium. The wage is w^* and demand equals supply. Now suppose the gov-ernment enacts a minimum wage law and sets the legal minimum wage

at w. Since $w < w^*$, standard economics would lead us to expect that this cannot possibly have any impact (Mincer 1976; Ashenfelter and Blum 1976). But in this model, where there are added worker effects, this legal intervention can have significant consequences.

Observe that if the wage were at w, there are three levels of supply that would satisfy rational expectations. These are we, wb, and wz. Sup-pose wb is the supply that actually occurs. Then supply exceeds de-mand and so wages have a tendency to fall, but the law will not allow it to fall. So the wage persists at w and there is open unemployment. Hence, point b depicts an equilibrium. Point e does not depict an equilibrium because, though it satisfies rational expectations, at e there is excess demand for labour and so the wage would rise. By this same logic, point z depicts an equilibrium. Of course the earlier equilibrium at E is still available. In other words, the minimum wage law gives rise to multiple equilibria and, in particular, a legal minimum wage, imposed at a level below the prevailing market wage, can result in a fall in the wage. Note that among b and z, b is an unstable equilibrium. A small rise in unem-ployment at b will result in more unemployment and the equilibrium would finally settle at z which is a stable equilibrium.

Let us now check what happens if the minimum wage is set above w^*, for instance at $\overline{w}$. Standard theory would predict an unemployment level of fg. But supply occurs at point g only if the probability of finding work is one. As soon as there is unemployment, supply will begin to change. Hence, our model predicts an unemployment level of fh.

Another interesting result arises if this model is combined with an efficiency wage model. Consider either a labour turnover model or a

Leibensteinian model (Fehr 1986; Leibenstein 1957; Mirrlees 1975; and Stiglitz 1974, 1976) in which a worker's productivity happens to depend on his wage, ignoring for now the fact that a part of this wage may go to feed other members of the household. The latter is discussed in Genicot (1998). We will, later in the paper construct a model which combines a model of household decision making, as discussed above, along with a theory of endogenous wage rigidity of a fairly standard kind. Let us for now suppose that the efficiency wage is at, w, and the aggregate demand for labour is wk. For wages above w, aggregate labour demand is given by the line Dk.

Let us suppose the supply conditions are as shown in Figure 3.2. Thus, the standard textbook supply curve is given by OA. Our first expectation may be that, since at the efficiency wage labour demand exceeds we, wage will rise above w, the efficiency wage, and there will be no involuntary unemployment. However, in our model, wage may persist at w with unemployment equal to kb or, more likely kz. Of course at this wage, workers will be willing to work for a lower wage, but employees will not accept such offers.

It should also be transparent that the aggregate supply curve of labour depends on the nature of the demand curve. To see this, suppose the wage is fixed at w (Figure 3.3) and the economy is at the equilibrium A. Consider a drop in the labour demand from D_1 to D_2. To w corresponds

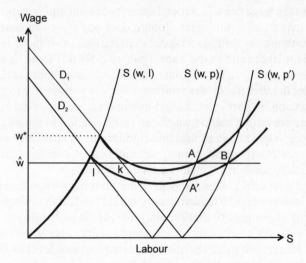

Fig. 3.3: Supply Depends on Demand.

a labour demand   smaller than k. Hence A no longer belongs to the actual aggregate supply curve since $\dfrac{w}{wA} < \dfrac{wk}{wA} = p$. The point on $S(w, p)$ which will translate in an actual probability of finding work of p is now A'. It is easy to check that a fall in demand will result in the supply curve moving down (everywhere to the right of the demand curve). Starting from A, a decrease in the demand worsens people's expectations about the likelihood of finding a job. In response they will increase their labour supply causing the unemployment to rise by more than the fall of demand and the economy will settle in a new equilibrium B.

UNEMPLOYMENT BENEFITS

Turning now to another important labour policy, we shall in this section study the effect of unemployment benefits on the kind of equilibrium obtained in the labour market.

Suppose in Figure 3.2 the wage has a floor at w. This can be because there is a minimum wage law or because w happens to be the efficiency wage. The exact explanation does not matter for our purpose here. There are then three possible equilibria—at points E, b, and z. Let us check on the welfare properties of these equilibria. Clearly, given that this is a competitive market, the equilibrium at E is the most efficient. At b and z there is greater output but this is caused by workers working excessively, for fear of unemployment. The household's welfare is the highest at E, since there is full employment and the wage is higher. Between the two other equilibria, our conjecture is that b dominates z.[3] Output and employment are the same at b and z, but there is more unemployment at z. As we switch to a more general formulation, where costs of effort vary across individuals, z becomes even more welfare dominated by b. The reason is that more people supply labour at z than at b. This means that, at z, workers whose effort is more costly supply labour. So a random selection of workers at z will contain more of these inefficient (in the sense of high cost) workers than a random selection at b. So the expected effort cost at z is more and this accentuates the welfare difference between both equilibria. Since z is the stable equilibrium and b is unstable, this is a worrying consequence of the added worker effect. In the absence of the added worker effect the equilibrium would move to E.

---

[3] For reasons similar to the argument in Rothschild and Stiglitz (1970).

This raises the question whether we can devise policies that counteract the tendency of workers to oversupply labour.

Since the oversupply is a consequence of the workers fearing that their household will be left without adequate employed members, any policy that combats this risk should improve matters.[4] An obvious candidate is a safety net for the unemployment. We shall here study a safety net at the level of the household, since it is the *household-level efficient decision making* which is the source of the problem (whether decisions are taken at by a unitary household or efficient bargainers). If this is properly designed the safety net may seldom have to be used. It is its mere presence that can change household behaviour favourably. So it need not cause any fiscal strain.

To see formally how this works, suppose that the government guarantees an income of G for each household. So any household whose income drops below G is given enough unemployment benefit for the household to consume G. If we use $\widetilde{W}$ to denote a household's expected welfare, then following a notation similar to that used in the second section, and staying for simplicity with the special case, were $d \geq c$, we may write:

$$\widetilde{W}(n, p, w, G) = \sum_{k=0}^{n} \pi(k|n, p) V(\max\{kw, G\}) - npc \qquad (3.5)$$

Given p, w, and G, the household's total supply of labour is defined as follows:

$$\widetilde{s}(p, w, G) = \arg \max_{n} \widetilde{W}(n, p, w, G) \qquad (3.6)$$

The question that we want to investigate is the effect of G on the supply of labour. Using Theorem 2 in Basu et al. (2002), we can tell that as G increases, $\widetilde{s}(p, w, G)$ decreases.

This implies that unemployment benefit can dampen the added worker effect. It may be checked that an implication of this theorem is that as G increases, the aggregate supply curve moves (weakly) upwards. Hence, for each wage, w, the largest supply of labour satisfying rational expectations must fall. Hence, for a given minimum wage, a rise in G can cause unemployment to fall (with total employment remaining

---

[4] It should be stressed that this is currently a conjecture since we have not yet proved formally that b dominates z.

unchanged). Further it is easy to see that if G is kept at a small level, the quasi supply, when p is 1, remains unaffected by the G. That is, $\tilde{s}\,(1, w, G) = s\,(1, w)$. In other words there is no shirking of labour. Hence, interestingly, what this demonstrates is that unemployment benefits may be justified without having to invoke equity reasons, but purely on grounds of efficiency. Moreover, the cost of this policy is very small, as its mere existence will discourage the oversupply of labour and, therefore, unemployment.

RACE, GENDER AND UNEMPLOYMENT

AFFIRMATIVE ACTION AND UNEMPLOYMENT

A well-known fact for most economies is that unemployment rates vary across different categories of labour more than can be dismissed as natural stochastic variations. Thus, we often hear how Black unemployment exceeds White unemployment by a wide margin, or how unemployment for some caste groups in India is markedly larger than for others.[5]

At first blush, it may appear that our model with its penchant for multiple equilibria may have an explanation for this. Indeed, it does offer an explanation but for reasons more roundabout than one may suppose initially. To see this, suppose first that employers are race-blind and caste-blind, that is, they select their workers randomly from among the unemployed without showing preference for any race or caste. Evidently, then the expected unemployment rates of Hispanics, Blacks, and Whites, and any sub-category for that matter, must be the same. This fact remains unchanged even if it were the case that more low caste workers supplied labour. In brief, this fact is independent of the supply responses of the different groups. If, on the other hand, employers set themselves, or are given, quotas for different castes, races, or other sub-categories, or have diversity norms for the workforce, the unemployment rate can vary across different sub-groups. What is interesting is that this can happen even if employers follow diversity norms that are 'fair'.

To understand this, assume that a fraction β of an economy's (working-age) population happens to be of a low caste, or 'Scheduled Caste', and the remaining $1-\beta$ are of a high caste. Let us suppose that the wage

---

[5] In Third World countries, child unemployment rates often differ markedly from adult unemployment rates. This can, however, have causes very different from the ones discussed here (see Basu 2000).

has a floor at w below which it will not go. This can be because of a minimum wage law or because of efficiency wage arguments. Let us also suppose that w is below the aggregate market-clearing wage w^*. So the situation is akin to the one shown in Figure 3.2. Now assume that the low caste and the high caste takes their household labour decisions based not on the aggregate employment rate p, but the race-specific employment rates, p_l and p_h.. Now it is entirely possible to have different unemployment rates for the two groups despite the fact of the employer following the norm of employing workers so that a fraction β of the workers are from the Scheduled Caste. The argument is easy to see. Suppose that disadvantaged caste workers conjecture that p_l is low, while high caste conjectures p_h to be high. Then this can create a relatively larger supply of the disadvantaged caste labour by bringing more of their family members into the labour force while high caste women and children stay at home and in school, thereby fulfilling the initial conjectures.

Note finally that we assumed that the employers use a fair norm not because they actually do so, nor because that is necessary for our argument, but because that is the assumption under which our result is least expected. If employers use a biased norm, variations in caste-specific unemployment rates are only to be expected.

It is interesting to note that the logic of sex-specific unemployment rates will have to be very different since most households consist of males and females, and so female labour supply will depend not just on p_f (the employment rate of females) but also on p_m (the male employment rate). And typically a larger male unemployment will cause a positive female labour supply response, resulting in a larger female unemployment rate as well. Our model suggests that at a macro level male–female unemployment rates will tend to move together, though unemployment rates can vary markedly across races.

This leads us to an interesting micro question. How do unemployment rates within households and across gender vary? That is the subject matter of the next sub-section.

DISCOURAGEMENT EFFECT AND SOME EMPIRICAL PARADOXES

A number of empirical studies of labour supply in the US have found the added worker effect to be feeble.[6] Other studies have pointed out

---

[6] See e.g. Mincer (1976), Maloney (1991).

that this effect may not be feeble but its net effect is weak because it is offset by a comparable discouragement effect pushing in the opposite direction.[7] As we know from Basu et al. (2002), the presence of search costs might explain a certain discouragement effect in the sense of a less active search. However, we are inclined to believe that in empirical studies the discouragement effect *appears* to be larger than it really is. We shall show this by assuming that there are no search costs and therefore, there is no discouragement effect. Hence, from here on we assume $d \geq c$ and $\theta = 0$. We will then show how with a small realistic modification of our model we can explain why it may be the case that the discouragement effect is overestimated.

The modification in question consists in allowing for the possibility that there are household-level factors that can influence a person's job prospect. This possibility is hinted at in a study by Layard et al. (1980) and discussed more explicitly by Lundberg (1985). It seems quite reasonable to suppose that there are many influences that occur at the level of the household. The empirical evidence of 'assortative mating' provides support for this assumption. In the US, in a typical household, both husband and wife are Black or both are White. Now if employers discriminate against Blacks, then either both members of an household will stand better chances on the market, or both will stand worse chances respectively. Likewise, if some locations provide better job opportunities, then again each member of one household may have better job prospects than each member of another household. The same is true if one's social network matters and if every husband and wife belong, or do not belong, to networks together.

To model this, let us assume that there are two types of households, 1 and 2. There are h_1 and h_2 households of each of these types and $h_1 + h_2 = h$. These two kinds of households are identical in every other way except that type 1 households are more likely to find jobs when there is unemployment. Let us model this by assuming that, when a type 1 individual (i.e. a person belonging to a household of type 1) applies for a job, he is $1 + \gamma$ times as likely to get a job as a type 2 individual, where $\gamma > 0$. It then follows that if K_1 and K_2 persons of types 1 and 2 supply their labour and there are J jobs going, then the probability of each type 2 person finding a job is given by (for simplicity, we assume that $K_1 + K_2 \geq J$):

---

[7] Cain (1966), Lundberg (1985), Tano (1993).

$$p_2(J, K_1, K_2) \equiv \frac{J}{(1+\gamma) K_1 + K_2} \qquad (3.7)$$

and the probability of each type 1 person being employed is given by:

$$p_2(J, K_1, K_2) \equiv \frac{(1+\gamma)J}{(1+\gamma) K_1 + K_2} \qquad (3.8)$$

The lottery process which gives us these probabilities may be thought of as follows. When the employment exchange gets K_1 and K_2 job applications from types 1 and 2, respectively, and has J jobs to allocate ($K_1 + K_2 \geq J$), earlier (that is, in the previous sections), the employment exchange may have been thought of as allocating $\dfrac{K_1 J}{K_1 + K_2}$ jobs to type 1 applicants and $\dfrac{K_2 J}{K_1 + K_2}$ to type 2. Now it sets aside $\dfrac{(1+\gamma)K_1 J}{(1+\gamma)K_1 + K_2}$ jobs for type 1 applicants and $\dfrac{K_2 J}{(1+\gamma)K_1 + K_2}$ for type 2, picking within each category by some unbiased lottery mechanism.

From here we can proceed along two alternative routes. First, we could assume that households are unaware of their differing probabilities of being employed and so both types use the aggregate employment rate as the expected probability of finding jobs. Second, we could assume that households are more discerning and compute their own probability of being employed as p_1 and p_2 depending on whether they are of type 1 or type 2. Both routes lead to the same conclusion but we illustrate the argument by making the second assumption. Then, given w, p_1, and p_2, we can as before, determine the supply of labour of a type i household to be given by

$$s_i = s(w, p_i), \qquad (3.9)$$

where the function $s(.,.)$ is the same as before. Then, given w, p_1, and p_2, the total supply of type i workers will be

$$S_i(w, p_i) = h_i s(w, p_i) \qquad (3.10)$$

As before, p_1^e and p_2^e are *rational expectations* of finding a job on the part of type 1 and type 2 households if and only if

$$p_i(D(w), S_1(w, p_1^e), S_2(w, p_2^e)) = p_1^e, \, i = 1, 2. \qquad (3.11)$$

Equilibrium, with or without minimum wage legislation, is defined as above.

Now, consider an equilibrium where there is unemployment. It will be found that in households where men are unemployed, the women will be more likely to be unemployed and in households where men are employed, the women will be more likely to be employed. This occurs despite the fact that the added worker effect is there for each household and there is no discouragement effect. Without denying that in reality there could be certain discouragement effects that result from search costs, empirical evidence supporting it, based on the fact that an unemployed person's spouse tends to be unemployed, might overstate this effect.

In addition, as stressed earlier, it seems important to measure the added worker effect as the households' and their secondary workers' labour supply response to the worsening job prospects of the primary worker, instead of the actual loss of employment of the primary worker used in much of the empirical literature.

A NOTE ON INFLATION

Our model sheds an interesting insight into the relation between unemployment and inflation. Suppose an economy has a legal minimum wage at w as shown in Figure 3.2 and suppose that the labour market equilibrates exactly at that wage with labour supply equal to wz and unemployment kz. It is usually the case that minimum wages are specified in nominal rather than real terms, and so let us assume that this is the case. Now, suppose that there is gentle inflation in the economy. This means that the minimum wage, in real terms, will slowly erode downwards. It seems reasonable to suppose that the equilibrium supply will move along the segment zr on the actual supply curve.[8] Note now that, as we go from z to r, we move from $S(w, p^3)$ to $S(w, p^2)$. From Theorem 1, we know that $p^3 < p^2$. Hence $1 - p^3 > 1 - p^2$. So as inflation occurs, unemployment will tend to fall. In other words, a minimum wage legislation, in the absence of automatic indexation, provides an explanation for a Phillips curve type relation, though inflation in our model results not just in lower unemployment but a falling *rate* of unemployment.

---

[8] In other words, though the labour supply correspondence is multi-valued around w, we are assuming that as w changes a little, supply varies continuously as long as that is possible.

CONCLUSION

Whenever decision-making occurs at the level of the household (whether we conceive the household as a single decision-making unit or an arena of bargain), it is natural that what is expected to happen to one person in the labour market will affect the behaviour of other members of his or her household. Hence, the aggregate labour supply curve cannot strictly be derived without knowledge of what the demand curve looks like.

This paper argues that in the presence of unemployment risk, there might be important added worker and discouragement effects. Households could send additional participants to the labour market in order to insure against the worst outcome of no labour income and there can also be situations where workers become despondent in the face of increased unemployment and cease to search for work. The empirical literature in labour economics has shown awareness of this interdependence and there is a body of writing that has looked into the 'supply response' to demand shifts. However, most existing empirical studies have tended to underestimate the added worker effect by focusing on actual employment status and neglecting expectations; we showed that they may have overestimated the discouragement effect of unemployment by ignoring household-level characteristics. It is also worth noting that increasing the labour supply is only one way to reduce the fluctuations in income due to unemployment—borrowing and dissaving constituting other options. Hence, while most empirical studies look at data for the United States or the United Kingdom, the added worker effect is likely to be stronger for developing countries and poor areas, where families are larger and credit or dissaving opportunities are more limited.

The added workers increase labour supply, possibly creating a downward sloping supply curve and giving rise to surprising phenomena. One of the most interesting insights concerns the response of the labour market to wage rigidity, whether it be from minimum wage legislation or some kind of efficiency wage. In particular, this paper has shown that a minimum wage law can result in an overall drop in wages.

The paper has also analysed the effect of a household-level income guarantee scheme which insures worker households against the worst ravages of an economic slump. It has been argued that such unemployment benefits can be justified not just in terms of equity but also efficiency.

The model developed here can be extended in several ways. For one, there are other policy interventions (for instance, differently designed guarantee schemes or unemployment benefits) that need to be examined. This can be useful in designing social welfare interventions. Secondly, in constructing our model, we kept coming up against matters that, essentially, involve dynamics or at least a modicum of intertemporal decision-making. People may, for instance, want to revise their labour supply decision *after* they learn what happens to the household. Of course, one then has to allow a third round of adjustment, and a fourth round and so on. Moreover, a household could try to smoothen its consumption not only by offering and withdrawing its secondary workers but by having its primary workers work more than usual when work is available and save for the rainy season. We have, in this paper, made strong assumptions and deliberately stayed away from these dynamic issues; but these will be worth researching into in the future.

REFERENCES

Ashenfelter, O. (1980), 'Unemployment as Disequilibrium in a Model of Aggregate Labor Supply', *Econometrica*, vol. 48, no. 3, pp. 547–64.

Ashenfelter, O. and J. Blum (1976), *Evaluating the Labor Market Effects of Social Programs, Industrial Relations Section* (Princeton, NJ: Princeton University).

Bardhan, P.K. (1984), *Land, Labor and Rural Poverty: Essays in Development Economics* (New York, NY: Columbia University Press).

Basu, K. (1999), 'Child Labor: Cause, Consequence and Cure, with Remarks in International Labor Standards', *Journal of Economic Literature*, vol. 37, pp. 1083–119.

Basu, K. (2000), 'The Intriguing Relation Between Adult Minimum Wage and Child Labor', *Economic Journal*, vol. 110, no. 462, pp. C50–C61.

Basu, K. and P.H. Van (1998), 'The Economics of Child Labor', *American Economic Review*, vol. 88, no. 3, pp. 412–27.

Basu, K., G. Genicot, and J.E. Stiglitz (2002), 'Household Labor Supply and Unemployment', *work-in-progress*.

Belton, M. F. and G. Rhodes (1976), 'Unemployment and the Labor Force Participation of Married Men and Women: A Simultaneous Model', *Review of Economics and Statistics*, vol. 58, no. 2, pp. 398–406.

Cain, G.G. (1966), *Married Women in the Labor Force: An Economic Analysis* (Chicago, Ill.: University of Chicago Press).

Cullen, J.B. and J. Gruber (2000), 'Does Unemployment Insurance Crowd out Spousal Labor Supply?' *Journal of Labor Economics*, vol. 18, no. 3, pp. 546–71.

Datta-Chaudhuri, M. (1990), 'Market Failure and Government Failure', *Journal of Economic Perspectives*, vol. 4, no. 3, pp. 25–39.

Fehr, E. (1986), 'A Theory of Involuntary Equilibrium Unemployment', *Journal of Institutional and Theoretical Economics*, vol. 142, no. 2, pp. 405–30.

Genicot, G. (1998), 'An Efficiency Wage Theory of Child Labor: Exploring the Implications of Some Ideas of Leibenstein and Marx', Department of Economics Working Paper No. 462, Cornell University.

Harris, J.R. and M.P. Todaro (1970), 'Migration, Unemployment and Development: A Two-Sector Analysis', *American Economic Review*, vol. 60, pp. 126–42.

Humphrey, D.D. (1940), 'Alleged Additional Workers in the Measurement of Unemployment', *Journal of Economic Studies*, vol. 48, pp. 412–19.

Layard, R., M. Barton and A.M. Zabalza (1980), 'Married Women's Participation and Hours', *Economica*, vol. 47, pp. 51–72.

Leibenstein, H. (1950), 'Bandwagon, Snob and Veblen Effects in the Theory of Consumers Demand', *Quarterly Journal of Economics*, vol. 64.

_____ (1957), *Economic Backwardness and Economic Growth: Studies in the Theory of Economic Development* (New York: Wiley).

Lundberg, S. (1985), 'The Added Worker Effect', *Journal of Labor Economics*, vol. 3, no. 3, pp. 11–37.

Maloney, T.J. (1987), 'Employment Constraints and the Labor Supply of Married Women: A Reexamination of the Added Worker Effect', *Journal of Human Resources*, vol. 22, no. 1, pp. 51–61.

_____ (1991), 'Unobserved Variables and the Elusive Added Worker Effect', *Economica*, vol. 58, pp. 173–87.

Mincer, J. (1966a), 'Labor-Force Participation of Married Women: A Study of Labor Supply', in J. Mincer, *Studies of Labor Supply: Collected Essays of Jacob Mincer 2* (Hants, England: Edward Elgard Publishing).

_____ (1966b), 'Labor-Force Participation and Unemployment: A Review of Recent Evidence', in J. Mincer, *Studies of Labor Supply: Collected Essay of Jacob Mincer 2.* (Hants, England: Edward Elgard Publishing).

_____ (1976), 'Unemployment Effects of Minimum Wages', *Journal of Political Economy*, vol. 84, pp. 87–104.

Mirrlees, J.A. (1975), 'A Pure Theory of Underdeveloped Economies', in L.G. Reynolds (ed.), *Agriculture in Development Theory* (New Haven, Conn.: Yale University Press).

Rothschild, M. and J.E. Stiglitz (1970), 'Increasing Risk I: A Definition', *Journal of Economic Theory*, vol. 2, pp. 225–43.

Schlicht, E. (1978), 'Labor Turnover, Wage Structure and Natural Unemployment', *Zeitschrift fur die gesamte Staatswissenschaft (JITE)*, vol. 134, pp. 337–46.

Shapiro, C. and J.E. Stiglitz (1984), 'Equilibrium Unemployment as a Worker Discipline Device', *American Economic Review*, vol. 74, no. 3, pp. 433–44.

Stiglitz, J.E. (1974), 'Alternative Theories of Wage Determination and Unemployment in LDCs: The Labor Turnover Model', *Quarterly Journal of Economics*, vol. 88, no. 2, pp. 194–227.

_____ (1976), 'The Efficiency Wage Hypothesis, Surplus Labor, and the Distribution of Income in LDCs', *Oxford Economic Papers*, vol. 28, no. 2, pp. 185–207.

Tano, D. (1993), 'The Added Worker Effect', *Economic Letters*, vol. 43, no. 1, pp. 111–17.

Veblen, T. (1991), 'The Theory of the Leisure Class', in *The Writings of Thorstein Veblen* (Fairfield, New Jersey: Reprints of Economic Classics).

Woytinsky, W.S. (1940a), 'Additional Workers and the Volume of Unemployment', Pamphlet Series No. 1 (Washington, DC: Committee on Social Security of the Social Science Research Council).

_____ (1940b), 'Additional Workers and the Volume of Unemployment', *Journal of Political Economy*, vol. 48, pp. 735–40.

4

Crouching Tiger, Lumbering Elephant

Pranab Bardhan

Over the last three decades, Mrinal and I have discussed at considerable length many issues of life in general, but if there is one theme that
we have come back to repeatedly it is that of political economy. I do not
mean here political economy only in the narrow sense of special interest
politics that seems to preoccupy most of the economists who write formally on the subject, but in the more general sense, involving some of
the organizing principles of social life. While the exigencies of my pro-
fessional life have often kept me busy with exploring the intricacies of
narrow theoretical models or managing large projects of data collection
and analysis, I have always been delighted by the opportunity to indulge
in long conversations with Mrinal on free-floating big-think issues in
general, and political economy in particular. This paper is on one such
unabashedly broad-brush topic, and I am sure bears the imprint of my
many conversations with him.

Many decades back when I was a student in Calcutta one of the politically challenging questions for us was the analysis of China–India
comparison in terms of the pace and pattern of development. More than
fifty years back these two largest countries of the world, now containing
between them nearly two-fifths of the world population, launched on
distinctly different paths of social, political, and economic development,
even though they were faced with similarly massive problems of poverty, disease, and illiteracy. Those paths have taken some twists and
turns over the decades, and at the beginning of the new century China
seems, on all accounts, to be crouching to leap to a leading position in
the world economy, while India lags far behind. When I was young we
were frequently told that the Chinese were better socialists than us, and
now we are told that they are better capitalists. It is partly the contention
of this paper that these two aspects are not as contradictory as

they sound, and that the political complexities behind India's lagging performance may also give us some clues about the long-run uncertainties in China's future.

The facts[1] about relative economic performance in the two countries are simple enough, notwithstanding the many deficiencies and comparability problems in the data in both countries (to our knowledge, there have been fewer reliability tests and internal consistency checks carried out on the Chinese data, compared to the Indian one). Over the last three decades, official data suggest that the average annual rate of growth of per capita income was about 7 per cent in China[2] and 2.5 per cent in India. Productivity per hectare in agriculture (say, in rice) has been much higher in China for centuries, but the relative progress in manufacturing in recent decades has been phenomenal. In the early 1950s, the total gross domestic product (GDP) in manufacturing in India was slightly below that in China; in the late 1990s, it was less than a quarter of that in China. In 1999, the manufacturing share of GDP was 38 per cent in China, while it was 16 per cent in India. Indian labour productivity in manufacturing was about 71 per cent of that in China in 1952; in 1995 it was 37 per cent.[3] Compared to India, total electricity use per capita is twice as high in China and teledensity (the number of telephones per thousand people) is several times higher. In 1999, the share of world trade (exports plus imports) in goods was 3.3 per cent for China, 0.7 per cent for India; in services the corresponding percentages were 2.1 and 1.2. The total amount (in dollars) of foreign direct investment in China was 18 times that in India in 1999. In the same year, gross domestic saving as a proportion of GDP was exactly twice as high in China as that in India.

The sustained high rate of growth of per capita income was expectedly accompanied by a decline of poverty in China of historic proportions, although the corresponding decline over the last quarter of century in Indian poverty has also been significant. According to the World Bank estimates (for whatever these necessarily crude estimates are worth), in 1999, 18.5 per cent of the population in China lived on less than a dollar

---

[1] Most of the data in this and the following paragraph are, unless otherwise mentioned, from the *World Development Indicators*, World Bank, Washington, D.C.

[2] Lardy (1998) suggests that the Chinese growth rates are overstated by about 1.0 to 1.5 per cent a year.

[3] See Lee and Rao (2001).

a day; the corresponding figure for India was about 44 per cent. According to the Chinese State Statistical Bureau data (reported in *The Economist*, 2 June 2001), the Gini coefficient of income in rural China was 0.34, and 0.29 in urban China in 1999 (it is not clear if the households were classified according to per capita income or household income). In India, the data from one of the very few income surveys, MISH (Market and Income of Households Survey data of the National Council of Applied Economic Research), suggest that the Gini coefficient of income in rural India was 0.40, and 0.42 in urban India in 1997–8.[4] What is striking (and has been so for some time) is the higher inequality in rural compared to urban China (the opposite of the pattern in India and most other countries), mostly due probably to the extreme regional disparity in rural China.[5] By most accounts overall income inequality in China, though low relative to India, worsened over the last two decades, whereas there is not much trend in Indian income inequality. The social or human development indicators all indicate the superior performance of China. The life expectation at birth is about 70 years in China, to India's 63. Under 5 child mortality (per thousand live births) was 37 in China and 90 in India in 1999. Female illiteracy for above age 15 was 25 in China and 56 in India in 1999.

So, after many years of quantitative comparisons and studies that have absorbed the energies of many social scientists the great game of guessing the China–India economic race is, for all practical purposes, over. By most criteria of standard economic measurements of levels of living and their growth, China has clearly won the race. The hue and cry raised by business in India these days—it will be even louder after China's entry into the WTO takes full effect—of the 'cheap' Chinese goods flooding the Indian market and the inevitable charge (by the weak against the strong) of 'dumping', lent receptive ears by the populist Indian politicians of the Left as well as the Right, are among the latest signs of Indian defeatism. In this paper, I want to go beyond the broad indicators of economic performance and look at some general issues of a society's ability to (a) resolve collective action problems and (b) to politically

[4] See Lal et al. (2001).

[5] See, for example, the analysis of rural household data covering 18 provinces in 1988 and 1995 in Gustafsson and Shi (2002); they find that most of income inequality in rural China in 1995 was spatial, and the uneven development of mean income across counties stood for most, but not all, of the rapid increase in income inequality.

manage conflicts. I will suggest that over the last few decades, China has, by and large, shown a better performance in the former, and India in the latter, and I shall speculate on some common reasons underlying both, and what they portend for the future in both countries.

I have been convinced for many years that both at the macro level of political economy and the micro level of management of public space in general and of common property resources in particular, one of the most serious problems that Indian society faces is that of collective action. At the macro level, collective action is necessary in formulating cohesive developmental goals with clear priorities and avoiding prisoner's di-lemma-type deadlocks in the pursuit of commonly agreed upon goals. When society is extremely heterogeneous (both in terms of ethnicity and wealth distribution) and conflict-ridden as in India, and no indi-vidual group is powerful enough to hijack the state by itself, the demo-cratic process tends to install an elaborate system of checks and bal-ances in the public sphere and meticulous rules of equity in sharing the spoils, at least among the divided elite groups. There may be what soci-ologists call 'institutionalized suspicion' in the internal organization of such a state and a carefully structured system of multiple veto powers. In the Indian case, this is enhanced no doubt by the legacy of the institu-tional practices of the colonial rulers suspicious of the natives, and an even earlier legacy of the Moghul emperors suspicious of the potentially unruly *subadars* and *mansabdars*, the local potentates.

Nearly two decades back, I had tried to analyse the (continuing) fis-cal crisis and developmental gridlock in India as an intricate collective action problem in an implicit framework of non-cooperative Nash equi-libria (see Bardhan 1984, 1998). I described how the system settled for short-run particularistic compromises among the clamouring groups in the form of sharing the spoils through an elaborate network of subsidies and patronage distribution, to the detriment of long-run investment and economic growth. Since then there has certainly been an increase in the diversity, fluidity, and fragmentation in the coalition of dominant inter-est groups, which has made some of the deregulatory reforms of the last decade more acceptable than before. But one should not underestimate the enormity and tenacity of vested interests in the preservation of the old political equilibrium. The mounting fiscal deficits (particularly rev-enue deficits), the staggering burden of various (implicit and explicit) subsidies, the near-bankruptcy of many state governments, the limited ability of the political system to bear the short-run costs of beneficial long-run reforms (in matters of relaxing foreign trade restrictions, de-reservation for small-scale industries, lifting restrictions on movement and storage of agricultural products, clearing the deck for unfettered operation of foreign investors in infrastructure, restructuring the management of the giant public sector corporations and giving them genuine autonomy in a framework of competition, easing on the stringent labour laws, etc.) and a continuing erosion of the institutional mechanisms that enable credible commitments to coherent long-term development policies—all testify to the extreme difficulties of resolving the collective action problems that the contending groups face in the matter of economic reform in India, even though most of these groups have the potential of benefiting from the reform in the long run. So in the coming years I expect Indian reform to lumber along, clumsily and haltingly, two steps forward and one step backward.

Over the last fifty years the Chinese economy has gone through tumultuous changes, from massive land reforms in the 1950s, the Great Leap Forward and the Great Famine, the Cultural Revolution and the associated great destruction of human capital, then decollectivization of agriculture, to the last two decades of international opening of the economy and the spectacular emergence of the non-state industrial enterprises (particularly the township and village enterprises, or the TVEs) under local government (and in some cases semi-private) control. If we concentrate on the policy changes in the last two decades alone, they have involved large restructuring decisions, often upsetting a whole range of apple-carts of vested interests. Allowing the massive inflows of foreign investment and prying open an economy hitherto largely closed to foreign trade must have involved wrenching dislocations and reorganizations of the domestic economy, as the cold wind of international competition blew over enterprises and activities nurtured by decades of Party control and established structures of patronage.

For example, consider the TVEs which formed the leading sector in the industrial economy in the last two decades. I believe that the clue to their dramatic success particularly in coastal China lay in three major elements of this unique institutional experiment: (i) there was intense competition among the TVEs run by different local governments; (ii) this competition had teeth (unlike, say, in the case of the competition of public sector banks in India) in the sense that there was a hard budget constraint imposed on them, so that by and large a failing TVE could not expect a bailout by the provincial or central government (although there was some cross-subsidization between enterprises within the same township or village); and (iii) when the TVE made money, the local authority was largely allowed to keep most of it (residual claimancy without private ownership was the novel institutional feature). In particular, to maintain a hard budget constraint on a (local) government-controlled enterprise requires a commitment, akin to resolving a collective action problem in the conservation of resources in the 'commons' of the public fisc. In India even announced commitments of non-bailout are usually not credible, as when 'push comes to shove' more often than not the government yields to some pressure group or other for a bailout programme, and the earlier collective resolve against it unravels. Of course, the vast state-owned enterprise sector in China is still as much of an albatross on the rest of the economy as in India, but even here the recent retrenchments of several millions of industrial workers from the overmanned public sector enterprises suggests a collective determination on a feat of harsh short-run sacrifice that is rare in India.[6]

To many commentators the superior Chinese ability to take (and stick to) hard decisions in contrast to India is simply a matter of authoritarianism versus democracy. I believe authoritarianism is neither necessary nor sufficient for credible commitment. That it is not sufficient is obvious from the cases, say, of many African dictators presiding over weak states and vacillating decisions. That it is not necessary is clear from examples of the post-Second World War history of Scandinavian or Japanese democracies where many coordinated macroeconomic adjustment decisions, rising above short-run political pressures, have been taken (although in the macroeconomic crisis of the last decade the famed Japanese ability to coordinate on hard decisions is looking a bit frayed). I think deeper issues than the formal pattern of the political regime are involved here, and my central point in this paper is that some of these deeper factors may simultaneously influence the nature of collective action in economic management and the pattern of political regime in a country.

---

[6] The Chinese government also seems to have been somewhat more innovative and experimental in the manner of downsizing the public enterprises. Apart from the voluntary retirement schemes similar to those in India, they have tried out policies like *xiagang* under which a worker is still officially employed (and entitled to some benefits like keeping the housing allocation) but not paid a wage, or a policy of *lungang* or rotating employment and labour sharing among the workers (with someone temporarily displaced still entitled to the fixed wage but not to the bonus which is a large part of the employed worker's compensation).

Much of the general empirical literature on collective action in economics and anthropology suggests that social heterogeneity and economic
inequality tend to have a negative effect on coordination and cooperation
in matters of collective action.[7] This has a bearing on the India-China
comparison even at the macro level (just as the better coordinating ability
of the Scandinavians and the Japanese may be linked to their remarkable
social homogeneity and economic equality). In terms of ethnicity, language, or religion, Chinese society is less heterogeneous than the Indian
(some of the social homogeneity is, of course, the artificial outcome of
the centuries-old domination of the Han Chinese and their forcible iron-
ing out of ethnic and linguistic differences[8]). Since the Revolution, the
Chinese economy, both rural and urban, has been characterized by far
less inequality in assets (land, financial assets, and human capital) and
income. Even in the last two decades, when inequality has been increasing sharply in China, as we have noted before, the levels so far seem to be
significantly below those in India. Other things remaining the same, this
relative social and economic homogeneity facilitates taking coordinated
action in long-term policies in China and makes it easier to enlist the
support of a broad range of social groups for necessary short-run sacrifices.[9] In particular, the imposition of the hard budget constraint on the
local governments, which is at the root of the phenomenal industrial success of the TVEs has been made tolerable, inspite of all the hardships and
disruptions of the competitive process, by the fact that China has had

---

[7]   For a summary discussion of this empirical literature relating to the local commons, see Bardhan (1993), and Bardhan and Dayton-Johnson (2002).

[8]   The sinologist and historian Jenner (1992, p. 4) writes on this issue:
Nowhere has the homogenizing effect been more successful than in creating the
impression that the Han Chinese themselves are a single ethnic group, despite the
mutual incomprehensibility of many of their mother tongues and the ancient hostility between such Han Chinese nationalities as the Cantonese and the Hakkas. While
the occupation of Tibet and East Turkestan has failed to persuade most Tibetans and
Uighurs that they are Chinese, so that they can be kept in the empire only by force,
historical myth-making has so far been remarkably effective not just in inventing a
single Han Chinese ethnicity but also, and this is a far bigger triumph, in winning
acceptance for it.

[9]   There is considerable historical and contemporary cross-country evidence on
this general phenomenon. A major institutional lesson that Morris and Adelman
(1989, p. 1417) draw from their historical research on the nineteenth-century development experience of 23 countries is the following:

some kind of a minimum rural safety net, made possible[10] to a large extent by one of the world's most egalitarian distributions of land cultivation rights that has followed the decollectivization since 1978 (the size of land cultivated by a household is assigned almost always strictly in terms of the demographic size of the household). In most parts of India, for the poor there is no similar rural safety net; and the more severe educational inequality makes the absorption of shocks in the industrial labour market more difficult (to the extent that education and training provide some means of flexibility in retraining and redeployment). Hence, the resistance to the competitive process that market reform entails is that much stiffer in India. It is in this sense that it may not be entirely flippant to state that compared to India the Chinese are better capitalists now *because* they were better socialists before: the egalitarian base has made the shocks of transition to capitalism more bearable. In fact the TVEs grew out of the old production brigades under the commune system, and, of course, the TVEs themselves may have formed a transitional stage in the institutional evolution towards private capitalism, as the last few years of increasing privatization of TVEs in coastal China portend.

'Favorable impacts of government policies on the *structure* of economic growth can be expected only where political institutions limit elite control of assets, land institutions spread a surplus over subsistence widely, and domestic education and skills are well diffused'.

Keefer and Knack (1997) provide some cross-country evidence that inequality and other forms of polarization make it more difficult to build a consensus about policy changes in response to crises, and result in instability of policy outcomes and insecurity of property and contractual rights. Rodrik (1999) cites cross-country evidence for his hypothesis that the economic costs of external shocks are magnified by the distributional conflicts that are triggered and that this diminishes the productivity with which a society's resources are utilized.

Campos and Root (1996) also emphasize this point in their study of the East Asian experience: 'In contrast with Latin America and Africa, East Asian regimes established their legitimacy by promising shared growth so that demands of narrowly conceived groups for regulations that would have long-term deleterious consequences for growth were resisted. In particular, broad-based social support allowed their governments to avoid having to make concessions to radical demands of organized labour'.

[10] This is a major oversight in the literature on the Chinese success story on the basis of what is called 'market-preserving federalism'; see, for example, Oi (1999) and Montinola et al. (1995). For a general critique of the latter paper, see Rodden and Rose-Ackerman (1997).

But China is far behind India in the ability to politically manage conflicts. I was in Beijing the day of the Tiananmen killings, and I had visited the Square two days before. The scale of (unarmed) demonstration there was something that Indian authorities routinely face everyday in several parts of the country. Large societies always generate many kinds of conflicts, and an extremely heterogeneous society like India with a great deal of economic disparities and social inequalities is always in some kind of turmoil somewhere. Yet it is remarkable how in the last fifty-plus years since Independence the Indian political system has been able to douse the fires and contain most of the conflicts,[11] starting with the language riots in the 1950s, to the armed rebellions of militant peasants or regional separatists, to the sporadic outbreaks of inter-caste and inter-community violence that continue to this day. Defying many dire predictions of the Indian state breaking up, the system has by and large managed conflicts in some ways even better than a far less heterogeneous and less poor Europe has fared over, say, the last two hundred years .

The standard comment is, of course, that democracy acts as a safety valve for the smouldering tensions, and this is no doubt true. But again I think there are some deeper forces involved. In my political economy book (1984, 1998), I suggested, on an admittedly speculative level, that the same heterogeneity of socio-economic groups which has hindered collective action in the matter of economic management of long-term policies and investment has also strengthened the demand for democratic rules in inter-group negotiations and bargaining, thereby contributing to the continued survival of democratic processes in India, against all odds. Social and economic cleavages can, of course, make compromise difficult and multiply the stresses and strains in the polity, but the Indian experience suggests that the contending groups may come to value the procedural usefulness of democracy as an impersonal (or least arbitrary) rule of negotiation and demand articulation inside the ruling coalition, and as a device for one partner to keep the other partners at the bargaining table within some moderate bounds. Thus, without minimizing the importance of a certain tradition of tolerance and pluralism in the Indian political culture and legal system and a degree of continuing commitment on the part of India's political and military officials, I have suggested that the general persistence of democracy and the form it has

[11] Kashmir and the North-East are two areas where the Indian state has repeatedly failed in accommodation and containment.

taken has also something to do with the political exigencies of bargaining within a divided coalition, and the constant need to absorb dissent and co-opt potential rebel leaders and groups. Even in far less conflict-ridden Western Europe, if one looks at the history of the rise of democracy in the nineteenth century, one sees some evidence of the divisions within the dominant classes playing an important role. In France, for example, Louis Napoleon shrewdly used the restoration of universal (male) suffrage to play the landed classes against the urban. He even reportedly[12] advised the Prussian government in 1861 to introduce universal suffrage because 'in this system the conservative rural population can vote down the liberals in the cities'. In mid-nineteenth century Britain, competition between the landed class and industrial capital led to significant extensions of franchise for the working class.

For many centuries, Chinese high culture, language, and political and historiographical tradition have not given much scope to pluralism and diversity, and a centralizing, authoritarian Communist Party has carried on with this tradition. Jenner (1992) in his provocative book, analysing the link between the 'history of tyranny' and the 'tyranny of history' in China, describes one of the most basic tenets of Chinese civilization as 'that uniformity is inherently desirable, that conflict is bad, that there should be only one empire, one culture, one script, one tradition', and that 'what is local and different is treated (by the high culture) as deviant'. Nurtured in this tradition, it is no wonder that not merely the Party mandarins considered the voices of dissent and disturbances of Tiananmen Square as a dire threat to their continuing control of the state, but even many non-Party Chinese intellectuals genuinely felt them as a threat to order and stability in the country, which supercede most other social goals.

It is in the context of this preoccupation with order and stability and the quickness to brand dissenting movements and local autonomy efforts as seditious, that one sees some dark clouds on the horizon for China's future. Not merely has the fast pace of economic growth created many inequalities and job disruptions and dislocations, coastal China is moving far ahead of the inland provinces.[13] Those left behind are bound to get restive, particularly as fiscal decentralization has meant that the

---

[12] See Anderson (1972), p. 115.

[13] The province of Guizhou, for example, is as poor as Bangladesh in terms of per capita income.

lagging regions cannot depend on central transfers, and have to live with large cuts in community services.[14] These tensions of fiscal federalism are increasing in India too. The better-performing state governments are now openly protesting large redistributive transfers to laggard states ordained by the Finance Commission. In the Indian democratic system, however, some of these laggard states (like Uttar Pradesh or Bihar) send a very large number of members to the Parliament, and the (shaky) coalition governments at the Centre can ill afford to alienate them. In China, however, the hard budget constraint bites and the laggard regions are largely left to fend for themselves.[15] This, along with arbitrary levies on farmers by corrupt local officials and large numbers of workers laid off from failing state enterprises (where they see the on-going rampant asset-stripping by managers) has explosive potential for the future. All this has been openly acknowledged in a startlingly frank report on the widespread 'collective protests and group incidents', recently released by the organization department of the Central Committee of the Party, as reported in The *New York Times,* 3 June 2001.

Of course, the leadership is trying campaigns and exhortations to paper over the cracks, with nationalism slowly replacing socialism as the necessary social glue. At the same time, the Party is also slowly relaxing some of its rigid controls. It would be heretical to say this in China, but in many ways mainland China in recent decades may be in effect following in the footsteps of Taiwan. Taiwan also had a highly disciplined authoritarian (organized on similar quasi-Leninist lines) ruling party—the Kuomintang—presiding over a capitalist transformation, with party committees playing an important role in economic management of enterprises. Taiwan also had a very large state-owned sector, and instead of drastic large-scale privatization of this sector, they allowed the non-state sector (often in small industries) to grow and gradually eclipse the importance of the state sector. As the economy gathered momentum in high

[14] This may be partially responsible for the remarkable reversal in the decline in female infant mortality rates since the early 1980s.

[15] An econometric estimate by Jin et al. (2001) on the basis of a panel dataset from 29 provinces in China suggests that while in the period 1970–9 the central government extracted about 83 per cent of any increase in provincial revenue, in the period 1982–91, with the implementation of the 'fiscal contracting system' (*caizheng chengbao zhi*) the percentage fell dramatically to about 25 per cent, and to that extent the central government's capacity to transfer from high-revenue to low-revenue provinces declined.

growth the prospering middle classes started demanding political and civic rights and gradually won them, until Taiwan became a full-scale democracy only recently. Things may not be as smooth in this transition process in mainland China, and their preoccupation with maintaining order and stability may make them over-react to difficult situations, sometimes with disastrous consequences.

However, it is interesting to note that China has already started allowing for some competitive elections[16] (with secret ballot) at the village level (though not yet at the more important township level) as long as the Party monopoly is not seriously challenged. Even without elections the Chinese local officials have sometimes displayed more accountability to the villagers than in many parts of India. This is illustrated by a comparative case study of two villages, one in North India and another in Eastern China, in the field of primary education, carried out by Dreze and Saran (1995). To this day large parts of India do not have effective local democracy, and the delivery (and financing) of many vital public services for the poor is still in the hands of, often corrupt, officials of the state and central governments. In China, even though the local Party officials are centrally appointed, in some sense there has been more devolution of authority to local governments, and with more financial responsibility thrust on them. Not surprisingly, the poor under the financially strapped local governments of laggard regions are bearing the brunt. With the unfreezing of the labour market, migration is a possible way out, as is evident from the size of the migrant population in the cities (estimated in the range of 80 to 130 million people for China as a whole), but they do not have household registration (*hukou*) and are often discriminated against.

By all accounts in the last two decades, and even earlier, Chinese economic performance has been much better than that of India. In this brief paper I have tried to probe underneath the contrasting performance of these two vast countries and offer some very broad speculative hypotheses. Economic reform and commitment to long-run policies require hard collective decisions (and follow-up collective actions), and I have tried to trace the relative difficulty for India to take these decisions and actions to India's more heterogeneous society and conflict-ridden polity. But Indian heterogeneity and pluralism have also provided the

---

[16] Some reports of conflicts between these elected village leaders and village party secretaries suggest that these elections may not be entirely a facade.

basis for a better ability to politically manage conflicts, which I am not sure China's overarching homogenizing bureaucratic state has so far acquired, even though this ability is likely to be sorely needed in the future years of increasing conflicts inevitable in a fast-growing internationally-integrated economy with mounting disparities and tensions. I argue that this requires looking at deeper social and historical forces than simply refering to an aggregative comparison of an authoritarian and a democratic political regime.

REFERENCES

Anderson, M.S. (1972), *The Ascendancy of Europe, 1815–1914*, (London: Longman).

Bardhan, P. 1984 (1988), *The Political Economy of Development in India* New Delhi: Oxford University Press, (expanded edition, 1998).

Bardhan, P. (1993), 'Analytics of the Institutions of Informal Cooperation in Rural Development', *World Development*, vol. 21, no. 4, pp. 633–9.

Bardhan, P. and J. Dayton-Johnson (2001), 'Unequal Irrigators: Heterogeneity and Commons Management in Large-scale Multivariate Research', in National Research Council, *The Drama of the Commons*, (Washington, DC: National Academy Press).

Campos, E. and H.L. Root (1996), *The Key to the East Asian Miracle: Making Shared Growth Credible* (Washington D.C.: Brookings Institution).

Dreze, J. and M. Saran (1995), 'Primary Education and Economic Development in China and India: Overview and Two Case Studies', in K. Basu, P. Pattanaik, and K. Suzumura, eds, *Choice, Welfare, and Development*: A Festchrift in Honour of Amartya K. Sen (Oxford: Clarendon Press).

Gustafsson, B. and L. Shi (2002), 'Income Inequality Within and Across Counties in Rural China 1988 and 1995', forthcoming in *Journal of Development Economics*, vol. 69, no. 1, pp. 179–204.

Jenner, W.J.F. (1992), *The Tyranny of History: The Roots of China's Crisis* (London: The Penguin Press).

Jin, H., Y. Qian, and B.R. Weingast (2001), 'Regional Decentralisation and Fiscal Incentives: Federalism, Chinese Style', unpublished.

Keefer, P. and S. Knack (1997), 'Does Social Capital have an Economic Payoff? A Cross-country Investigation', *Quarterly Journal of Economics*, vol. 112, no. 4, pp. 1251–88.

Lal, D., R. Mohan, and I. Natarajan (2001), 'Economic Reforms and Poverty Alleviation: A Tale of Two Surveys', *Economic and Political Weekly*, vol. 36, no. 12, pp. 1017–28.

Lardy, N. (1998), *China's Unfinished Economic Revolution* (Washington, DC: Brookings Institution).

Lee, B.L. and D.S. Prasada Rao (2001), 'Comparisons of Purchasing Power, Real Output and Productivity of Chinese and Indian Manufacturing, 1952–1995', unpublished, Queensland University of Technology, Brisbane, Australia.

Montinola, G., Y. Qian, and B.R. Weingast (1995), 'Federalism, Chinese Style: The Political Basis for Economic Success in China', *World Politics*, vol. 48, no. 1, pp. 50–81.

Morris, C.T. and I. Adelman (1989), 'Nineteenth-Century Development Experience and Lessons for Today', *World Development*, vol. 17, no. 9, pp. 1417–32.

Oi, J.C. (1999), *Rural China Takes Off: Institutional Foundations of Economic Reform* (Berkeley: University of California Press).

Rodden, J. and S. Rose-Ackerman (1997), 'Does Federalism Preserve Markets', *Virginia Law Review*, vol. 83, no. 7.

Rodrik, D. (1999) 'Where Did All the Growth Go? External Shocks, Social Conflicts, and Growth Collapses', NBER Working Paper No. 6350, Washington, DC.

5

Government Failures: A Political Economy Perspective

Bhaskar Dutta

INTRODUCTION

The relative roles of the market and government in promoting social welfare has been an active topic of research and debate for several decades. Proponents of centralized planning argue that the market can fail to reach efficient outcomes unless the economy satisfies a set of very stringent conditions. However, empirical evidence indicates that many economies of countries which adopted centralized planning have also performed rather poorly, suggesting that there can also be instances of *government failure*.

Much of this discussion assumes that the government is *benevolent*, so that its sole objective is to maximize the welfare of the representative individual.[1] Of course, this *normative* view of government behaviour is an important tool of analysis. However, it can often be a sterile exercise if it completely ignores the institutional constraints and rigidities in which policy-making occurs. The presence of these constraints makes it important to analyse the *positive* theory of government behaviour, or in other words to explore what policies governments *actually* pursue, rather than the policies that they are supposed to follow.

The recent public choice literature discusses various political features which crucially influence government behaviour, and which drive a

I am most grateful to Sugato Dasgupta, Arunava Sen, and Rohini Somanathan for helpful discussions.

[1] An exception is Krueger (1990), who point out that 'political pressures often shape economic programs'. Datta-Chaudhuri (1990) also emphasizes the role of socio-political characteristics in influencing development processes.

wedge between what 'real' governments actually do and what a benevolent government would choose to do. Typically, political power is dispersed, either across different wings of the government, or amongst political parties in a coalition, or across parties that alternate in power through the medium of elections. The desire to concentrate or hold on to power will in general contribute to inefficient policies being implemented, that is to *government failure*.

For instance, lobbying by various interest groups together with the ruling party's wish to remain in power often results in policy distortions being exchanged for electoral support.[2] Several papers also emphasize the presence of political cycles in economic policy formulation. In the aptly named opportunistic models, policymakers are interested solely in maximizing their probability of surviving in office, so that the resulting character of government is very far away from the benevolence assumed by more traditional normative theories of government behaviour.[3] In contrast to opportunistic models, partisan models specify that political parties are almost exclusively concerned with furthering the interests of their own support groups.[4] There is also a sizeable and growing literature on special interest politics.[5] Again, the conclusions which follow from this class of models are very different from the benevolent government models.

This paper uses two simple models to illustrate how political factors can cause governments to choose inefficient policies in two different contexts. The first model focuses on the nature of the government. In particular, the rent-seeking behaviour of single-party and coalition governments is contrasted and it is shown that the latter will typically be more predatory. The framework used is one in which the incumbent government extracts rents to the maximum extent possible, subject to being re-elected—the incumbent wants to be re-elected because of the ego rents associated with being in power. However, if the ego rents have to be shared between the members of a coalition government, then each

[2] See Bardhan (1984) for an illuminating account of this process in the Indian context.

[3] Nordhaus (1975) was amongst the first to develop this class of political cycle models. See also Rogoff (1990) and Rogoff and Sibert (1988).

[4] See Alesina (1987).

[5] Grossman and Helpman (1996), Dixit and Londregan (1996, 1998), Lindbeck and Weibull (1987) constitute a small sample of this literature. See Persson and Tabellini (2000) for additional references.

party in the coalition will attach a lower weight to re-election. Hence, the total amount of rent extracted by coalition governments will be higher than the amount extracted by a single party government.

The second model compares the behaviour of an incumbent government under two different electoral systems. The incumbent has to choose levels of government expenditure in three identical regions. Since tax rates are fixed, voters in each region prefer higher levels of expenditure as these result in higher levels of employment. So, the incumbent earns additional goodwill amongst the voters in any region where it spends more than the expected level. However, given an overall budget constraint, higher spending in one region must be compensated by lower spending in some other region. In the latter region, it loses goodwill. Given these trade-offs, how will it allocate expenditure? Under the proportional system, where seats captured are proportional to votes won, the incumbent has no incentive to spend heavily in some regions at the expense of reduced spending in other regions. However, the electoral incentive in the first-past-the-post system is quite different. Under this system, the incumbent has an incentive to increase spending in a majority of regions by slashing expenditure in a minority of regions. This increases the incumbent's probability of winning a majority in the legislature. Hence, the latter system may well result in unbalanced development and exacerbate regional inequalities.

ELECTORAL ACCOUNTABILITY AND COALITION GOVERNMENTS

A possible interpretation of the electoral process is that the voters offer a 'contract' to the winning party or politician to administer them for a fixed term. The contract is renewed—that is, the incumbent is re-elected for another term—if a majority of the electorate is satisfied with the performance of the incumbent. As far as the incumbent is concerned, there is a cost in providing better governance. This cost could arise due to a variety of reasons. For instance, better governance may be possible only if the incumbent puts in more effort. Alternatively, the level of governance may be inversely related to the amount of rent extracted by the incumbent. So, if current performance had no bearing on future electoral prospects, then the incumbent would have no incentive to provide satisfactory administration. However, the incumbent prefers to be in power (possibly because of the scope for extracting some level of rents in the future), and so the threat of being voted out of office provides them with an incentive to provide better governance. Thus, elections act as an incentive device.

In this section, a simple model[6] is constructed to show that the threat of being voted out of power loses potency if the incumbent is a coalition government. Consider an economy in which there are two goods, a private good and a public good. The public good, which is produced by means of the private good, is supplied by the government. Assume that the production function (transforming the private good into the public good) satisfies constant returns to scale. With appropriate choice of units, one can also assume that one unit of the private good is converted into one unit of the public good.

The electorate consists of a continuum of identical individuals of unit mass. Each individual has pre-tax income y. The incumbent government has to decide on a level of public good provision and a tax rate. However, we will assume that the government has no flexibility in so far as the tax rate is concerned. For instance, the tax rate may have been announced as part of the pre-election platform of the parties constituting the government. Let T be the total government tax revenue. The government can use this to finance the provision of public goods. However, a fraction of government revenues can also be 'captured' by the parties constituting the government. This type of rent is best interpreted as the resources which are diverted to the party funds or possibly into the pockets of politicians of the ruling parties.

Letting g and R denote the quantities of public goods and aggregate rent, the government's budget constraint is given by:

$$g + R = T \tag{5.1}$$

The system also generates another kind of rent: an exogenous *ego rent* of E, which reflects the value of holding office. An important distinction between these two kinds of rent is that the ego rent does not enter the government budget constraint. If the government is made up of n parties, assume that these parties share the ego rent equally.

Assume that the parties together cannot extract more than the total government revenue as rent. So, If party i demands r_i and $\sum_{i=1}^{n} r_i \leq T$, then

[6] Persson and Tabellini (2000) use a similar model to illustrate the role of elections as a disciplinary device, but restrict attention to single-party governments.

each party i gets what it demands, while the remainder is spent on the provision of public goods. However, if the aggregate demands of the parties exceed T, then the parties have to be rationed. Assume that the demands are scaled down proportionately. Hence, letting $\bar{r}_i$ denote party i's share,

$$\bar{r}_i = \begin{cases} r_i & \text{if } \sum_{i=1}^{n} r_i \le T \\ \dfrac{r_i}{\sum_{j=1}^{n} r_j} T & \text{Otherwise.} \end{cases} \tag{5.2}$$

Notice that if the individual demands of the parties add up to more than T, then the entire government revenue is extracted as rent, and there is no public good provision.

Given any vector of rent demands $\mathbf{r} = (r_1, \ldots, r_n)$, let $g(\mathbf{r}) = T - \sum_{i=1}^{n} \bar{r}_i$.

Then, $g(\mathbf{r})$ represents the amount of public good produced.

While the voters do not care directly about the rent extracted, they do care about the amount of public good provided by the government. Following Persson and Tabellini (2000), I assume that the voters coordinate their voting strategies, and decide to re-elect the government, if public good provision does not fall short of a cut-off level $\bar{g} > 0$. Conversely, voters decide to punish the incumbent government if $g < \bar{g}$. Assume that this cut-off level is known to all political parties.[7]

The parties constituting the coalition government have to decide on the level of public good provision and the rent extracted by each party. Suppose that the n parties (simultaneously) announce the vector $\mathbf{r} = (r_1, \ldots, r_n)$. Then, $g(\mathbf{r})$ represents the level of public good produced. So, given any cut-off level $\bar{g}$, the incumbent is re-elected with probability one if $g(\mathbf{r}) \ge \bar{g}$, and is defeated with probability one if $g(\mathbf{r}) < \bar{g}$. Clearly, the individual payoffs to each party i corresponding to any vector of announcements $\mathbf{r}$ is given by:

[7] I will describe shortly how the voters decide on the level of $\bar{g}$.

$$\pi_i(\mathbf{r}) = \begin{cases} \dfrac{E}{n} + r_i & \text{if } g(\mathbf{r}) \geq \overline{g} \\ \overline{r_i} & \text{if } g(\mathbf{r}) < \overline{g}. \end{cases} \tag{5.3}$$

This has an obvious interpretation. If the demands of the parties are 'moderate', so that the quantity of public good produced does not fall short of the cut-off mark, then the incumbent is re-elected. In that case, the parties share the ego-rent E equally in the next period. Moreover, each party also gets r_i, the rent demanded in the current period.[8]

However, if $g(\mathbf{r}) < \overline{g}$, then voters punish the incumbent by defeating it in the next election. So, the incumbent parties do not get any share of the ego-rent R in the next period, and their payoffs are restricted to $\overline{r_i}$, the amount of rent they can extract in the current period. Note that $\overline{r_i}$ can be less than r_i if the aggregate demands exceed T.

Given any $\overline{g}$, we now have a well-defined normal form game in which the players are the incumbent parties. Each party can announce any non-negative rent demand not exceeding T. The payoffs corresponding to any vector of demands is given by (5.3). We now analyse the Nash equilibria of this game.

If there is more than one party in the government, then one Nash equilibrium is for each party to demand T. In this case, each party receives $\dfrac{T}{n}$. This is an equilibrium because no single party can deviate and ensure re-election of the government. Neither can a party extract a higher level of current rent, given the rent demands of the other parties.

However, this is not an 'interesting' equilibrium. In what follows, we focus attention on equilibria in which the incumbent government is re-elected. We call these *re-election equilibria*.

Definition: A *re-election equilibrium* corresponding to $\overline{g}$ is a vector of demands $\mathbf{r} = (r_1, \ldots, r_n)$ such that

(i) $g(\mathbf{r}) \geq \overline{g}$.

(ii) For all i, $\pi_i(\mathbf{r}) \geq \pi_i(r_{-i}, r'_i)$ for all r'_i.

The first part of the definition ensures that when parties' rent demands are given by $\mathbf{r}$, then the incumbent government is re-elected. The second part ensures that no party can ensure itself a higher payoff by a unilateral deviation to a different rent demand.

---

[8] Since $\overline{g} > 0$, the aggregate rent demands are strictly less than T, and so $\overline{r_i} = r_i$ in this case.

Let us call $\mathbf{r} = (r_1, \ldots, r_n)$ a *symmetric* re-election equilibrium if $\mathbf{r}$ is a re-election equilibrium with $r_i = r_j$ for all i, j.

Henceforth, we will restrict attention to symmetric re-election equilibria. Fix $\bar{g}$, and r_{-i}, an $(n-1)$-tuple of demands of all parties other than i. How should party i respond to these demands? Notice that it cannot be in i's interest to demand a level of rent which is too 'low'. In particular, it will never want to produce a level of public good which exceeds $\bar{g}$. If it chooses to get re-elected, it chooses $r_i = T - \bar{g} - \sum_{j \neq i} r_j$, ensuring a payoff of $\dfrac{E}{n} + r_i$. [9]

Alternatively, party i wants to maximize current rent and forego $\dfrac{E}{n}$. In this case, it demands T since $\bar{r_i}$ is strictly increasing in i's announcement. In this case, its payoff will be $\dfrac{T^2}{T + \sum_{j \neq i} r_j}$.

Hence, provided that $\sum_{j \neq i} r_j \leq T - \bar{g}$, i prefers re-election if

$$\frac{E}{n} + (T - \bar{g} - \sum_{j \neq i} r_j) \geq \frac{T^2}{T + \sum_{j \neq i} r_j} \tag{5.4}$$

Following Persson and Tabellini (2000), we also assume that voters choose the cut-off mark of public good so as to maximize their welfare.

Suppose that $\dfrac{E}{n} \geq T$. Then, voters should certainly set $\bar{g} = T$. Although parties cannot extract any current rent and gain re-election, an equal share of the ego-rent is still large enough for them to opt for re-election. For suppose all parties set $r_i = 0$. Then, all parties get $\dfrac{E}{n}$. This will still be a re-election equilibrium. To see this, note that if a party deviates and demands T as the rent, its payoff will still not exceed an equal share of the ego rent.

The following assumption ensures that the ego rent is small enough for there to be some rent extraction at a re-election equilibrium.

---

[9] Of course, this option may not be available if the aggregate demand of the other parties exceeds $T - \bar{g}$.

Assumption 1: $\dfrac{E}{n} < T$.

Voters do not want to choose $\bar{g}$ to be too high. If they do so and given that Assumption 1 holds, it may be in the interest of the parties to deliberately choose to be defeated at the next election in order to maximize current rent extraction.

On the other hand, the voters should not choose $\bar{g}$ to be too low. Clearly, $\bar{g}$ is an upper bound on the public good provision at a Nash equilibrium. Given the demands of the others, a re-election equilibrium must entail party i maximizing current rent extraction subject to producing $\bar{g}$. Hence, only $\bar{g}$ will be produced at a re-election equilibrium and nothing if parties deliberately opt to be defeated in the electoral contest in order to maximize current rent extraction.

How high can the voters set $\bar{g}$? We derive below the highest possible level of public good which can be produced at a symmetric re-election equilibrium. Thus, this specification of $\bar{g}$ seems to be the natural answer to the question posed here.

Let $r^* > 0$ be a solution to the equation:

$$\frac{E}{n} + r = \frac{(T)^2}{T + (n-1)r}. \tag{5.5}$$

We can rewrite this as:

$$Ar^2 + Br + C = 0, \tag{5.6}$$

where $A = (n-1)$, $B = \dfrac{(n-1)}{n} E + T$, $C = -T\left(T - \dfrac{E}{n}\right)$. Note that $A > 0$, $B > 0$, and $C < 0$. This ensures that there is one and only one positive solution for r in (5.6)—that is, r^* is well-defined and unique.

It is easy to check that:

$$r^* < \frac{T}{n}. \tag{5.7}$$

Choose g^* such that:

$$g^* + nr^* = T \tag{5.8}$$

It follows from (5.7) that $g^* > 0$.

Theorem: The unique symmetric re-election equilibrium corresponding to $\bar{g} = g^*$ is given by $r_i = r^*$ for all i. Moreover, the aggregate rent extracted at this equilibrium is strictly higher when the incumbent is a coalition equilibrium.

Proof: Suppose $\mathbf{r} = (r^*, \ldots, r^*)$. It follows from (5.8) that $g(\mathbf{r}) = g^*$. So, in order to prove the first part of the theorem, we only need to show that no party can gain by a unilateral deviation to any $r_i \neq r^*$.

Note that

$$\pi_i(\mathbf{r}) = \frac{E}{n} + r^* \tag{5.9}$$

Clearly, since $g(\mathbf{r}) = g^*$, a higher rent demand by i implies that the incumbent government will not be re-elected.[10] If party i prefers to maximize current rent extraction, then it should demand T. From (5.2) and (5.3), its payoff will then be $\dfrac{T^2}{T + (n-1)r^*}$. But, from (5.5), this equals $r^* + \dfrac{E}{n} = \pi_i(\mathbf{r})$. This shows that $\mathbf{r}$ is indeed a symmetric re-election equilibrium.

From the construction of r^* and g^*, it is also clear that there is no symmetric re-election equilibrium corresponding to any $\bar{g} > g^*$.

Persson and Tabelini (2000) show that the rent extracted by a single party incumbent government is $(T - E)$. We want to show that $r^* > \dfrac{T - E}{n}$.

Suppose $r_j = \dfrac{T - E}{n}$ for all $j \neq i$. We want to show that by demanding T, i can get a payoff which is strictly higher than $\dfrac{T}{n}$, which is the payoff that i will obtain by demanding $\dfrac{T - E}{n}$ and getting re-elected.

Indeed, when i demands T, then

$$\pi_i(r) \geq \frac{(T)^2}{T + (n-1)\left(\dfrac{(T - E)}{n}\right)} \tag{5.10}$$

Note that (5.10) follows because the right-hand side of (5.10) is the current rent that i can extract by demanding T. It is easy to check that right-hand side of (5.10) exceeds $\dfrac{T}{n}$. Hence, $\pi_i(r)$ exceeds the payoff

---

[10] Of course, we need not consider deviations to lower rent demands.

that i would get if $r_i = \dfrac{T-E}{n}$ was the demand of i at the re-election equilibrium.

This establishes that $r^* > \dfrac{T-E}{n}$.

The above proof also provides an intuitive explanation for the reason why current rent extraction is higher at the re-election equilibrium when the incumbent is a coalition government. While the single party government captures the entire ego-rent E, each party in the incumbent coalition government gets only the share $\dfrac{E}{n}$. So, re-election is a less attractive proposition for members of the coalition government. In particular, if the current rent demand is pegged at $\dfrac{(T-E)}{n}$ by each party, then it becomes profitable for a deviant party to demand T and maximize the current rent extraction. On the other hand, a higher current rent demand by each party sustains a re-election equilibrium for two reasons. First, it makes re-election more profitable. Second, it reduces the gain from deviating to a demand of T.

TACTICAL REDISTRIBUTION UNDER ALTERNATIVE ELECTORAL SYSTEMS

Several recent papers discuss the patterns of redistribution which emerge as a result of electoral competition.[11] In particular, competing parties may design electoral platforms or incumbent governments may choose policies so as to win the support of *swing voters*. These are voters who are undecided or indifferent between the two parties and are thus more easily won over. Hence, parties have an electoral compulsion to design policies or tactical redistribution programmes which are particularly attractive to the swing voters. These papers typically assume a given electoral system. The focus of this section is to compare the patterns of tactical redistribution programmes under two alternative electoral systems—the *proportional* and *first-past-the-post* (henceforth FPTP) systems.

In a parliamentary system, it is natural to assume that the objective of each party is to gain at least a majority of the seats in the legislature

---

[11] See, for example, Dixit and Londregan (1996, 1998), Lindbeck and Weibull (1987), and Grossman and Helpman (1996).

since that enables it to form the government. In a proportional system, the number of seats won is proportional to the number of votes captured by the party. This *linear* relationship between votes and seats implies that if there are several identical groups of voters, then a party has no incentive to favour one group at the expense of another.

The FPTP system leads to a completely different electoral calculus. Consider, for instance, a legislature which consists of three seats elected from three identical constituencies. A party can gain a *majority* of the seats by winning just over a *third* of the total votes polled. This can happen if it wins slightly more than half the votes on two of the constituencies and none in the third. While this is an extreme example,[12] it is clear that the relationship between votes won and seats captured is far from proportional under the FPTP system.

This in turn provides an incentive to incumbent governments to implement policies favouring some constituencies while neglecting others. For instance, in the example given above, the incumbent government may want to concentrate resources in *two* of the three constituencies since it is sufficient to win two seats to get a majority in the legislature. The unfortunate implication is that this may well result in an *unequal* utilization of resources.

In this section, I develop a simple model in order to verify this intuitive conclusion. The basic features of the model are easily described. Consider a 'country' which consists of three regions. Each region consists of a continuum of voters of unit mass. There are two political parties A and B. Suppose an election is held in every time period, so that the incumbent is in power for exactly one period unless it is re-elected. Without loss of generality, assume that B is the incumbent party. The *normal* level of government expenditure in each region is $\overline{g}$. However, the government has some discretion about the *actual* level of expenditure in any region, subject to the overall budget constraint. So, it can deviate slightly and implement projects so that total expenditure in region i is $\overline{g} + g_i$, where g_i £ e for some $e > 0$. Of course, the overall budget constraint implies that

---

[12] But, note that the Congress Party in India captured as many as 415 out of the 517 seats that it contested in the 1984 Lok Sabha elections, although it won only 48 per cent of the votes.

$$\sum_{i=1}^{3} g_i = 0. \tag{5.11}$$

Assume that the additional expenditure of g_i generates a goodwill of dg_i for the incumbent (party B) amongst voters in region i. This formulation represents the idea that voters in each region expect a level of expenditure of $\bar{g}$. However, higher government expenditure (not financed by additional taxation) is always welcome since it creates additional jobs and public goods. Conversely, a reduction of public expenditure below the norm of $\bar{g}$ incurs the wrath of the electorate. So, if $g_j < 0$, then the loss in goodwill amongst voters in region j is dg_j. I will assume that de, the maximum goodwill which can be generated by additional expenditure is bounded above by $\dfrac{1}{2}$.

Towards the end of any period, parties A and B also announce electoral platforms x_A and x_B respectively from some compact set X. This announcement takes place after the incumbent party has implemented expenditure levels $\bar{g} + g_i$ in each of the regions. Also, both parties observe these regional expenditure levels.

Voters have identical (continuous) utility functions over X. Let $u(x_A)$, $u(x_B)$ represent the levels of utility corresponding to platforms x_A, x_B, respectively. A voter in region i bases her decision of which party to support on the basis of the announcements x_A, x_B, the goodwill dg_i earned or lost by the incumbent B, as well as the ideologies of the two parties and the general popularity of the incumbent. Hence, voter j in region i votes for party A rather than B if

$$u(x_A) > u(x_B) + dg_i + \sigma_{ij} + \delta \tag{5.12}$$

Here, σ_{ij} measures the ideological bias in favour of party B of voter j in region i, while δ is the average popularity of party B in the population. Assume that σ_{ij} is uniformly distributed on $\left[-\dfrac{1}{2\phi}, \dfrac{1}{2\phi} \right]$ and δ is uniformity distributed on $\left[-\dfrac{1}{2\psi}, \dfrac{1}{2\psi} \right]$.

Suppose party B has implemented a particular vector of regional expenditure levels $(\bar{g} + g_1, \bar{g} + g_2, \bar{g} + g_3)$. Let us analyse the choice of electoral platforms x_A, x_B by the two parties under the two electoral systems. This requires identification of the swing voter in each region.

Since the swing voter is indifferent between the two parties, we must have

$$\sigma_j = u(x_A) - u(x_B) - dg_j - \delta, \qquad (5.13)$$

where σ_j denotes the ideological bias of the swing voter in region j. So, given (x_A, x_B), the share of votes won by party A in region j is given by

$$\pi_j^A (x_a, x_B) = \phi\sigma_j + \frac{1}{2}$$

$$= \phi[u(x_A) - u(x_B) - dg_i - \delta] + \frac{1}{2}. \qquad (5.14)$$

Of course, this is a random variable since the value of δ is not known when parties choose x_A, x_B. Party A's overall expected vote share is

$$\pi^A (x_a, x_B) = \frac{1}{3} \sum_{j=1}^{3} \pi_j^A (x_a, x_B). \qquad (5.15)$$

Let us first consider the parties' choices of x_A, x_B under the proportional system. Then, it makes sense to assume that each party's objective is to maximize the probability of winning at least 50 per cent of the votes.

The probability that party A will win at least 50 per cent of the votes is given by Prob $[\pi^A (x_A, x_B) \geq \frac{1}{2}]$. Using (5.11), (5.14), and (5.15), we get:

$$\text{Prob } [\pi^A (x_A, x_B) \geq \frac{1}{2}] = \text{Prob } [u(x_A) - u(x_B) \geq \delta] \qquad (5.16)$$

$$= \frac{1}{2} + \psi \ (u(x_A) - u(x_B)). \qquad (5.17)$$

Two points need to be noted about (5.17). First, notice that the pattern of g_i does not enter the equation. This is because each π_i^A is a *linear* function of dg_i. So, the effect of an increase in vote share in say region i due to higher government expenditure of γ is exactly offset by the effect of a decrease in vote share due to lower expenditure of γ in region j. Given the overall budget constraint represented by (5.8), this means that the incumbent government *cannot* allocate expenditure amongst the regions so as to increase the probability of electoral success. Hence, there is no reason to expect any unequal distribution of government expenditure to materialize under proportional voting.

Second, note that both parties will end up choosing that platform which maximizes u over X. Hence, the policy convergence will ensure that each party has an equal chance of winning a majority of the votes. Of course, this is not surprising—the model has been specified in such a way that the two parties are symmetric in every respect, except for the fact that B is the incumbent. But, since the incumbent cannot adjust regional government expenditure so as to improve its electoral prospects, the parties are symmetric in every relevant sense. This explains why the parties have an equal chance of capturing a majority of the seats in the legislature.

We now examine the parties' electoral prospects under the FPTP system. For every pattern of expenditure $g = (g_1 + \bar{g}, g_2 + \bar{g}, g_3 + \bar{g})$, we assume that each party i choose x_i given the choice x_j of the other party so as to maximize its probability of winning a majority of seats in the legislature.

Let $p_j(x_A, x_B | g_j)$ denote the probability that party A wins the seat in region j.

Then,

$$p_j(x_A, x_B | g) = \text{Prob} \left[\pi_j^A (x_A, x_B) \geq \frac{1}{2} \right]. \tag{5.18}$$

Notice that whatever the choice of x_B, party A maximizes $p_j(x_A, x_B)$ by choosing x^* where $x^* = \text{argmax}_{x \in X} u(x)$. Similarly, party B minimizes $p_j(x_A, x_B)$ by choosing x^* for each choice of x_A. Hence, irrespective of the choice of (g_1, g_2, g_3), both parties choose x^*. Hence, the (equilibrium) probability that A wins the seat in region j depends simply on g_j. Let $p_j (g_j)$ denote this probability. Using (5.14), we get:

$$p_j(g_j) = \text{Prob} [\phi (-dg_j - \delta) \geq 0] = \frac{1}{2} - \psi dg_j. \tag{5.19}$$

Equation 5.19, makes it clear that the choice of government expenditure will influence the probability of party A winning a seat in any given constituency, and hence it will also affect the overall probability of party A winning a majority of the seats in the legislature. Given any distribution $g = (g_1, g_2, g_3)$ satisfying the overall budget constraint, let $p_s(g)$ denote the probability that party A wins at least two seats in the legislature:

$$p_s(g) = p_1(g_1) p_2(g_2) + p_1(g_1) p_3(g_2) + p_2(g_1) p_3(g_2)$$
$$- 2p_1(g_1) p_2(g_2) p_3(g_3). \tag{5.20}$$

Clearly, the incumbent party B should choose g so as to minimize $p_s(g)$ subject to g satisfying (5.11).

Routine calculation yields that B should equate government expenditure in any two of the three regions. Without loss of generality, let $g^* = (g_1^*, g_2^*, g_3^*)$ be such that $g_1^* = g_2^* = k$ and $g_3^* = -(g_1^* + g_2^*)$. Making the necessary substitutions, we can write $p_s(g^*)$ with some abuse of notation as $p_s(k)$. Again, routine calculations yield:

$$p_s(k) = -4k(\frac{1}{2} - k)^2 + 2(\frac{1}{2} - k)(\frac{1}{2} + 2k) = \frac{1}{2} - 4k^3. \qquad (5.21)$$

Equation 5.20 shows that $p_s(k)$ *decreases* with k. This shows that the incumbent will exercise its discretion over regional expenditure to an extreme level—it will push up government expenditure as far as possible in two of the three regions, and balance its budget by cutting back expenditure in the third region. That is, we will have $g_1^* = g_2^* = \epsilon$, and $g_3^* = -2\epsilon$. That is, the distribution of government expenditure will be as unequal as possible given that the government cannot increase expenditure in any region beyond $\overline{g} + \epsilon$.

This model demonstrates another context where political institutions influence the nature of economic policies. In the process, the model illustrates once again the importance of a proper specification of political constraints in the analysis of government behaviour. Of course, these constraints will typically imply that government failure will be more endemic than is realized in the debate on 'market failure versus government failure'.

REFERENCES

Alesina, A. (1987), 'Macroeconomic Policy in a Two-Party System as a Repeated Game', *Quarterly Journal of Economics*, vol. 102, pp. 651–78.

Bardhan, P. (1984), *The Political Economy of India's Development* (Oxford: Basil Blackwell).

Datta-Chaudhuri, M. (1990), 'Market Failure and Government Failure', *Journal of Economic Perspectives*, vol. 4, pp. 25–39.

Dixit, A. and J. Londregan (1996), 'The Determinants of Success of Special Interests in Redistributive Politics', *Journal of Politics*, vol. 58, pp. 1132–55.

_____ (1998), 'Ideology, Tactics, and Efficiency in Redistributive Politics', *Quarterly Journal of Economics*, vol. 113, pp. 497–529.

Grossman, G. and E. Helpman (1996), 'Electoral Competition and Special Interest Politics', *Review of Economic Studies*, vol. 63, pp. 265–86.

Krueger, A.O. (1990), 'Government Failures in Development', *Journal of Economic Perspectives*, vol. 4, pp. 9–23.

Lindbeck, A. and J. Weibull (1987), 'Balanced Budget Redistribution as the Outcome of Political Competition', *Journal of Public Economics*, vol. 51, pp. 195–209.

Persson, T. and G. Tabellini (2000), *Political Economics: Explaining Economic Policy*, (Cambridge Mass.: MIT Press).

Nordhaus, W.D. (1975), 'The Political Business Cycles', *Review of Economic Studies*, vol. 42, pp. 169–90.

Rogoff, K. (1990), 'Equilibrium Political Business Cycles', *American Economic Review*, vol. 80, pp. 21–36.

Rogoff, K. and A. Sibert (1988), 'Elections and Macroeconomic Policy Cycles', *Review of Economic Studies*, vol. 55, pp. 1–16.

6

On the Notion of Optimality in Welfare Economics

David Fairris and Prasanta K. Pattanaik

INTRODUCTION

The notion of optimality is at the heart of welfare economics[1] and is an integral part of the conceptual foundation of a large literature relating to the role of the state in a market-based economy. In this paper, we analyse the formal structure of this concept; we also discuss how some components of this structure have been interpreted in diverse ways in welfare economics and the theory of social choice, and how this diversity gives rise to different notions of optimality. The analysis allows us to clarify some ambiguities and identify the differences in intuition that underlie certain debates on the role of the state.

The plan of the paper is as follows. In the second section, we discuss the structure of the general 'criterion of efficiency', and its special version in welfare economics, namely, the principle of Pareto optimality. Three distinct features of this structure are identified: the notion of a universal set of options, the notion of feasibility of options, and, finally, the notion of rankings of the options in terms of the relevant criteria. The third, fourth, and fifth sections respectively, discuss how these three aspects permit alternative interpretations; the fourth section also discusses how specific interpretations of the notion of feasibility of a social state

David Fairris would like to thank Lee Alston, Doug North, and John Weymark for initiating and sustaining his interest in the issues addressed in this paper. Prasanta K. Pattanaik would like to acknowledge his enormous intellectual debts to Wulf Gaertner, Amartya Sen, and Kotaro Suzumura.

[1] In this paper, we shall use the term 'welfare economics' so as to include the theory of social choice within its scope.

can have implications for one's views regarding the role of the state in the context of 'market failures'. Concluding remarks are presented in the sixth section.

THE GENERAL PRINCIPLE OF EFFICIENCY, AND ITS SPECIAL CASE, THE PRINCIPLE OF PARETO OPTIMALITY

THE GENERAL PRINCIPLE OF EFFICIENCY

Consider an agent who may be a single individual or a group of individuals, such as the society. Suppose, at different times, the agent has to choose from different sets of mutually exclusive, feasible options which are assessed by the agent in terms of a multitude of criteria. At any given point of time, the agent's problem of choice can then be formally characterized by the following basic features:

(i) the universal set of all conceivable (mutually exclusive) options, X = $\{x, y, z, \ldots \}$;

(ii) the set, A, of all options, which are feasible at the given point of time, A being a non-empty subset of X; and

(iii) a set of orderings, $H_1, \ldots, H_m$, over X, m being the number of 'criteria' used by the agent to assess the options, and the ordering H_t $(t = 1, \ldots, m)$ being interpreted as the ranking of the options in X in terms of the t-th criterion (for all options x and y in X, $x H_t y$ denotes that x is at least as good as y in terms of the t-th criterion).

Suppose, our agent is faced with a choice problem as specified above. We say that an option x in X *dominates* another option y in X if and only if x is at least as good as y in terms of every criterion t, and x is strictly better than y in terms of some criterion t'.[2] Further, given a non-empty subset B of X, we say that x belonging to B is *undominated in B* if and only if there does not exist y in B such that y dominates x. The notion of an alternative in the feasible set of options, which is undominated in the feasible set of options, leads us to *the principle of efficiency* (or, synonymously, *the criterion of efficiency*), which simply requires that the option chosen by the agent from the set of feasible options should be

---

[2] As usual, x is better than y in terms of criterion t if and only if $x H_t y$ and not $y H_t x$.

undominated in that set. At the risk of emphasizing the obvious, we would like to mention that the criterion of efficiency prescribes only a necessary condition for choice; it does not lay down any sufficient condition for the agent's choice.

Note that the formal framework of a choice problem, outlined above, is general enough to be able to accommodate a multitude of interpretations. For example, the framework can be interpreted in terms of the standard problem of multicriterial decision-making by an individual. Thus, X may be the set of all conceivable, 'perfectly certain', and mutually exclusive options, say, the set of all conceivable alternative careers for the individual under consideration; A may be the set of careers feasible for the agent; and the orderings may be the rankings in terms of the different criteria, such as pay, job satisfaction etc., that the agent uses to assess the alternative careers. Alternatively, the choice problem can be interpreted as an agent's problem of choice under uncertainty, in which case, the options are the alternative actions of the agent, n is the number of possible states of the world, and the ranking H_t is the agent's ranking of the actions, given the t-th state of the world. Yet another interpretation of the choice problem can be in terms of social decision-making (see the next sub-section). In this paper, we shall be concerned exclusively with the interpretation of the general choice problem in terms of social decision-making and the corresponding interpretation of the criterion of efficiency.

Note that, whatever the interpretation, if one accepts the characterization of the choice problem—namely the specifications of the universal set of options, the set of all feasible options, and the set of rankings of the options, interpreted as the rankings in terms of all the relevant criteria—then it is difficult to see how one can object to the principle of efficiency, that is, the requirement that the chosen option must be undominated in the set of feasible options. It is, of course, possible that one may object to the specification of the options in the choice problem or the specification of the set of feasible options as inappropriate. One may also object to the set of criteria for judging the options and the corresponding rankings of the options on the ground that the set of criteria considered includes inadmissible criteria or excludes some relevant criteria. However, if one does not raise any of these different types of objections to the specification of the choice problem, then the prescription coming from the efficiency criterion seems to be unexceptionable.

THE PROBLEM OF SOCIAL CHOICE

Much of welfare economics is concerned with a specific interpretation of the general problem of choice outlined in the previous sub-section, namely the interpretation in terms of social choice on the basis of individual preferences. Here the agent making choices is, of course, the society; the universal set of options is the set of all conceivable social states, the set of feasible social states at any given point of time being a non-empty subset of the universal set; and the relevant criteria for judging the social states are typically assumed to be the preferences of the individuals constituting the society so that the orderings defined over the universal set of options are the preference orderings, $R_1, \ldots, R_n$, of the individuals in the society, where n is the number of individuals . Given this interpretation, the notion of 'domination' is simply the standard notion of 'Pareto superiority' of one social state over another; and the notion of a feasible option that is undominated in the feasible set is simply the notion of a Pareto optimal social state. Then the general criterion of efficiency takes the specific form of the *principle of Pareto optimality* (PPO), which requires that, given the set of all feasible social states, the society should choose a Pareto optimal social state.

As we noted earlier, if one accepts the specifications of the options, the set of feasible options, the criteria for assessing the options, and the corresponding rankings of the options, then there can hardly be disagreement about the prescription that the option chosen from the feasible set must be undominated in the feasible set. Therefore, if there are objections to PPO, then it must be for one or more of the following reasons: (i) the interpretation of the social states is found unacceptable; (ii) the notion of feasibility of a social state is unacceptable; and (iii) the relevant criteria, the preferences of individuals, for judging the social states are found to be unacceptable or incomplete. In what follows, we discuss, under the three categories listed above, various concerns that have been raised in connection with PPO.

THE CONCEPT OF SOCIAL STATES

First, consider the notion of a social state. How does one specify a social state? One can take a very broad view of the social state, so that the specification of a social state includes the specification of 'every' relevant feature of the society over time (see Bergson 1938; Samuelson

1947). Alternatively, one can take a rather narrow view of a social state. For example, in the literature on the two basic optimality theorems and related issues, the social state is just an allocation, that is, a specification of a consumption plan for each consumer and a production plan for each producer (see Debreu 1959). The specification of an allocation in this sense does not tell us anything about the institutional arrangements in the society. In particular, in view of the considerable recent interest of welfare economists in rights and liberties as important criteria for assessing social well-being, it is worth noting that the specification of an allocation, as it is conventionally defined, does not give us any information about the rights and liberties enjoyed by the individuals in the society

The question then arises as to whether one should use a narrow conception of the social state as in the literature on the basic optimality theorems, or a more comprehensive conception of a social state—a conception that would include a description of the institutions in the society. The answer to this question would depend on our view of the value of institutions. There are two distinct issues relating to institutions, which need to be distinguished here. First, there is the issue of whether, in assessing the well-being of a society, institutions have any intrinsic importance independently of the outcomes that may be realized through them. Secondly, there is the issue of institutions being instruments for achieving specific outcomes. As we will discuss later, the purely instrumental role of institutions may be an important issue in deciding which outcomes are 'really' feasible, but, if institutions are no more than just instruments for achieving social outcomes defined in a narrow sense, then there would not be any need for incorporating the description of the institutions into the specification of a social state. However, not only do we care about social outcomes or social states in the narrow sense of the term, but we also often value institutions in their own right. The consumption bundles that the individuals in a society actually consume do matter for our assessment of social well-being, but so do the extent of each individual's freedom to choose his/her consumption bundle[3] as well

---

[3] The recent literature on the ranking of opportunity sets has developed around the idea that the set of options from which the agent makes his/her choice matters independently of the option actually chosen by the agent (see, among others, Jones and Sugden 1982; Sen 1987, 1991; Pattanaik and Xu 1990, 1999; Puppe 1996; and Sugden 1998).

as each individual's right to practise the religion of his/her choice.[4] Rights, liberties, and procedural fairness are examples of concerns which are basically related to institutions and their intrinsic value, and are not very well captured by a narrow definition of a social state as an allocation or, more generally, as an outcome in the conventional sense of the term.[5]

It is true that, even if welfare economists attach intrinsic values to certain institutions, they do not necessarily have to bring institutions into their analysis if what they happen to be interested in does not have any institutional implications. Thus, if we are concerned with the choice between an income tax and an excise tax or between a tariff and a quota, there may not be any reason to lumber ourselves with an unnecessarily broad notion of a social state involving the details of the rights structure, political institutions, etc. In such cases, the welfare economist can reasonably assume the institutions of the society to be given and to remain unaffected by the choice of a tariff over a quota or of the excise tax over the income tax. However, if economists are interested in comparisons of social well-being as between different societies, then institutions cannot be assumed to be fixed, and, in that case, if we believe that institutions embodying rights, freedom, procedural fairness, etc. are relevant for assessing individual and social well-being, then a framework focusing on narrowly defined social states turns out to be restrictive. Similarly, when one considers the effect of liberalization of a formerly planned or semi-planned economy, it may be unrealistic to assume that the social and political institutions will remain unchanged, and, in that case, it may be necessary to use a broader notion of a social state if one attaches intrinsic importance to such institutions.[6]

Assuming that we want to use a broad notion of a social state that will incorporate a description of institutions, how does one capture the institutional features in our model? One possible way of modelling

[4] It is Sen's (1970a, 1970b) pioneering contributions that, in welfare economics, first emphasized the importance of individual rights in assessing social welfare.

[5] The conventional notion of an outcome typically does not incorporate the features of the mechanism or the institution through which the outcome is realized.

[6] For some illuminating comments on what we call the broad notion of a social state, see Arrow (1963, pp. 90–1). Following the basic idea suggested in these comments, Pattanaik and Suzumura (1996) have developed a detailed formal structure of the theory of social choice.

institutions is to visualize them as game forms.[7] For example, game forms have been extensively used by many social choice theorists to model the structure of rights in a society.[8] However, for our purposes, the following very simple way of incorporating institutions into the analysis will suffice. Let S denote the class of all conceivable social outcomes defined in the narrow fashion, and G denote the class of all conceivable institutional structures. Then $S \times G$ is the universal set of social alternatives interpreted in a broad sense.

The basic intuitive point we wish to make is that, for many normative points of view, a narrow definition of a social state can be severely inadequate, and, therefore, the notion of Pareto optimality developed in this framework may have limited appeal in such contexts. In such cases, one would like to capture, besides other features such as the allocation, the specification of the institutional structure in the description of the social state.

THE FEASIBILITY OF SOCIAL STATES

In the context of the normative problem of social choice, PPO prescribes that the society must choose a Pareto optimal social state, a social state x being defined to be Pareto optimal if and only if it is feasible and there does not exist any other feasible alternative y which is Pareto superior to x. Thus, the application of PPO presupposes that one has identified the set of all feasible alternatives from which the society is to make a choice. However, the notion of feasibility is by no means straightforward, and some of the debates centre precisely around the issue of what constitutes the feasibility of a social state. In this section, we focus on this issue.

THE CONCEPT OF A FEASIBLE ALLOCATION

To start with, assume that our sole concern is with allocations (as defined in the standard theory of general equilibrium), and that nothing beyond allocations matters for social well-being. Thus, we are in the

---

[7] Intuitively, a game form is the formal structure that we are left with when we discard, from the specifications of a game, the specifications of the players' preferences. For the definition of game forms, see Osborne and Rubinstein (1994, pp. 178–9 and p. 201).

[8] For models of rights as game forms, see Gardenfors (1981), Sugden (1985), Gaertner et al. (1992), and Pattanaik (1994).

domain of 'conventional' welfare economics where a social state is simply an allocation. Recall that, in the classical literature on the two optimality theorems of welfare economics, an attainable or feasible allocation is defined to be an allocation where the consumption bundle of each consumer belongs to his/her consumption set, the production plan of each producer belongs to that producer's production set, and the total amount of each commodity consumed by all consumers is equal to the total amount of that commodity figuring in the production plans of all the producers plus the total initial endowment of that commodity. Thus, the definition of an attainable or feasible allocation is entirely based on a *physical* concept of feasibility that does not take into account anything more than the constraints imposed by the technologies of the producers, the constraints represented by the consumption sets of the consumers, and, finally, the constraint that the total consumption of each commodity must be equal to the total available amounts of that commodity.

Note that this notion of feasibility does not ask the question whether there exists any known institutional structure that is capable of achieving the allocation. In order to distinguish this notion of feasibility from other possible notions of feasibility, in what follows, we shall call an allocation that is feasible in the physical sense (that is, in the sense of Debreu 1959, outlined above) a *feasible* (Type I) allocation. A feasible (Type I) allocation such that no other feasible (Type I) allocation is Pareto superior to it will be called Pareto optimal (Type I), and the principle of Pareto optimality based on the notion of feasibility (Type I) of allocations will be called PPO (Type I). Thus, PPO (Type I) prescribes that the society should choose a Pareto optimal (Type I) social state.

We know that, given the assumptions underlying the first optimality theorem of welfare economics, a competitive equilibrium allocation will be Pareto optimal (Type I), that is, a competitive equilibrium allocation will be feasible (Type I), and there will not exist another feasible (Type I) allocation which would be Pareto superior to the competitive equilibrium allocation. We also know that, when we discard certain assumptions, such as the existence of complete markets and perfect information, this result no longer holds necessarily, and we may have 'market failure'. What exactly is the significance of such market failure? What such market failure implies is that, as compared to the competitive equilibrium allocation α, there exists some other *physically feasible* allocation α' that can make some consumers better off without making any consumer worse off.

However, an important question that needs to be raised here is the following: Is there any institutional structure that can achieve this physically feasible allocation α', and, more generally, is there any institutional structure that can achieve an allocation that is Pareto superior to α? Given that any institutional structure must confront the information imperfections and incompleteness of markets characteristic of this competitive equilibrium, and must devote resources which would otherwise be used for direct production to overcoming such problems, it is not clear why α' or any other feasible (Type I) allocation which is Pareto superior to α will be necessarily achievable through some institutional framework. Suppose, moreover, that, although the competitive equilibrium allocation α is Pareto inoptimal (Type I),[9] one also cannot conceive of any other institutional arrangement that can achieve an allocation which is Pareto superior to the competitive equilibrium allocation. Then, it seems to us that the competitive equilibrium allocation is not inoptimal in any significant intuitive sense, even though, according to our formal definition, it happens to be Pareto inoptimal (Type I). The point is this: The fact that the competitive equilibrium allocation is Pareto inoptimal (Type I) only means that the market mechanism has, in some sense, failed to attain the full *physical* potential of the society. However, this can hardly be the basis of an indictment of the market mechanism in terms of the Pareto criterion, if one cannot think of any institutional set-up, which, in similar circumstances, can possibly improve the situation in the sense of Pareto.

To illustrate, consider the failure of the market in the presence of classical Pigovian externalities. We know that externalities are really examples of the non-existence of markets for certain relevant commodities (see Arrow 1969). We also know that the non-existence of a market is often due to the high cost of acquiring the information necessary for identifying the users of the relevant commodity and the extent of their use of the commodity, as well as the cost of excluding those who would not pay the price. Thus, when there is market failure because, for example, the use of chemical fertilizers in fields pollutes the sources of drinking water, analytically one can identify the problem with the non-existence of a market for this effect on the drinking water. One possible reason for the

[9] A social state is said to be Pareto inoptimal (Type I) if and only if it is not Pareto optimal (Type I). Similarly, we shall also talk of Pareto inoptimality (Type II).

non-existence of such a market may be the high cost of gathering the information about whose use of fertilizer pollutes the water, and to what extent—information which is essential if the relevant market is to come into existence. However, if that indeed happens to be the problem, how does one overcome the problem without using valuable resources to collect the relevant information and/or to enforce the optimal use of fertilizer by the relevant producers? For example, proposing the institution of a Pigovian tax-subsidy scheme to correct the failures of the market mechanism raises the issue of how the state collects the information necessary for devising the Pigovian tax-subsidy scheme and how the state enforces such a scheme. If valuable resources have to be used for collecting such information and to enforce the scheme, then, like the free market mechanism, the combination of the tax-subsidy scheme and the market mechanism will also fail to achieve a Pareto optimal (Type I) allocation. Moreover, it is possible that, in the presence of the costs of information and enforcement, no Pigovian tax-subsidy scheme will be able to attain an allocation that is Pareto superior to the initial competitive equilibrium allocation. If every possible institutional structure that one can think of fails to achieve an allocation which is Pareto superior to the competitive equilibrium allocation, then one can plausibly argue that the Pareto inoptimality (Type I) of the competitive equilibrium allocation, in itself, is not a reason for serious worry about the market mechanism.

This basic criticism of conventional market failures analysis—that the Pareto inoptimality (Type I) of the competitive equilibrium under conditions of incomplete markets or imperfect information tells us nothing about whether this equilibrium can be improved upon—is acknowledged (if not as clearly as one might like) in both the property-rights/transaction-costs literature (for example, Coase 1960; Demsetz 1969) and in the literature on the new institutional economics (for example, Stiglitz 1985). However, in neither of these literatures do we find a careful treatment of the notion of optimality under conditions of incomplete markets or imperfect information, nor, as a consequence, a consistent answer to the question of whether the competitive equilibrium can be improved upon. Thus, many property-rights/transaction-costs economists incorrectly conclude that the competitive equilibrium under incomplete markets or imperfect information is necessarily optimal, whereas some practitioners of the new institutional economics incorrectly conclude that the competitive equilibrium under such circumstances is necessarily inoptimal.

In the property-rights/transaction-costs literature, the argument regarding efficiency in the context of imperfect information or incomplete markets often starts with the valid point that, if the competitive equilibrium allocation happens to be Pareto inoptimal (Type I), then it must be due to the presence of transaction costs, since, in the absence of these costs, the agents could always move out of the Pareto inoptimal allocation by voluntarily engaging in mutually beneficial trade. However, from this it is often concluded that, even though the competitive equilibrium allocation may be Pareto inoptimal (Type I), since there does not exist any further possibility of mutually advantageous voluntary trade among the agents, there is no genuine inoptimality. The question that arises here is why the exhaustion of all possibilities of mutually advantageous trade in the basic framework of the market system should be considered to be a criterion of 'genuine' efficiency or optimality. This presupposes that private negotiations and exchanges constitute the only available institutional structure for attaining an optimal allocation.[10]

Consider the type of externality created when every household in a town sweeps out the household garbage onto the street in front of the house. In this case there may not be any difficulty in getting the information about who is littering the street, and to what extent. Despite this, private negotiations and agreement may not come about because of the cost of negotiation to reach an agreement among a large number of individuals. However, the state with its coercive powers *may* find it much less costly to enforce an anti-litter law. In that case, state intervention *may* be able to achieve an allocation, which, even if it is not Pareto optimal (Type I), is Pareto superior to the allocation that can be attained in the absence of such state intervention. Thus, simply because, given the transaction costs and costs of collecting information, all possibilities of further mutually advantageous trade between private parties have been exhausted, it does not necessarily follow that no modification of the institutional framework of free markets, property rights, and private negotiation and trade can ever bring about an allocation that is Pareto superior to the allocation that will be achieved in the absence of such

---

[10] Alternatively, it presupposes that the other background institutional arrangements are already efficient, presumably based on some (unexplained) mechanism for the selection of efficient institutions. Oliver Williamson's approach to institutions often displays this characteristic. For a criticism of Williamson on this point, see Dow (1987).

modification. An equilibrium allocation α, that results from the exhaustion of all mutually-advantageous exchanges, is not necessarily optimal when optimality is redefined with reference to allocations which are institutionally, as well as physically, feasible [see below the definition of what we call 'Pareto optimality (Type II)'].

By the same token, nor is it the case that the competitive equilibrium allocation a, characterized by imperfect information or market incompleteness, is necessarily inoptimal, as is maintained in the famous Greenwald–Stiglitz Theorem (1986), which claims that competitive equilibrium outcomes of this sort can always be improved upon by the actions of government. To illustrate their argument, consider the case of moral hazard and insurance. The problem with the existence of insurance is that the insured have inadequate incentive to prevent the occurrence of the event they have insured against. For example, those who possess health insurance may take less than adequate care of their physical well-being, by, say, smoking and partaking of too much alcohol. By providing the insured persons protection against unfavourable outcomes, the system of insurance may adversely affect their incentive to take suitable precautions. The central insight of Greenwald and Stiglitz is that a simple government tax on cigarettes and alcoholic beverages can lead to an improvement in welfare: the efficiency gain by the reduced 'moral hazard' will more than offset the efficiency loss (that is, deadweight loss) due to the distortionary taxes.

What seems to be overlooked in this analysis, however, is the resource cost of devising and administering these taxes. State intervention does not take place in a vacuum: virtually every form of state intervention requires scarce resources to ensure its actual implementation. Further, the state functions through individual human beings, and their motivations and incentives need to be considered in determining whether state intervention can achieve an allocation not achievable by the system of free markets in a private ownership economy. Although the quantity will vary with the set of institutional arrangements proposed, a certain amount of valuable resources must be devoted to addressing the problems created by informational asymmetries, no matter what institutional mechanism is proposed as a possible solution. If the opportunity cost of the resources required for government intervention outweighs the benefits thereby attained, the free market competitive equilibrium under conditions of asymmetric information or incomplete markets may well be optimal when optimality is redefined with reference to allocations which are institutionally, as well as physically, feasible [see below the definition of what we call 'Pareto optimality (Type II)'].

Now let us be clear about the precise meaning we attach to the term 'optimal' in our discussions above. It is clear that we do not have in mind here the notion of Pareto optimality (Type I), but rather an alternative formulation of the notion of Pareto optimality based on an alternative notion of a feasible allocation. Under this alternative formulation, an allocation α will be called feasible (Type II) if and only if it is feasible (Type I) and there exists some institutional structure that can achieve it;[11] and an allocation α can be called Pareto optimal (Type II) if and only if it is feasible (Type II) and there does not exist any other feasible (Type II) allocation α' which is Pareto superior to α. It seems to us that, when social states are simply allocations, the really meaningful formulation of the efficiency criterion in the context of social choice is that the society should choose a Pareto optimal (Type II) allocation rather than that the society should choose a Pareto optimal (Type I) allocation. Note that this involves a comparative search for the set of institutional arrangements that results in a Pareto optimal (Type II) allocation.

To summarize, in the conventional literature on market failure, the fact that a competitive equilibrium allocation is Pareto inoptimal (Type I) tells us nothing about whether it can be improved in the sense of Pareto. The presumption in that literature that it is *always* possible to achieve a Pareto superior feasible (Type I) allocation through an alternative

---

[11] One point may be worth noting here. The set of feasible (Type I) allocations can be determined without any reference to individual preferences over the allocations; this is because the notion of feasibility (Type I) is an entirely physical notion of feasibility. In contrast, when we consider the notion of feasibility (Type II), not only do we take account of the physical feasibility of the allocation under consideration, but we also consider whether there exists any institutional set-up through which the allocation can be attained. However, the attainability of a physically feasible allocation through any given institutional structure may not be independent of the preferences of the individuals. To take a straightforward example, an allocation may be a competitive equilibrium allocation in a private-ownership economy for some orderings, $R_1, \ldots, R_n$, of the consumers but not if the consumers' orderings happen to be, say, $R'_1, \ldots, R'_n$. Thus, it follows that the set of feasible (Type II) allocations may depend on the preferences of the individuals in the society though the set of feasible (Type I) allocations is independent of such preferences. For a detailed discussion of this point, when institutions are visualized as game forms, see Pattanaik and Suzumura (1996).

institutional framework, usually assumed to be some combination of government intervention and the market mechanism, is almost certainly incorrect because valuable resources must be devoted to overcoming the information imperfections or market incompleteness that are the basic cause of the Pareto inoptimality (Type I). The appropriate formulation of the question of the existence of a Pareto superior alternative is whether there exists a Pareto superior alternative that is feasible (Type II).

Both property-rights/transaction-costs economists and those economists associated with the new institutional economics movement appear to be aware of this basic criticism of conventional market failures analysis. However, neither tradition extends the analysis of efficiency in the context of market incompleteness or information imperfections in a convincing way. The claim by many property-rights/transaction-costs economists that whatever equilibrium allocation is reached through the free market mechanism cannot be improved upon is as misleading as the counter-claim made in the new institutional economics literature that every such competitive equilibrium allocation can be improved upon through clever state intervention. The essential inadequacies of both these traditions arise from the same source: neither of them possesses an adequate treatment of institutions, and especially an adequate analysis of the benefits and costs of state intervention in the functioning of the market mechanism. Once again, the appropriate formulation of the question of existence of a Pareto superior alternative is whether there exists a Pareto superior alternative that is feasible (Type II).

THE FEASIBILITY OF SOCIAL STATES INTERPRETED IN A BROAD SENSE

Suppose we interpret the notion of a social state in a broad sense so that $S \times G$ is the set of social states. Under this interpretation, a typical social state is an ordered pair (s, g), where s is a narrowly defined social outcome and g stands for the set of institutions. As in the case of allocations, one can say that (s, g) belonging to $S \times G$ is feasible (Type I) if and only if s is physically feasible and g represents a possible institutional structure; and that (s, g) is feasible (Type II) if and only if (s, g) is feasible (Type I) and s can be attained through g.[12] If we have individual

---

[12] We have deliberately left undefined the notion of the attainability of s through g. This is because it is not possible to provide a precise definition of this concept in

preference orderings defined over $S \times G$ (see the next section), then we can formulate, in terms of such orderings, definitions of Pareto optimality (Type I) and Pareto optimality (Type II) of an ordered pair (s, g) belonging to $S \times G$; such definitions will be analogous to the definitions of Pareto optimality (Type I) and Pareto optimality (Type II) of an allocation in the preceding section. For reasons similar to those discussed earlier, here also we believe that Pareto optimality (Type II) is a more fruitful notion of optimality for the elements of $S \times G$, that is, for social states interpreted in a broad fashion.

THE CRITERIA FOR EVALUATING SOCIAL STATES

Irrespective of how one interprets the social alternatives, there remains the issue of the set of criteria on the basis of which these alternatives are to be judged in assessing their social desirability. Traditionally, in welfare economics, narrow interpretations of social states (often visualized as allocations) have been combined with an acceptance of the individuals' preferences with respect to these social states as the exclusive basis for judgements about social welfare, the individual preferences being interpreted in terms of desire fulfilment. Since the narrowly defined social states do not contain information about the institutions, the framework itself is rather ill suited for articulating any concern that one may have for institutional features such as the rights of individuals, their freedom of choice, and procedural fairness. However, even when one does not attach any intrinsic values to institutions, one can still object to the position where individual preferences over the narrowly defined social states constitute the sole basis of social assessment of these alternatives.

Suppose that the social states are interpreted as allocations. Institutions do not have any intrinsic value, and every allocation that is feasible (Type I) is also feasible (Type II). One can think of possible objections to PPO (Type I) even under these stipulations. Consider a situation where there are exactly two feasible (Type I) allocations, α and α' and everyone in the society strictly prefers α to α'. It is possible to argue for social

the absence of a specific formal model of institutions, and, in this paper, we have not committed ourselves to any such formal model. For a definition, when institutions are formally modelled as game forms, see Pattanaik and Suzumura (1996).

Note that, as in the case of an allocation (see fn. 11 above), the feasibility (Type II) of (s, g) may also depend on individual preferences; the example given in fn. 11 can be readily adapted to illustrate this.

choice of α' over α, if, for example, α is characterized by a much greater degree of inequality (measured in some acceptable fashion) of distribution than α'. Should the greater degree of inequality matter if everybody in the society really prefers α to α'? Is it not paternalistic to say that, even though everybody in the society strictly prefer α to α', the society should choose α' because α' is a more egalitarian allocation?

It seems to us that, to some extent, the answer depends on what exactly we mean when we say that everybody strictly prefers α to α', that is, on the interpretation of the preference orderings used in defining Pareto optimality. Suppose these preference orderings reflect the 'self-interests' of the individuals, but their moral values attach a very high weight to the degree of equality prevailing in the society. Then α can be Pareto superior to α' when Pareto superiority is defined in terms of individual preferences based on self-interest, while α' can be Pareto superior to α when Pareto superiority is defined in terms of their morality-based preferences. It is not entirely obvious that one should necessarily take the individual preference orderings based on their self-interests as the basis for social judgement or that it is necessarily paternalistic to take people's moral judgements, rather than their preferences based on self-interest, as the basis of social choice.[13] In general, welfare economics has not always paid adequate attention to the fact that the same individual may have different types of preferences, that the appeal of basing social choice on individual preferences may depend on the exact nature and content of these preferences, and that it is not necessarily paternalistic to argue that one type of preferences of an individual may be a more appropriate basis of social choice than another type of preferences of the same individual.

A different objection to PPO (Type I) is based on the endogenous nature of individual preferences. Individual preferences over social states are often moulded by the social states that prevailed in the past (see Gintis 1974; Sen 1987, p. 11), and, in such cases, the sanctity of such endogenously determined individual preferences as the basis of social choice may be in doubt. For example, if the individual preferences, which underlie the notion of Pareto optimality (Type I) of competitive equilibrium allocations, are themselves the consequence of the initial distribution of property rights or of the institution of the market mechanism

---

[13] This is, of course, reminiscent of Harsanyi's (1953, 1955) well-known distinction between subjective and ethical preferences. See also Sen's (1977) distinction between the aggregation of individual interests and individual judgements.

itself, then the principle of Pareto optimality (Type I) based on such preferences may not appear as compelling as it would be otherwise. While this line of reasoning does have some validity, it is, however, not clear whether one can ever find any type of individual preferences which are completely 'exogenous'. Rejection of all individual preferences on the ground that almost invariably individual preferences, however interpreted, are to some extent endogenous, would seem to be as imprudent as completely uncritical acceptance of whatever individual preferences may have resulted from the social states that prevailed in the past.

So far in this section, we have interpreted social states in the narrow sense. How do we visualize the criteria for the social evaluation of the social states when $S \times G$ is assumed to be the universal set of social states? One can, of course, assume that every individual has a preference ordering over $S \times G$, and then define PPO (Type I) as well as PPO (Type II) in terms of these preference orderings over $S \times G$. However, when institutions matter, and, therefore, social states are interpreted as elements of $S \times G$, one can pose the problem of social choice somewhat differently and, in that context, visualize a version of the principle of efficiency that does not take the form of the principle of Pareto optimality. We illustrate this with the help of an example. Suppose, each individual i ranks the elements of S in terms of an ordering R_i that simply reflects the ordinal desires of individual i. Simultaneously, assume that the only aspect of the institutional structures belonging to G which are of interest are the different degrees of freedom that these institutions offer to the different individuals, and that, for each individual i, we have an ordering T_i over G, where, for all g and g' belonging to G, $(g\ T_i\ g')$ denotes that g offers to i at least as much freedom as g'.[14] Then, given that we have n individuals in the society, there are $2n$ orderings: $R_1, \ldots, R_n, T_1, \ldots, T_n$. For every individual i, let P_i denote the strict relation 'better than' corresponding to R_i and let V_i be the strict relation 'offers more freedom than' corresponding to T_i.[15] We can then formulate a version of the efficiency principle as follows:

the society must choose an element (s, g) of $S \times G$, such that (s, g) is feasible (Type II) and there does not exist a feasible (Type II) element, (s', g'), of $S \times G$ such that [for all i in $\{1, 2, \ldots, n\}$, $s'\ R_i\ s$ and $g'\ T_i\ g$] and ([for some i in $\{1, 2, \ldots, n\}$, $s'\ P_i\ s$] or [for some i in $\{1, 2, \ldots, n\}$, $g'\ V_i\ g$]).[16]

---

14 See the literature on the ranking of opportunity sets, referred to earlier in fn. 3.

15 More formally, P_i and V_i are, respectively, the asymmetric factors of R_i and T_i.

In our example, we have singled out freedom as the only relevant institutional feature that is of intrinsic value. However, one can have an analogous formulation of the efficiency principle, given any set of well-specified institutional features which generate rankings over $S \times G$. It is clear that the principle of efficiency formulated in this fashion will be different from the principle of Pareto optimality in so far as it would be based on rankings generated by criteria other than the preference orderings of the individuals in the society.[17]

CONCLUDING REMARKS

The main points that we have tried to make in this paper may be summarized as follows. First, the principle of Pareto optimality is a specific interpretation of the principle of efficiency. The latter seems unexceptionable, once one accepts the specification of the options, the definition of feasible options, the specification of the criteria for assessing the options and the orderings of the options in terms of these criteria. Therefore, objections to the principle of Pareto optimality can arise only if one has objections to: (a) the specific notion of a social state, or (b) the notion of feasibility of social states, or (c) the individual preferences as the sole basis of the assessment of social states.

Second, a narrow concept of social states which does not include institutional specifications may prove too restrictive if we attach intrinsic

---

[16] From a strictly formal point of view, the formulation of the efficiency principle here is not quite tight. This is because the orderings $R_1, \ldots, R_n$ are defined over S and the orderings $T_1, \ldots, T_n$ are defined over G, while, in our formulation of the efficiency principle in the second section of the paper, the rankings underlying the efficiency principle are defined over the universal set of options (note that, in the present case, $S \times G$ is the universal set of options). However, this is not a serious problem. Given the orderings, $R_1, \ldots, R_n$, over S one can define orderings, $R^*_1 \ldots, R^*_n$, over $S \times G$, such that, for every individual i and for all (s, g) and (s', g') in $S \times G$, $(s, g) R^*_i (s', g')$ if and only if $sR_i s'$. Similarly, given the orderings, $T_1, \ldots, T_n$, one can define orderings, $T^*_1, \ldots, T^*_n$, over $S \times G$, such that, for every j in $\{1, 2, \ldots, n\}$ and all (s, g) and (s', g') in $S \times G$, $(s g) T^*_j (s', g')$ if and only if $gT_j g'$. The efficiency principle can then be formulated in terms of the orderings $R^*_1 \ldots, R^*_n$, $T^*_1, \ldots, T^*_n$.

[17] Note that, insofar as individual preference orderings will be a basis (if not the sole basis) of any reasonable formulation of the criterion of efficiency in the context of social choice, the difficult issues relating to the type of individual preferences that one should take into account and the possible endogenous nature of individual preferences, however interpreted, are likely to arise under all such formulations.

values to institutional features, such as rights, freedom of choice, and procedural fairness.

Third, one can distinguish between two types of feasibility of a social state: feasibility (Type I) which refers to 'physical' feasibility only, and (ii) feasibility (Type II), which, in addition to physical feasibility, takes into account the achievability of the physically feasible outcome through an institutional set-up. Intuitively, the notion of Pareto optimality (Type II), based on feasibility (Type II) of a social state, seems more appealing than the notion of Pareto optimality (Type I), based on feasibility (Type I). However, an effective use of the notion of Pareto optimality (Type II) requires careful analysis of alternative institutions; the absence of such analysis is often a major lacuna in the literature on the efficiency of the market mechanism.

Fourth, in the context of social choice, individual preferences based on self-interest may be inadequate as the (exclusive) basis for the principle of efficiency.

REFERENCES

Arrow, K.J. (1963), *Social Choice and Individual Values*, second edition (New York: Wiley).

Arrow, K.J. (1969), 'The Organization of Economic Activity: Issues Pertinent to the Choice of Market versus Non-market Allocation', in Joint Economic Committee, United States Congress, *The Analysis and Evaluation of Public Expenditures: The PPB System*, vol. 1 (Washington, DC: Government Printing Office).

Bergson, A. (1938), 'A Reformulation of Certain Aspects of Welfare Economics', *Quarterly Journal of Economics*, vol. 52, no. 2, pp. 310–34.

Coase, Ronald (1960), 'The Problem of Social Cost', *Journal of Law and Economics*, vol. 3, pp. 1–44.

Debreu, G. (1959), *Theory of Value* (New York: Wiley).

Demsetz, Harold (1969), 'Information and Efficiency: Another Viewpoint', *Journal of Law and Economics*, vol. 12, no. 1, pp. 1–22.

Dow, G.K. (1987), 'The Function of Authority in Transaction Cost Economics', *Journal of Economic Behavior and Organization*, vol. 8, no. 1, pp. 13–38.

Gärdenfors, P. (1981), 'Rights, Games and Social Choice', *Noûs*, vol. 15, no. 3, pp. 341–56.

Gaertner, W., P.K. Pattanaik, and K. Suzumura (1992), 'Individual Rights Revisited', *Economica*, vol. 59, no. 234, pp. 161–77.

Gintis, H. (1974), 'Welfare Criteria with Endogenous Preferences', *International Economic Review*, vol. 15, no. 2, pp. 415–30.

Greenwald, B. and J.E., Stiglitz (1986), 'Externalities in Economics with Imperfect Information and Incomplete Markets', *Quarterly Journal of Economics*, vol. 101, no. 2, pp. 229–64.

Harsanyi, J.C. (1953), 'Cardinal Utility in Welfare Economics and in the Theory of Risk Taking', *Journal of Political Economy*, vol. 61, no. 5, pp. 434–5.

_____ (1955), 'Cardinal Welfare, Individualistic Ethics, and Interpersonal Comparisons of Utility', *Journal of Political Economy*, vol. 63, no. 4, pp. 309–21.

Jones, P. and R. Sugden (1982), 'Evaluating Choice', *Review of Law and Economics*, vol. 2, no. 2, pp. 47–65.

Osborne, M.J. and A. Rubinstein (1994), *A Course in Game Theory* (Cambridge, Mass.: The MIT Press).

Pattanaik, P.K. (1994), 'On Modelling Individual Rights: Some Conceptual Issues', in K.J. Arrow, A.K. Sen, and K. Suzumura, eds, *Social Choice Re-examined* (London: Macmillan).

Pattanaik, P.K. and K. Suzumura (1996), 'Individual Rights and Social Evaluation: A Conceptual Framework', *Oxford Economic Papers*, vol. 48, no. 2, pp. 194–212.

Pattanaik, P.K. and Y. Xu (1990), 'On Ranking Opportunity Sets in Terms of Freedom of Choice', *Recherches Economiques de Louvain*, vol. 56, no. 3–4, 383–90.

_____ (1999), 'On Ranking Opportunity Sets in Economic Environments', mimeograph; forthcoming in *Journal of Economic Theory*.

Puppe, C. (1996), 'An Axiomatic Approach to "Preference for Freedom of Choice"', *Journal of Economic Theory*, vol. 68, no. 1, pp. 174–99.

Samuelson, P.A. (1947), *Foundations of Economic Analysis* (Cambridge, Mass.: Harvard University Press).

Sen, A.K. (1970a), *Collective Choice and Social Welfare* (Amsterdam: North-Holland).

_____ (1970b), 'The Impossibility of a Paretian Liberal', *Journal of Political Economy*, vol. 78, no. 1, pp. 152–57.

_____ (1977), 'Social Choice Theory: A Re-examination', *Econometrica*, vol. 45, pp. 53–89.

_____ (1987), *The Standard of Living* (Cambridge: Cambridge University Press).

_____ (1991), 'Welfare, Preference and Freedom', *Journal of Econometrics*, vol. 50, no. 1–2, pp. 15–29.

Stiglitz, Joseph E. (1985), 'Information and Economic Analysis: A Perspective', *Economic Journal*, vol. 95 (supplement), pp. 21–41.

Sugden, R. (1985), 'Liberty, Preference and Choice', *Economics and Philosophy*, vol. 1, no. 2, pp. 213–29.

_____ (1998), 'The Metric of Opportunity', *Economics and Philosophy*, vol. 14, no. 2, pp. 307–37.

7

Markets versus State: A Sterile Controversy?

Dilip Mookherjee

INTRODUCTION

Mrinal Datta-Chaudhuri, or MDC as he has been known through generations of successive Delhi School of Economics students, first introduced me to the modern literature on growth, development, and information economics. It was the year 1976: at that time the compulsory subject of 'Planning and Policy' in the first year of the MA curriculum was team taught by a variety of professors, eventually leading up to an exposition of the various five year plan models. MDC went early in the sequence, laying the groundwork for the theory of development planning, as it was then known. He delivered eight or nine lectures, spanning Rosenstein-Rodan's big push theory, Scitovsky's 1954 article on externalities, surplus labour, and Harris–Todaro style migration models. This was a wide new world for me. I was struck by the logical connection between development economics and resource allocation theory that we had learnt in our microeconomics classes: I saw that it was possible to discuss development issues analytically using microeconomic tools. I remember spending long hours in the library reading well beyond the list of prescribed readings: numerous articles about the foundations of development economics, from classics like Lewis, Ranis-Fei, and Sen, to more modern treatments of surplus labour such as Dixit, Lefeber, and Marglin, and of development planning from Chenery to Chakravarty. Lacking the requisite theoretical grounding, I found it difficult to absorb it all. Some of the models incorporated microeconomic resource allocation as well as growth, capital, and dynamics, while the plan models were remarkably sparse of any behavioural or institutional content. Later in the year, when we got to the plan models part of the course on which others professors lectured, we were referred to turnpike theory that was supposed to provide the behavioural foundation of the input–output models. In these planning models, the social planner knew the technology and could decree any level of output he or she wanted in any sector of the economy, as long as it satisfied the material balance conditions imposed by the technology. We suspended our scepticism and focused on passing the course exams.

MDC came back later in the macro sequence and delivered an elegant series of lectures on growth theory, built around the Solow model. This was conceptually more straightforward, and the logic was linear, though its connection with the world outside our windows was more tenuous. Turnpike theory was however too advanced for the class—it was a compulsory class after all, rather than an elective—and so we continued to remain in the dark about the foundations of the five year plan models.

The following year I approached MDC for help in suggesting a line of research that I could propose in my application for an Inlaks scholarship. I was interested in the microeconomics of development. He suggested I read the new literature on asymmetric information and what it was doing to neoclassical price theory, particularly the work of Akerlof and Stiglitz. He gave me a copy of Akerlof's 1970 article on the market for lemons, and the QJE 1976 symposium, containing papers by Akerlof on caste and the rat race, Spence on job market signalling, Jaffee and Russell on credit rationing, and Rothschild and Stiglitz on equilibrium non-existence in insurance markets. This was a new world, but one that I could relate to much better. While the models were absurdly simple, they dealt with phenomena one saw around oneself in India all the time, manifest imperfections of the market mechanism that bore no relation to the pristine textbook world of traditional resource allocation theory.

This potpourri of ideas and literatures whetted my appetite for trying to understand underdevelopment in terms of market imperfections, stemming from underlying informational and enforcement problems. It was my extraordinary luck to win an Inlaks scholarship to the London School of Economics, where George Akerlof had just been appointed to the Cassell chair. MDC and Akerlof happened to be chums from their MIT graduate student days, so MDC wrote to George and arranged for him to be my advisor. And I was launched on a journey to explore the meaning of underdevelopment as market failure and coordination failures of various sorts, and what they implied for the role of the state in the development process.

I started my thesis trying to model Scitovsky's (1954) idea of pecuniary externalities arising from missing markets and asymmetric information, and the role of a government in ensuring coordination of investment plans across industries. I ended up with a piece that bore only a passing resemblance to the original question, which I never published. A large part of the problem was to explain why certain financial markets were missing, and especially so in developing countries, as Scitovsky had originally suggested. This remains one of the thornier questions even today in general equilibrium theory; Acemoglu and Zilibotti (1997) made a substantial advance on formalizing related ideas only a few years ago.

Later, in collaboration with Charles Kahn, I worked on general equilibrium models with imperfect information, which produced unemployment, effective demand problems, Keynesian multipliers, dual economies and so forth (Kahn and Mookherjee 1988), many of which I had first come across in MDC's courses at the Delhi School. The *ad hoc* assumption of sticky wages of Keynesian macro models, fix-price general equilibrium theory of the Dreze–Benassy kind, and dual economy development models of the 1960s could finally be avoided, while retaining some of their conclusions concerning the efficacy of state interventions. This was the era of implicit contract and efficiency wage theory, of which there were many exponents: Azariadis (1983), Grossman and Hart (1983), and Shapiro and Stiglitz (1984) being the best known. Bulow and Summers (1986) explored some of their policy implications, and were perhaps the first to point out that these models provided support for interventionist policies of all sorts. Greenwald and Stiglitz (1986) and my papers with Kahn developed this theme further. It seemed then that the theoretical basis for an activist state in developing countries was just around the corner.

An alternative route was via imperfect competition. Hart (1982) and Weitzman (1982) constructed general equilibrium models of imperfect competition which exhibited Keynesian features. This was developed further by Shleifer (1986) in his thesis, by Basu (1984) in his book on the less-developed economy, and eventually the well known Murphy–Shleifer–Vishny (1989a, 1989b) models of coordination failure formalizing Rosenstein-Rodan's big push ideas.

Yet this promised theory of development planning failed to materialize. Prescott and Townsend (1984) had meanwhile published an extension of the classical welfare theorems concerning the invisible hand to asymmetric information contexts. Using an alternative, rather esoteric formulation of markets for lotteries over incentive compatible contracts, they showed that the results relating Pareto efficient allocations and competitive equilibria continued to hold. Prescott came one summer to the Stanford Summer Institute and presented a paper with Andrew Hornstein showing how this construction could be applied to the model I had developed with Kahn. So there were two alternative formulations of competitive equilibria of the same asymmetric information economy, with entirely different implications for the role of government policy! It was all very confusing, and Kahn and I subsequently embarked on a project trying to understand the sources of this discrepancy. As MDC remarks in his 1990 *Journal of Economic Perspectives* article, the state–market debate continued to remain unsettled.

MDC's 1990 article refers to this literature as 'sterile'. What have we really learned from this literature? Where does one go from here, then? MDC's answer is to engage in comparative analysis of actual development experiences of different countries, which he illustrates in the article with a comparison of Indian and Korean development in the last half century. The answer, he suggests, involves an understanding of the political economy of these two respective societies. It also involves changing our perception of the role of market institutions—not as a set of decentralized price signals that permit resource allocation, nor as a Lange–Lerner–Hurwicz information exchange mechanism, but rather as a set of credible rewards and penalties around economic activities. And the activities that matter for development involve learning about new markets and technologies, becoming cost and quality conscious, in which the state has an important role to play as facilitator. Whether and how it discharges this role is a matter of political economy, of the interest groups that control or influence state policy, and the extent to which their interests are aligned with the broader development of that society.

From the perspective of a theorist, this is a far distance from the earlier literature in development economics that MDC had taught and the profession practised just a little over a decade ago. His 1990 article is replete with examples and anecdotes. While unsatisfying in the lack of a theoretical framework that helps organize the new thinking—MDC explicitly rues that 'social scientists do not as yet have the tool-kit to explain these differences satisfactorily, but it is not difficult to see how the dominance of the landed aristocracy in the political economy of the Philippines hindered the creation of a dynamic capitalist economy' (1990,

p. 36)—it is rich in institutional detail, and reads more like an essay in comparative politics rather than neoclassical economics.

Indeed, this exemplifies a shift in the thinking and research of mainstream economists. Subsequent to the appearance of MDC's article, we have witnessed a resurgence of models of inequality, political economy, governance and institutions in what is perhaps becoming the dominant research paradigm in development economics today. This currently ongoing literature attempts to develop the analytical tool kit whose absence was mentioned by MDC, and to empirical applications to understanding comparative development experience. Egged partly by the dismantling of the Soviet bloc in the late 1980s, and the worldwide shift to market mechanisms with privatization, deregulation, and globalization being the contemporary buzzwords in policy circles worldwide, attention has shifted considerably away from the normative and theoretical market versus state debate. There is almost a consensus among economists of different ideological hues on what the appropriate role of the state ought to be in developing countries. No longer is there any argument about the virtues of public enterprise dominating the commanding heights of the productive sector of the economy. Even large chunks of infrastructure are being privatized and deregulated. The traditional role of the state in these sectors has been redefined to the status of a regulator and facilitator, besides filling in the gaps left by the private sector. The shift in state priorities is towards redistribution and the social sector: social security, education, health, sanitation and so on. More fundamentally, it is towards creating good governance institutions. From a descriptive standpoint, then, the key question is understanding what MDC posed as: 'Can a government be relied upon to do the "right" thing and avoid doing the "wrong" thing? It is impossible to give a context-free answer to this question.' (1990, p. 38).

On reflection, the shift in thinking in a little over two decades is truly amazing. How did this new-found consensus emerge? Was the old market versus state debate truly sterile, focused on the wrong questions, using a flawed approach? Is there nothing to be learned from that literature? In particular, should we continue to teach it to our students? If it was sterile, what was the root cause?

This essay provides me an opportunity to reflect on these questions. While identifying some sources of 'sterility' in the old literature, I will argue that the old literature (suitably interpreted) is actually complementary to the new literature, rather than a substitute: there is no paramount inconsistency between them. Indeed, they represent two faces of the same coin. Specifically, the theoretical–normative market-versus-state literature provides a fairly clear set of areas of the economy subject to 'market failure', defined as areas where the government has an important *potential* role to play. Whether and how the government actually discharges this role is the other side of the coin—that of 'government failure', where matters of positive political economy and related institutions are paramount. In this context, normative analysis is treacherous (as MDC reminds us frequently in the 1990 article). Clearly, explaining actual development experiences of different countries will involve understanding the political economy and governance institutions of those respective societies, as the source of actual differences in the role played by the state. Whatever scope for normative analysis there is concerns the role of underlying institutions that affect the nature of governance—which is the most important factor in the development process, even in market-based economies. The role of good governance in the functioning of a market economy has of course been stressed in the treatises of Alice Amsden and Robert Wade on East Asian industrialization. The highlight has been intensified by the transition woes faced by Russia and the Eastern European countries in the 1990s, as well as the structural problems faced by many of the poorest African countries. If there is scope for normative prescriptions, it is at the level of constitutional and institutional design, embracing fundamental political, administrative, legal, and media reforms.

THE TRADITIONAL MARKET FAILURE PARADIGM

In accounting for this shift in terms of a natural progression from the logic of the traditional market failure paradigm, it is appropriate to recount the way that the question has traditionally been posed. First, one describes the outcome of a decentralized market economy by a suitable notion of equilibrium (Walrasian equilibrium, or Nash equilibrium, or core). Then the following question is asked: is this equilibrium constrained Pareto-efficient? In other words, could a benevolent central planner, subject to the same resource, technology, information, and enforcement constraints as market agents in the decentralized economy, be able to effect a Pareto improvement (whereby somebody could be made better off without making anybody else worse off)?

Three aspects of this question need to be noted at the outset. The benevolent central planner is obviously a fiction, a mere benchmark.

Not only must such a planner act in the best interests of society, it must also have unlimited computational abilities of a kind that is clearly unrealistic, as Hayek and von Mises pointed out repeatedly in the context of the famous 1930s debates on socialism. To which Lange, Lerner and Hurwicz retorted with the possibility of decentralizing the computational task of the central planner via iterative communication mechanisms. Nevertheless the central planner has been seen as a theoretical benchmark, representing an upper bound to what real governments might possibly achieve. If the market economy turns out to be constrained efficient, that is a strong indictment indeed, since it says that the market achieves the very best that a government may conceivably achieve in terms of Pareto efficiency.

Second, imposing equivalent constraints on the central planner as those faced by market agents is crucial in ensuring a level-playing-field comparison. If the central planner is assumed to have access to superior technology than market agents, it is obvious that the government would be ahead in the race. More important, the theory does not explain the source of the difference in access to technology that forms the basis for the differential performance: why does one mode of economic organization have a technological advantage? There may be many reasons to expect that the performance of market firms with respect to fostering and implementing technological change is vastly different from that in a socialist economy. But if this is true, one would like the theory to be able to explain it. Indeed, much of the usual explanation rests in terms of behaviour and related incentives of agents to conduct research and development (R&D), develop new products, and assimilate new technologies under the two respective systems—all of which is what the theory ought to be able to explain. What is meant by 'technology' obviously pertains to a broader notion of technological opportunity, which is commonly available to different economic systems at any given point of time. The same goes also for information and enforcement capabilities, an issue to which we will return in more detail below.

Third, the normative criterion employed is Pareto-efficiency. This excludes any welfare judgments concerning redistribution, as well as various non-welfarist criteria based on freedoms and entitlements. The idea is to separate issues of the size of the social pie from the way it is distributed. However, a correspondence between the notion of Pareto efficiency with measures of collective income or wealth such as per capita income or consumption obtain only under restrictive assumptions concerning the existence of feasibility of monetary transfers or compensations. I shall argue shortly that in most realistic settings such transfers are not feasible; accordingly the normative criterion is hopelessly weak and fails to accommodate commonly held notions of collective welfare that are implicit in many policy discussions. And the 'sterility' of the debate owes partly to the use of this criterion.

Having described the nature of the question posed, turn now to the answers provided by the theory. The first classical theorem asserts that competitive (Walrasian) equilibria are Pareto efficient, provided the following assumptions hold: (a) there are a complete set of markets; (b) there are no (technological) externalities or public goods; (c) there are no significant economies of scale; (d) there are no asymmetries of information or problems in enforcing contracts. Each of these assumptions represents a potential source of failure of the theorem to apply. Whether they amount to market failure is however not obvious, as one has to re-examine the question afresh whenever there is a departure from this pristine set of assumptions.

TECHNOLOGICAL EXTERNALITIES

Suppose that a factory emits smoke which affects neighbouring residents. Or that the cows of one farmer stray into the fields of other farmers, trampling upon the latter's crops in the process. Common property resources are frequently overexploited in the tragedy of the commons. In urban metropolitan areas, millions of commuters decide whether to drive to work rather than take public transport, the collective implications of which affect emission of greenhouse gases that cause local smog and delete the earth's ozone layer. These forms of interdependencies across decisions of different agents in a decentralized economy are not mediated via markets. Self-interested behaviour fails to incorporate the wider social implications of such decisions. Consequently, Walrasian equilibria fail to be Pareto efficient. As Pigou argued, there appears to be a compelling case for the state to step in and levy corrective taxes in order to restore efficiency. This is the basis of the common view that the state has a role in regulating or taxing externalities: every market economy needs environmental, safety, and land use regulations. Moreover, similar externalities arise in the process of technological diffusion and learning, suggesting the role of the state in encouraging these in developing countries.

This orthodoxy came to be challenged by Coase in his celebrated 1960 article on the problem of social cost. The narrower version of this critique came to be encapsulated in the form of the so-called Coase Theorem, which was based on restrictive assumptions concerning the existence of monetary side-transfers. Coase argued that in a decentralized society, neighbours would efficiently resolve disputes resulting from externality-causing activities amongst themselves, without any need for state interventions in the form of corrective Pigouvian taxes. All that is needed is for property rights to be well-defined and enforced by the courts. Indeed, the Theorem asserts that in the presence of monetary side-transfers, the ultimate outcome would not just be Pareto efficient, but also independent of the exact manner in which property rights are defined. If the cattle owner has the right to let his cows wander, the wheat farmer whose crops get trampled will bribe the cattle owner in order to prevent such intrusions. Otherwise, the cattle owner will bribe the wheat farmer to earn the right of letting his cows stray. Property rights affect distribution of welfares across agents, without affecting externality-causing decisions. Accordingly, to ensure efficiency, it suffices for the state to play the role of 'nightwatchman' and enforce property rights, nothing more.

The broader version of the Coase Theorem that applies in the absence of existence of monetary side transfers is less sharp: in that case property rights may affect externality-causing decisions. But the outcomes still happen to be Pareto efficient; in that sense there is still no market failure. The Pareto efficiency result is actually a tautology, as it holds under the assumption of 'zero transaction cost', the definition of which is actually in terms of ensuring that the outcome is Pareto efficient. These transaction costs include the cost of communicating, negotiating, and enforcing an agreement between the concerned parties. The idea goes back to Edgeworth's notion of a 'contract', a binding agreement between a number of parties, which makes no reference to prices or markets. The logic is absurdly simple: the outcome of such an agreement could not be Pareto inefficient; otherwise the parties could write a different agreement which makes all of them better off.

The Coase objection in its broadest sense amounts to questioning the suitability of Walrasian equilibrium as a valid description of the functioning of a decentralized economy. Agents do not just react to impersonal price signals and interact with one another solely through organized markets. They search, contact, and make 'deals' with one another directly, on whatever terms they happen to negotiate with one another and find mutually agreeable. Some would consider this to be a truer description of a decentralized economy. Organized markets can be entirely bypassed. And even if organized markets for certain commodities do not exist, agents can make up for this deficiency with suitable bilateral or multilateral trading agreements. Since externalities are after all a manifestation of missing Lindahl markets (as pointed out by Arrow 1970), the Walrasian depiction of economic interaction is simply too narrow. Many public goods are organized and provided within the private sector by voluntary associations: coordination problems with respect to overgrazing or overharvesting of common property resources are frequently regulated by cooperatives or other forms of self-governing local groups. Ostrom (1990) and others have emphasized that such community organizations have traditionally managed common property resources quite successfully; instead, it is intervention by the state that has frequently undermined local voluntary cooperation and (particularly in the case of poorly informed and administered states) led to a tragedy.

How does one model voluntary contract formation? Edgeworth formulated the notion of the *core*, an allocation which is stable with respect to the formation of any contract among any coalition of agents in the economy. In the usual formulation of this notion, *any* coalition is free to form and go its own way. This embodies the extreme assumption of zero transaction cost. In this extreme form, it tautologically follows that every core allocation must be Pareto efficient, since if it were not so, the grand coalition of all agents in society would form and shift to a Pareto improving contract.

This alternative version of a decentralized economy must therefore satisfy the first Welfare Theorem by definition. Accordingly, it is worthwhile to ask whether and when this version is more plausible than the Walrasian one. The notion of voluntary agreements between coalitions seems plausible at the level of a small number of agents that happen to be located close to one another: neighbours, or even small local communities that voluntarily create mutual agreements and associations to regulate externality-causing activities within the neighbourhood. Even there, some communities and neighbourhoods appear to be better organized than others, and some not at all. What determines the efficacy of local collective action with respect to management of common property resources is a topic which has seen a fair amount of research, both theoretical and empirical, in recent years (stimulated by the classic work on the logic of collective action by Olson 1965). Bargaining even between a single pair of agents is subject to problems of asymmetric information concerning the relevant costs and benefits of the externality, resulting in possible breakdowns of agreement. In larger groups, characteristics such as group size, socio-economic heterogeneity, and existence of enforcement mechanisms, besides many others, are key determinants of their success. Groups that are large and heterogeneous typically have a harder time organizing and regulating themselves. These are clear manifestations of non-trivial transaction costs, that are excluded by the definition of the core.

When it comes to externalities that transcend local neighbourhoods and communities, the scope for voluntary agreements to spontaneously regulate these activities seems even more remote. Many environmental externalities are national and even global in nature. It seems absurd to think of commuters in any reasonably sized metropolis voluntarily agreeing to a common code of behaviour embodying self-restraint in the use of private transportation. Even if all parties could somehow get together in one place and at one time to negotiate such a multilateral agreement, the enforcement of such an agreement would be doomed: how would compliance be monitored and penalized if necessary, in the absence of a state-like coercive mechanism? And in the case of environmental goods such as climate change, the lives of future generations are at stake—the fact that they do not occupy the planet at the same time as current generations physically prevents them from offering any Coasian bribes to the latter. How can such externalities be regulated without the state acting on behalf of the interests of unborn generations?

The ability of decentralized behaviour to efficiently resolve externalities thus depends on the seriousness and magnitude of these transaction costs, which vary widely with the context. Many of these transaction costs also afflict state action. How does the government acquire the information concerning costs and benefits to know what corrective regulations or taxes are appropriate? How does it monitor and enforce these regulations? Collective policing of individual behaviour, and coercive enforcement of sanctions can limit the nature of free-riding within voluntary coalitions. But it introduces other hazards: poorly informed and designed regulations might do more harm than good; these problems are exacerbated by corruption of government inspectors that frequently accompanies state regulation. There is, therefore, a need to compare the respective transaction costs of either organizational mode. Indeed, this is essentially what is involved in resolving the appropriate domains of markets and the state.

Nevertheless, in answering the original market failure question, recall that the comparison was between markets and an ideal, benevolent government both subject to the same resource constraints and technological opportunities, including those involving monitoring and enforcement. Costs that pertain to potential governance failures are not supposed to be factored in. One, therefore, needs to separate technological from behavioural sources of transactions cost.

Ultimately, of course, the comparison must involve realistic models of the market as well as of the government, in particular an assessment of their respective behavioural transaction costs. Much of the research on institutions and governance in the last two decades deals with precisely this question. While this literature has focused more on the boundaries between firms and markets, similar principles are involved in the market–state controversy. And we are very far from a general theory in this respect, with much of the analysis being very specific to given contexts. This is essentially what makes it all very unsettled and contentious, with proponents of either mode failing to convince the other.

Returning to the market failure question, which does not necessitate an assessment of the governance hazards of state action, we need to focus on the likely ability of decentralized coalitions to successfully resolve externality problems. If at all there is scope for generalization in this respect, it pertains to the size and scope of the externality. When it comes to externalities spanning countries and generations, it is unlikely that voluntary contracts between concerned parties will be effective. In addition, economies of scale with respect to information gathering, monitoring of behaviour, and enforcement of sanctions further tip the balance in favour of state action. Voluntary agreements may be more effective in regulating externalities whose scope is purely local in nature, limited to agents located within a narrow geographic area and at the same point of time.

From this standpoint, then, one would assess that the following areas would be prone to market failure, where there is the *potential* for useful state intervention: regulation of the environment whenever its scope extends beyond a local community, regulation of safety of products used by large numbers of consumers, workers, or patients, and of patterns of land-use and traffic in large metropolitan communities. Activities with public good characteristics would also be included in this list: defence, law and order, public health, flood control and large scale irrigation systems, and scientific and technological research, to name a few. There is also a potential role for the government in aiding the diffusion of new technologies, which involve significant learning spillovers, such as agricultural extension services, and marketing and infrastructural services of value to large number of farmers or small industrial units. The governments of many successful market economies have traditionally played a significant role in all of these activities, and developing countries today would be no exception.

ECONOMIES OF SCALE

As Alfred Chandler (1977, 1990) has reminded us with his pioneering historical work on industrial capitalism in the USA and other developed countries, economies of scale and scope are the essential characteristic of modern capitalism. While this was particularly so in the heydey of manufacturing, and somewhat attenuated in today's world of information technology, even this sector continues to be dominated by Microsoft, Intel, AOL and so on. Some of the largest business corporations in the world are bigger than the entire economy of many mid-sized countries, and markets for many commodities and services are dominated by a few giants with considerable market power. Infrastructure areas such as transport, power, and communication are similarly dominated by large multinational entities that are exploring global markets. This is very far from the world of atomistic competition that the originators of competitive equilibrium theory were thinking about.

Murphy, Shleifer, and Vishny (1989a) have argued in their influential paper that economies of scale of infrastructure are characterized by economy-wide pecuniary externalities of the sort that Rosenstein-Rodan (1943) and Scitovsky (1954) had originally written about. Is this the appropriate context to think about development planning? How did the early industrializing countries overcome these coordination problems? Essentially through the creation of private industrial conglomerates which spanned many diverse lines of business, including upstream infrastructure and downstream industrial products. Such conglomerates have dominated the industrial economy of South Korea and Japan as well.

This returns us back to the Coasian point. Industrial conglomerates are a manifestation of the benefits of coordinated action across diverse lines of business. The same pecuniary externalities which motivate mergers and conglomerates in the private sector are the ones which may justify a 'big push' by the state. How then are we to draw a line to distinguish between the two?

It may be argued that there are some significant economy-wide externalities that will be insufficiently incorporated in the decision-making activities of large firms. First, there are limits to the extent of consumer surplus that can be extracted by firms, even those with a great deal of market power. This stems from the heterogeneity of customer needs and abilities to pay for their products and the impossibility of firms regulating the resale of their products by consumers. Consequently consumers will still be able to appropriate a large part of economic surplus from industrial goods; these consumer surpluses will be affected by business decisions of large firms involving product, technology, and pricing choices. This is the familiar monopoly distortion: firms with market power will tend to overprice their products. And as Arrow argued in his famous 1962 article on the economics of R&D, this implies a tendency for firms to engage in too little R&D, as a large part of the benefits of new inventions will accrue to consumers rather than innovators. Second, even in economies with large conglomerates, it is rare for a single conglomerate to dominate the entire economy, one that will internalize the implications of its business decisions on other firms in the economy. This owes to the operation of certain diseconomies of scale and scope beyond some large level, besides antitrust actions of the government. Then the effect of actions of any large firm on other firms will not be internalized. While some inter-firm externalities can be regulated through industry associations and cartel agreements, it is unlikely that diffuse economy-wide externalities pertaining to worker training, technological change, or network complementarities will be efficiently mediated through such voluntary inter-firm agreements. Acemoglu and Pischke (1998, 1999), for instance, offer a theoretical model and related empirical evidence concerning worker training externalities across firms.

Accordingly, there is a potential for government intervention with respect to (i) anti-trust actions, regulating pricing and other sources of potential anticompetitive conduct, (ii) stimulating and coordinating R&D activity, (iii) coordinating technology choices and facilitating learning and spillovers, and (iv) helping development of infrastructure with economy-wide implications and whose benefits are difficult to appropriate by private entrepreneurs. One would add the possible scope for selective interventions with respect to trade policy that might aid

learning-by-doing, or those that reallocate rents towards domestic producers and consumers and away from foreign entities (though as the
literature on strategic trade policy has indicated, it is difficult to make an
overarching case for such interventions). In the context of infrastructure, the state's role may be limited to providing a facilitating, coordinating and financing role for private investment, rather than directly
investing and producing the services itself. There is little guidance from
the theoretical market failure literature concerning the relative merits of
privatization and public sector investment: the arguments usually hang
on comparative assessment of respective governance failures.

MISSING MARKETS, ASYMMETRIC INFORMATION, AND IMPERFECT ENFORCEMENT

The 'information economics' revolution of the past three decades, led by
the work of Akerlof and Stiglitz, accounts now for a theory of distorted
and missing markets in credit and insurance, as well as in a large swathe
of other areas of the economy: agrarian contracts, labour markets and
education, entrepreneurship, occupational choice, organizational form of
industries, accounting and certification, and so on. It is clear that
informational imperfections cause myriad, pervasive distortions, such as
dual economies, non-market clearing, credit rationing, and contracts
interlinking transactions in multiple goods. Indeed, the non-existence of
some of these markets can be explained in terms of such information and
enforcement problems. If development economics is about the systematic study of market distortions, then the economics of information ought
to provide a microfoundation for the subject. Akerlof (1970) and many
others since have argued that this perspective may also help explain why
these problems are more pervasive in developing countries, in terms
of their weaker information infrastructure and contract enforcement
mechanisms.

While this literature certainly helps explain a wide variety of particular features of underdeveloped economies, the implications for market
failure are less clear. Recall the way the market failure question is typically posed: the central planner must be bound by the same informational
and enforcement constraints as market agents are in the decentralized
economy. Whether such a planner can generate a Pareto improvement
relative to market agents in a decentralized economy is the question. It
is not sufficient to point towards the apparent distortions such as

unemployment, credit rationing, or market non-existence and infer from their widespread prevalence in a developing country that the state has a potential role to play in alleviating these problems. Development 'led' by the state may be similarly crippled by these information and enforcement problems, possibly in different ways. If observed market distortions stem from underlying information and enforcement problems that equally afflict markets and the state, we need to extend the classical theory carefully before pronouncing judgment. I have surveyed much of the relevant literature on this topic elsewhere (Mookherjee 1994), but it is appropriate to recount some of the main lessons that have emerged.

Take for instance the context of credit rationing arising from moral hazard. The default risk of a borrower will depend on the total amount, duration, and terms on which he is able to obtain credit. Too much debt will reduce the incentive of the borrower to prevent default. Accordingly, the borrower may be rationed with respect to the amount of credit; lenders need to regulate the financial transactions of their clients with other lenders, and attempt to control their actions. Here there is an obvious pecuniary externality between different potential lenders: additional lending by one of them will affect the risk that other loans outstanding will be defaulted on. This pecuniary externality is the basis of the argument of Greenwald and Stiglitz (1986) for market failure from moral hazard.

Prescott and Townsend (1984) offer a different model of competitive equilibrium with moral hazard, in which they are able to extend the first Welfare Theorem. In their construction, all borrowers transact with a single firm-intermediary, causing all interlender pecuniary externalities to be internalized. The set of firms and commodities is primitive in Walrasian theory, so one cannot actually question why there are not more firms in their model. Implicit in their formulation is the Coasian premise that in the presence of inter-firm externalities, different firms would merge to internalize them. Banks or other financial intermediaries may be viewed as playing such a role.

A more serious problem with the Greenwald–Stiglitz argument is that it presumes an asymmetry between enforcement capacities of the state and market agents. How can the state correct or regulate the pecuniary externality across lenders? This requires the state to monitor the transactions of the borrower across different lenders. The presence of such monitoring does not necessarily imply a role for state regulation or public provision: the state can alternatively provide the information concerning financial transactions between different parties generated by its monitoring activities to concerned borrowers and lenders, or put it at the disposal of courts that enforce private contracts. Alternatively, the same monitoring functions could be performed by private credit rating agencies or other information networks among lenders. This will permit lenders to enter into exclusive lending contracts, or those that condition terms of lending on transactions of the same borrower from other lenders. Once such private contracts can be enforced, competitive equilibria would indeed implement constrained Pareto-efficient outcomes, as my work with Kahn has shown (Kahn and Mookherjee 1995a). And the same result holds when there is no public information available about financial transactions of borrowers with other lenders. In other words, if market agents and the central planner have access to the same monitoring and enforcement structures, there would be no market failure at all (in the moral hazard context). The Greenwald–Stiglitz argument must therefore be based on an implicit assumption of superior enforcement and monitoring capacity of the state.

Matters are somewhat more complicated in the presence of adverse selection rather than moral hazard as a role of credit imperfections. For instance, Prescott and Townsend (1984) were not able to satisfactorily extend their arguments to an adverse selection setting, and Kahn and Mookherjee (1995b) constructed a model of market equilibrium in an adverse selection insurance economy exhibiting Pareto inefficiency. In the latter model all coalitions of market agents are permitted to enter into contracts in a Coasian fashion, but these contracts are subject to the hazard that contracts entered simultaneously by *other* coalitions may not be observable. With a suitable extension of the notion of coalition-proof Nash equilibrium to a simultaneous offer contracting game, the market economy is vulnerable to the phenomenon of 'cream skimming', wherein firms try to lure away each others' profitable clients. The market thus fails to sustain any kind of cross-subsidization across insurance customers of differential risk types: each type gets an actuarially fair contract with restricted quantities of insurance to ensure suitable incentives for different types to self-select into different contracts. The amount of insurance available to low risk customers may need to be reduced very substantially, to prevent high risk customers from masquerading as low risk customers to avail of the lower rates offered to the latter. This reduction in the quantum of insurance (akin to rationing in the credit market) applies, irrespective of the relative proportions of the two types in the economy. Even if there is only one high risk customer for every million low risk customers, all of the latter must receive a small fraction of their efficient levels of insurance, just in order to prevent the one high risk customer from taking advantage of the low-risk low-price contract. All customers would be better off in this economy if there were a single contract designed for all types of customers, which is almost the same as the actuarially fair contract for the low risk customers (it offers full insurance but at a slightly higher price, in order to pay for the losses incurred on the high risk customers). Such provision of uniform cross-subsidized insurance (or credit) is feasible for the government (since it is not subjected to competitive market pressure) but not the market.

It is however difficult to create an overarching argument for state intervention based on adverse selection problems. The non-existence of competitive equilibrium, first pointed out by Rothschild and Stiglitz (1976), has led to many reformulations of equilibrium and of the under-lying market game, most of which yield distinct predictions. Institutional details of the market matter accordingly: there is no consensus concerning the 'correct' notion of competitive equilibrium, or the timing and sequence of moves in suitable game-theoretic models of the market. Logi-cally consistent formulations of competitive equilibria that are constrained efficient have been constructed, such as Hammond's (1989) model of 'perfected option' markets in the Prescott–Townsend (1984) tradition.

These ambiguities have spilled over to models of financial crises and the role of state regulation of financial activity. The Diamond and Dybvig (1983) theory has been influential with respect to thinking of financial crises as sunspots, or embodying coordination problems among diverse investors and their beliefs concerning the viability of institutions they invest in, which can be costlessly resolved via forms of state-provided deposit insurance. The experiences of the last two decades with the sav-ings and loan crises in the US and the financial crises in East Asia have now driven home the various forms of moral hazard that equally attend deposit insurance or fixed exchange rates (whose failure to adjust to investor expectations can cause liquidity crises similar to the bank runs in the Diamond–Dybvig model). Recent models of financial crises such as by Allen and Gale (2001) can accommodate the periodic occurrence of such crises which are consistent with constrained Pareto efficiency. Indeed, such models can be used to view crises as forms of constrained optimal risk-sharing between borrowers and lenders, which preclude the need for prudential supervision by state agencies.

In summary, then, no compelling and overarching case for market failure can be based on the existence of information and enforcement constraints. Much of the ambiguity stems from the attendant theoretical complications in obtaining a suitable definition of equilibrium. The problem is not the absence of equilibrium models, but instead the proliferation of alternative models yielding conflicting results. Particular formulations do suggest the scope for benign state interventions, but it is possible to quibble over the formulation and to present alternative ones where no such scope exists. It is not easy to settle on the right formulation (for example, are contracts signed *ex ante* or *ex post*?) on the basis either of theory or empirical evidence: it is ultimately a matter of one's subjective judgement what the right formulation is.

Most of the arguments commonly advanced for market failure are implicitly based on superior information and enforcement capabilities of the state relative to market agents. Take, for instance, the argument of Galor and Zeira (1993) who provide a model of credit market imperfection from the possibility that the borrower may 'take the money and run'. They argue that the state can better enforce credit contracts, owing to its capacity to impose and collect taxes. So while private loan markets may not fund the education investments of poor children owing to the risk that such loans will not be repaid, a state can provide public education and fund such education by taxes that are assumed to be non-evadable by students once they graduate and earn incomes later in their lives.

Note that the argument for state intervention here is based on superior enforcement capacity of the state over market agents. It does not qualify as an argument for constrained Pareto inefficiency of the market outcome: recall that the market failure question is posed as comparing markets and governments with identical information and enforcement capabilities. In similar vein, as explained above, the Greenwald–Stiglitz (1986) arguments and most others of its genre concerning market failure in the presence of imperfect information are based implicitly on the superior ability of the state to monitor and regulate activities that generate pecuniary externalities. These examples include engaging in transactions in related markets (for example, purchase of fire extinguishers or cigarettes by insurance purchasers affect fire risk) or with related agents (for example, supplemental loans borrowed from alternative sources). These are not *bona fide* arguments for constrained inefficiency of the market outcome. Instead they must be viewed as arguing that the state has a comparative advantage with respect to information gathering and enforcement of contracts.

Even if this argument were granted, an issue we discuss subsequently, it would give rise to the question of why the state does not limit itself to specializing in gathering and making public information on which private contracts can be based, and enforcing such contracts efficiently. That would effectively limit the state to its 'nightwatchman' role.

In addition, whether the state has a comparative advantage over market agents with respect to information and enforcement is debatable in many contexts. For instance, it has been argued that a principal reason for the robust ability of informal lenders to survive massive infusions of low cost formal credit in many developing countries is the limited information and enforcement capacity of lenders in the formal sector of the credit market. Informal lenders rely on community and social networks both to access key information about borrower characteristics that help predict their default risks, as well as to impose social sanctions in the event of default. Formal lenders have no recourse but use of marketable assets as collateral to limit default risk. So the credit market is segmented owing to these differences in information and enforcement mechanisms: those owning sufficient collateralizable assets access low cost formal credit, and all others access high cost informal credit. Often the wealthy who belong to the former category borrow at low cost from the formal sector, and re-lend these monies at higher interest rates (and higher default risk) to the less wealthy. Such segmentation creates a complementarity between the two segments of the credit market. The effects of expanding supplies of subsidized formal credit are complicated: much of the benefits accrue to the wealthy borrowers who can access the formal system, with the 'trickle down' benefit to borrowers in the informal system appearing to be negligible (see, for instance, the discussion and evidence cited in Hoff and Stiglitz 1993). The argument for state intervention in such contexts is tricky, and there is no compelling empirical evidence yet that the massive expansion of subsidized rural credit in many developing countries in the past half century have achieved much of their original goals.

SUMMARY OF THE TRADITIONAL MARKET FAILURE PARADIGM

The traditional paradigm assigns a potential role for state intervention on the basis of market failure arising principally from large-number externality problems, and of economies of scale that generate significant market power for private firms. These include areas such as (i) regulation of externalities, such as environment, product safety, traffic, land zoning, and so on; (ii) support for pure public goods, including national defence, law and order, basic science and technology research, technological diffusion, infrastructure, and marketing services (such as roads or export marketing) involving large fixed costs and widespread benefits, whose providers have difficulty in appropriating the benefits users derive from such services; (iii) regulating the use and consequences of market power in concentrated industries, for example, entry, mergers, pricing, and standardization of technologies with network externalities.

In the context of market distortions arising from imperfect (asymmetric) information or contract enforcement problems, in contrast, there is no overarching argument for market failure, in the form that this term is traditionally defined. There is a potential scope for the state to intervene only if it has a comparative advantage with respect to information concerning client characteristics or behaviour, or with respect to contract enforcement, which would have to be persuasively argued in any given context. Moreover, the appropriate nature of such intervention would need to be discussed. For example, if the state can enforce credit contracts better owing to its power to track and impose coercive sanctions on defaulters, should it be in the lending business itself, or should it limit its role to providing such information to private lenders and enforcing the contracts they enter into?

This summary of what the traditional market paradigm has to offer seems to be quite specific in its normative recommendations. Apart from the three broad areas (i)–(iii) described above, if there is no clear case for market failure, relative even to as ideal, benevolent government, then there would be even less a case when we factor in all the possible 'government failures', stemming from limited responsiveness and accountability of governments. The appropriate role of the state would be in the regulation of large-number externality problems, of antitrust action in concentrated industries, and in the support and facilitation of the provision of public goods subject to widespread and diffuse benefits. In this light, the redefinition of the role of the state in various 'liberalization' and 'market reforms' that have swept the developing world in the past two decades are moves in the right direction. There is little basis for the public sector to be directly involved in the production of a large number of goods and services which do not have any significant public good or externality component, and this indeed is the nature of a large number of sectors (for example, steel, chemicals, aviation, hotels, credit, insurance, and so on) in which the state has traditionally been involved in developing countries. Limiting itself to defence, law and order, infrastructure, technical and marketing support to small scale units, and regulation of antitrust and the environment, is very much in line with the massive privatization and deregulation initiatives of the 1990s. The traditional market paradigm indeed seems to fall in the line with the 'Washington consensus'; whichever way one may criticize it, 'sterility' interpreted as absence of specific policy implications seems inappropriate.

SOME QUALIFICATIONS: THE FUNCTIONAL ROLE OF INEQUALITY

The usual critique of the 'Washington consensus' centres around its neglect of social and distributional implications. In countries with highly unequal distributions of land, physical and human capital, a return to unbridled *laissez faire* would likely increase inequality and poverty in great measure. After all, one of the main responsibilities of the state has been to redistribute across socio-economic classes and across regions within a country. Even in developed countries where inequality is on average lower than in developing countries, the operation of governmental tax transfer programme such as education, health, social security, and antipoverty or welfare programme occupy a much larger share of the gross domestic product (GDP).

The usual response of defenders of the Washington consensus is built around two points. At a practical level, they argue (justifiably) that many redistributive programme in less developed countries have been poorly designed and targeted—benefits have been appropriated by the wealthy and the middle class rather than the poor for whom they were intended, and have given risen to large leakages and corruption.

At a broader, philosophical level, their response is based on an implicit separation of efficiency from redistribution issues. This separation is rooted in the ideal neoclassical world where the two theorems of Welfare economics apply. It is strengthened by Coasian considerations, where lumpsum side-transfers can be relied on to compensate losers from any efficiency enhancing policy change, a justification for ignoring their distributive consequences. For the more enlightened, there is the notion (bred by most introductory economics textbooks) of a trade-off between efficiency and equality, based on distorting incentive effects (on labour supply and savings) of most redistributive tax-transfer programmes. Added to this is the notion that the efficiency costs rise non-linearly with the size of the intervention (for example, the size of the relevant 'Harberger' triangles are proportional to the square of the tax rate), and the corruption and poor design of the public benefit programmes—the net implications are that the actual redistributive benefits, if any, are too costly in terms of their efficiency implications.

This faith is seriously undermined by a significant amount of recent theoretical research on asymmetric information economies, which explains why compensatory side-transfers are the exception rather than the rule in the real world, and that in many contexts (of particular relevance in developing countries) there may be no equality–efficiency trade off at all.

One difficulty in deciding on appropriate compensations is knowing the actual costs and benefits that actually result from any given externality or policy change. It is not enough to be able to calculate the average costs and benefits, where one may hope that various errors of approximation and measurement would wash away. The detailed distribution of costs and benefits is of the essence here, in deciding how much each affected individual or community is entitled to. No one knows better than the concerned agents themselves what these actual costs and benefits are. The fundamental problem is that there is no feasible way of eliciting this information from them, owing to incentive problems. In large populations these incentive problems compound: Mailath and Postlewaite (1990), Rob (1989), and Neeman (1998) have shown how relying on voluntary compensation mechanisms (such as bargaining over pollution rights) become entirely worthless in large populations, as transfers vanish asymptotically and the outcome is pinned down entirely by the original allocation of property rights.

Further difficulties arise in implementing transfer mechanisms from a legal and political standpoint. To uphold a proposed transfer mechanism, the courts will be concerned with the fairness of the outcome, both procedural and substantive. Differential compensations to different parties whose observed characteristics are the same would violate the norms of horizontal fairness. So would inconsistency of treatment of those affected by a current policy with all those affected by similar policies in the past.

From a political standpoint, there may be concerns about the credibility of the transfer mechanism. For one, paying the entire transfer in a lump-sum may involve a large increase in the government debt. For instance, if a switch to free trade involves closing down some old unprofitable industries, the new industries whose development may be the principal benefit may take some time to materialize. Ideally these industries should pay for the compensatory transfers to the old industries that were shut down, but it is difficult for anyone to predict where these new industries will crop up and who their owners and workers will be. Hence, the state will have to run up large levels of debt if it were to immediately pay transfers to those laid off. If the capacity of the state to raise its debt substantially is limited (as it typically is in bad times), the compensations will have to be staggered over time. In that case those laid off will have good reason to suspect that they will ever be paid in full. For one, governments can rarely commit to future fiscal policy, particularly beyond the term of current office. And for another, the political economy of fiscal policy may well change by then: the policy changes will create new interest groups such as workers and owners of the new industries who would be expected to resist implementation of the compensatory mechanism that they fund. Dixit and Londregan (1995) have developed a formal political economy model that explains this problem in particular detail. Other related explanations based on the political economy of reform have also been provided by Fernandez and Rodrik (1991) and Besley and Coate (1998).

Finally, imperfections in credit markets restrict the extent to which compensatory transfers can be paid by market agents. It is well known that the poor have little or no access to credit; combined with their poverty and high consumption needs relative to their incomes which leave little room for saving, they would be unable to finance the transfers they might wish to make in order to purchase assets, compensate real estate developers, or contribute to political lobbies that might subsequently be prepared to represent their interests in the political arena. We shall come back to this issue below.

If for a combination of all these reasons compensatory side-transfers are the exception rather than the norm, many efficiency-enhancing reforms with serious distributive consequences would be unable to tackle these problems the way neoclassical economists have traditionally (and rather unrealistically) supposed. It is difficult to think of any major arena of economic policy that lacks important distributive consequences. Even the policy approaches that typically command the most universal support from economists of all persuasions—trade liberalization, or imposition of emission taxes—give rise to significant losses for important sections of the economy. If the losers are not and cannot be adequately compensated, then the justification for these policies cannot be based on 'value-free' notions of Pareto efficiency alone.

Yet these policies command a level of support from neoclassical economists of a surprisingly wide range of leanings across the political spectrum. When it comes to prescribing free trade or the levy of Pigouvian environmental taxes, the profession at large does not resist making interpersonal utility comparisons, at least implicitly. Yet, their justification is in terms of the notion of 'economic efficiency'. Most neoclassical economists are really utilitarians at heart: what they mean by 'increasing efficiency' or 'increasing the size of the pie' is really about increasing a utilitarian measure of social welfare, where the losses of the few can be overwhelmed by the greater gains of the many. Or they will (implicitly or explicitly) invoke the Kaldor–Hicks 'compensation tests', wherein gainers can hypothetically compensate the losers, and it is not essential that the compensations be actually paid.

Similar judgments are involved when making the argument that new technologies or more open societies lead to faster rates of growth, which compound over time to produce dramatic differences in the standard of living for a large majority of citizens. Along the way some people inevitably get hurt: the Luddites and medieval craft guilds were indeed worse off as a result of the Industrial Revolution, as were English farmers when early nineteenth century Britain repealed the Corn Laws imposing tariffs on food imports from Europe. Yet these sacrifices see justified for the greater good of the British in the long run. Indeed, historians such as Mokyr (2001) and Rosenberg and Birdzell (1986) argue that the single most important reason the West grew richer than all other civilizations since the sixteenth century was its unwillingness to restrict the spread of new technology owing to opposition from threatened interest groups. In the long haul, the path of economic progress has rarely taken the form of Pareto improvements.

Practical economists are prone to evaluating economic welfare and progress in terms of per capita measures of income or consumption or wider measures of the standard of living, supplemented by attention to measures of inequality. Broader assessments embracing notions of human development may additionally incorporate health and education indicators, other notions of entitlements and freedoms as advocated by Sen's work, or equality of opportunity. All these approaches embody a sharper welfare criterion than Pareto efficiency. Economic changes that both increase per capita incomes and reduce income inequality will typically be considered 'win–win' propositions, even if they are accompanied by deteriorating living conditions for sections of the population.

Prominent examples of such policies that typically command wide support from economists are land reforms and educational provision to children in poor families. There are numerous theoretical and empirical reasons to believe that such reforms would correct underinvestments by the poor that arise from credit market imperfections (for a recent survey see Benabou 1996). Hence these policies, if successfully implemented and targeted to the poor, constitute 'win–win' changes, where per capita incomes would rise, income inequality and poverty would drop, and entitlement measures of human development would be expected to improve at the same time. Yet such policies, which fall squarely within the ambit of the state's responsibility, would not qualify as constituting a Pareto improvement, since they make some well-to-do groups (landowners or taxpayers that end up financing public education) in society worse off. Indeed had such changes been Pareto improving, a Coasian would have expected spontaneous pressures within a market economy for them to come about without need for any kind of state intervention.

Consider land reforms, wherein land owned by large landowners and farmed either by tenants or supervised wage labour is broken into small parcels and sold to landless peasants, that subsequently farm them using family labour. Small family farms have typically been found to be more productive than tenant or wage labour farms in many developing countries, a fact frequently explained by the incentive problems associated with either of the latter two modes of production. One might then expect it to be profitable for large landowners to split up the lands they own and sell them off to the landless or to their own tenants. The land market would then itself resolve the underproduction resulting from incentive problems inherent in tenancy or wage labour: there would be no need for any state-sponsored land reform initiatives. Yet in many societies with highly unequal landownership patterns, such as South Africa, South America, or parts of South East Asia, the land market is typically thin, with relatively few land sales from large landowners to small ones. Most of the sales move the land distribution in the opposite direction, taking the form of distress sales by small landowners. Presumably there are important credit market imperfections that prevent such equalizing land sales, a phenomenon which I have tried to explain theoretically elsewhere (Mookherjee 1997).

Similar credit market imperfections cause poor households to underinvest in schooling for their children. Human capital investments in developing countries are typically believed to yield a rate of return considerably in excess of their social cost. Available evidence concerning educational wage premia suggest substantially higher premia in developing countries compared with developed countries. Even higher rates of return are implied by cross-country evidence concerning growth rates of per capita income. Increased provision of schooling for the poor would most likely have a beneficial effect in terms of reducing inequality of wages and consumption, and promoting social mobility. Additional external benefits in terms of reduction in fertility rates following increased schooling for girls, an increased sense of political awareness and social responsibility of poorer citizens that would be likely to enhance government accountability, and the value of the increased sense of empowerment *per se*, add to the social value of education. On all accounts, thus, increased educational opportunities for the poor would be a 'win–win' proposition, despite the fact that well-to-do taxpayers that foot the bill may be rendered worse off.

In either case, well-to-do groups such as landowners and taxpayers that are worse off as a result of land reform or increased public provision of education would be expected to resist the introduction and expansion of such policies. It is no surprise then that the ability of the state to introduce and implement such policies depends heavily on the nature of the political mechanism. The most conspicuous examples of successful land reforms—in Korea and Japan, respectively—were carried out by foreign occupational authorities, while others have resulted from violent peasant revolutions. It is no accident that democracies rarely produce successful instance of land reforms. Educational reforms are more common, however, though exactly how the political process operated in the late nineteenth century in Europe and the United States to produce this outcome is an active area of current research (see, for instance, Galor and Moav 2001) and not very well understood yet. Yet historians believe that such reforms played a key role in the growth experience of these economies in the twentieth century (see, for example, Goldin and Katz 1999, 2001, who argue that the earlier expansion of public schooling in the United States compared with Europe is a key reason for its industrial pre-eminence in the twentieth century).

If we thus enlarge the notion of market failure from the Pareto criterion to include 'win–win' propositions such as land reforms and expansion of public education which simultaneously increase per capita wealth and distribute it more equitably, the appropriate areas of potential responsibility of the state in a market economy are considerably widened. By limiting itself to use of the Pareto criterion, the traditional market failure paradigm has indeed been somewhat sterile. One would clearly want to add to the list of activities identified in the previous section (externalities, public goods, and antitrust action) to include distributions of primary assets (such as land or human capital). Other examples may be efforts by the state to sponsor reforms in ownership and participation by small producers in marketing cooperatives, which reduce the market power of traditional middlemen. Indeed, the logic could be extended to include programmes of a purely redistributive nature, as long as they do not involve excessive efficiency costs, such as social security programmes.

The importance of reducing extreme inequality from this standpoint is further highlighted by a newly burgeoning literature on the *functional* role of inequality in hindering development. It is argued that even if one were normatively unconcerned about inequality, it is important to avoid high levels of inequality to prevent hindrances to growth from appearing. This literature, best associated with the theoretical models of Galor and Zeira (1993) and Banerjee and Newman (1993), is typically based on the consequences of credit market imperfections for the dynamics of inequality and growth. Households that are initially poor have limited access to credit markets, and hence underinvest in relevant productive or human assets, thus perpetuating their poverty. Additional growth-retarding implications of high inequality can stem from the external effects on local neighbourhoods, crime, and other social problems. The wider political effects of limited participation of the poor in democracies reinforce the initial inequalities by increasing the resistance of the well-to-do to redistributive reforms. The result can be deeply polarized and unstable societies, where even the well-to-do do not feel secure. In particular, the economic and social hysteresis effects can imply that a society with sufficiently high initial inequality can be locked into an underdevelopment trap, with lower per capita income and higher inequality that persists far into the future. Engerman and Sokoloff (1997) have recently provided historical evidence explaining divergent patterns of development across different countries of North and South America in terms of their early colonial origins. In particular, South American countries were naturally suited to plantation crop cultivation based on slave labour, which led to the development of deeply unequal colonial societies that grew (and continue even to this day to grow) slowly owing to restrictions on education and forms of democratic participation. Acemoglu et al. (2001) and Easterly (2001) have provided cross-country empirical evidence in support for similar hypotheses on a wider scale. What we see emerging in this literature, in effect, are theoretical and historical explanations of the kind of phenomena that MDC alluded to in discussing the role of the landed aristocracy in the Philippines in hindering the creation of a dynamic capitalist economy.

CONCLUDING REMARKS

Has the market failure paradigm been sterile? Is there a continuing lack of consensus concerning the role of the state *vis-à-vis* the market? My assessment differs in form, but not in substance, from that of MDC. I have argued here that the traditional paradigm has deliberately engaged in a one-sided analysis of markets, pitting their outcome against that of a hypothetical central planner working for the public interest without any weaknesses in governance. The aim was to identify areas where the hypothetical planner can effect a Pareto improvement over market outcomes, despite being constrained by the same resources, technologies, and information. The aim was to identify the set of areas where there is a *potential* role for the state, a potential which may or may not be realized depending on the nature of governance and bureaucratic failures that corresponding real governments may be subject to.

Relative to this (perhaps uneven and modest) goal, the literature provides some clear answers in some respects, though not in others. For only a few areas (economy-wide externalities, public goods, and antitrust) can an overarching case for potential Pareto improving state intervention be made. This includes the traditional domains of the state: defence, law and order, infrastructure, basic science and technology, and antitrust. Outside these, there is no clear general argument, even for a hypothetically benign social planner, to effect Pareto improvements over the market.

And even within its traditional domain, there is plenty of opportunity for governments to utilize the benefits of a private sector that is more cost conscious and innovative than most public enterprises. There is much empirical evidence supporting the hypothesis that private enterprise is typically more cost effective than public enterprise, across a wide swath of products, industries, and countries (see Megginson and Netter (2001) for a recent survey). Hence even if there is a compelling argument for public provision of some good or service, the state can limit itself to financing and contracting out the production to more cost effective private producers. Exceptions could be made only for products or services whose quality involves some social dimension that private providers would not internalize but public agencies might, and which is publicly non-verifiable (and so is difficult to contract out or regulate) such as in schools or prisons—as argued by Shapiro and Willig (1990), or Hart, Shleifer, and Vishny (1997) in their analyses of privatization.

From these standpoints, therefore, the theory provides support for recent waves of privatization observed throughout the developing world in sectors where the state has no potential role even in the absence of any governance or corruption problems. This pertains to many of the manufacturing sectors where the state historically dominated in the era of development planning. In the financial sector, the argument for subsidized supply of credit to rural areas or regulation of private financial entities has to be made on the basis of a clear understanding of institutional specificities and a reasoned assessment of the way in which incentive problems operate in the market *vis-à-vis* state agencies, rather than any generally applicable logic of market failure.

On the other hand, the traditional market failure paradigm can be criticized for being too narrow in terms of its preoccupation with the Pareto criterion as the basis of normative recommendations. Once one embraces a utilitarian perspective (or a more inequality-averse social welfare function), an additional set of responsibilities could naturally arise for the state in highly unequal, underdeveloped societies. In such societies, credit market imperfections and other social and political externalities can create a risk of historical lock-in to poverty traps and a low level of development. The state has an important potential role in redistributing productive assets such as land which reduce divergence between ownership and control, and in providing wide access to education. These have the potential of reducing inequality and stimulating productive efficiency at the same time, besides contributing to wider goals of human development.

Taken together with considerations based on the Pareto criterion, the normative recommendations of the traditional approach would be entirely in line with shifting the role of the state from producer of a wide variety of goods, to its role as regulator of private activity and provider in the 'social' sector.

Whether and to what extent the state will be effective in realizing its potential role is a topic that is not addressed by the market failure paradigm. That was never its goal. Nor is conventional microeconomics well-suited to such an enterprise. Insofar as the role of the state is an important determinant of the character and pace of development, it is no surprise that wider political, legal, and bureaucratic institutions—besides historical and social factors—play a crucial role in the development process. In terms of normative analyses, the relevant question concerns the nature of these institutions that are most likely to lead to good governance. As MDC rightfully pointed out, normative analysis is dificult when it comes to matters of political economy, and economists have to widen their horizons to understand broader social and political processes. Fortunately this has already begun to happen, where the real debates lie in the years ahead.

REFERENCES

Acemoglu, D. and F. Zilibotti (1997), 'Was Prometheus Unbound by Chance? Risk, Diversification and Growth', *Journal of Political Economy*, vol. 105, no. 4, pp. 709–51.

Acemoglu, D., S. Johnson, and J. Robinson (2001), 'Reversal of Fortune: Geography and Institutions in the Making of the Modern World Income Distribution', mimeo, Department of Economics, MIT.

Acemoglu, D. and S. Pischke (1998), 'Why Do Firms Train? Theory and Evidence', *Quarterly Journal of Economics*, vol. 113, pp. 79–119.

—— (1999), 'The Structure of Wages and Investment with General Training', *Journal of Political Economy*, vol. 107, pp. 539–72.

Akerlof, G. (1970), 'The Market for Lemons: Qualitative Uncertainty and the Market Mechanism', *Quarterly Journal of Economics*, vol. 84, pp. 488–500.

Allen, F. and D. Gale (2001), 'Banking and Markets', mimeo, Department of Economics, New York University.

Amsden, A. (1989), Asia's Next Giant: South Korea and Late Industrialization (New York: Oxford University Press).

Arrow, K. (1970), 'The Organization of Economic Activity: Issues Pertinent to the Choice Between Market and Non-Market Activity', in R. Haveman and J. Margolis, eds., *Public Expenditures and Policy Analysis* (Chicago: Markham).

Azariadis, C. (1983), 'Employment with Asymmetric Information', *Quarterly Journal of Economics*, Supplement, vol. 98, pp. 157–72.

Banerjee A. and A. Newman (1993), 'Occupational Choice and the Process of Development', *Journal of Political Economy*, vol. 101, no. 2, pp. 274–98.

Basu, K. (1984), *The Less Developed Economy: A Critique of Contemporary Theory* (Oxford: Blackwell).

Benabou, R. (1996), 'Inequality and Growth', Ben S. Bernanke and Julio Rotemberg, eds., *NBER Macroeconomics Annual 1996* (Cambridge: MIT Press), pp. 11–74.

Besley, T. and S. Coate (1998), 'Sources of Inefficiency in a Representative Democracy: A Dynamic Analysis', *American Economic Review*, vol. 88, no. 1, pp. 139–56.

Bulow, J. and L. Summers (1986), 'A Theory of Dual Labor Markets with Applications to Industrial Policy, Discrimination and Keynesian Unemployment', *Journal of Labor Economics*, vol. 4, pp. 376–414.

Chandler, A. (1977), *The Visible Hand: The Managerial Revolution in American Business* (Cambridge, Mass.: Harvard University Press).

——— (1990), *Scale and Scope: The Dynamics of Industrial Capitalism* (Cambridge, MA: Harvard Belknap).

Coase, R. (1960), 'The Problem of Social Cost', *Journal of Law and Economics*, vol. 3, pp. 1–44.

Datta-Chaudhuri, M. (1990), 'Market Failure and Government Failure', *Journal of Economic Perspectives*, vol. 4, no. 3, pp. 25–40.

Diamond, D.W. and Philip H. Dybvig (1983), 'Bank Runs, Deposit Insurance, and Liquidity', *Journal of Political Economy*, vol. 91, no. 3, pp. 401–19.

Dixit, A. and J. Londregan (1995), 'Redistributive Politics and Economic Efficiency', *American Politial Science Review*, vol. 89, no. 4, pp. 856–66.

Easterly, W. (2001), 'The Middle Class Consensus and Economic Development', World Bank Discussion Paper.

Engerman, S. and K. Sokoloff (1997), 'Factor Endowments, Institutions and Differential Paths of Growth among New World Economies: A View from Economic History of the United States', in Stephen Haber, ed., *How Latin America Fell Behind* (Stanford, Stanford University Press).

Fernandez, R. and D. Rodrik (1991), 'Resistance to Reform: Status Quo Bias in the Presence of Individual-Specific Uncertainty', *American Economic Review*, vol. 81, no. 5, pp. 1146–55.

Galor, O. and J. Zeira (1993), 'Income Distribution and Macroeconomics', *Review of Economic Studies*, vol. 60, pp. 35–52.

Galor, O. and O. Moav (2001), 'Das Human Kapital', Center for Economic Policy Research Paper No. 2701.

Goldin, C. and L. Katz (1999), 'The Shaping of Higher Education: Formative Years in the US 1890 to 1940', *Journal of Economic Perspectives*, vol. 13, no. 1, pp. 37–62.

Goldin, C. and L. Katz (2001), 'The Legacy of US Educational Leadership: Notes on Distribution and Growth in the 20th Century', *American Economic Review Papers and Proceedings*, May 2001.

Greenwald, B. and J. Stiglitz (1986), 'Externalities in Economies with Imperfect Information and Incomplete Markets', *Quarterly Journal of Economics*, vol. 101, pp. 229–64.

Grossman, S. and O. Hart (1983), 'Implicit Contracts under Asymmetric Information', *Quarterly Journal of Economics*, Supplement, vol. 98, pp. 123–56.

Hammond, P. (1989), 'Perfected Option Markets in Economies with Adverse Selection', Working Paper, Department of Economics, Stanford University.

Hart, O. (1982), 'A Model of Imperfect Competition with Keynesian Features', *Quarterly Journal of Economics*, vol. 97, pp. 109–38.

Hart, O., A. Shleifer, and R. Vishny (1997), 'The Proper Scope of Government: Theory and an Application to Prisons', *Quarterly Journal of Economics*, vol. 112, no. 4, pp. 1127–62.

Hoff, K. and J. Stiglitz (1993), 'Imperfect Information in Rural Credit Markets: Puzzles and Policy Perspectives', in A. Braverman, K. Hoff, and J. Stiglitz, ed., *The Economics of Rural Organization: Theory, Practice and Policy* (London: Oxford University Press).

Kahn, C. and D. Mookherjee (1988), 'A Competitive Efficiency Wage Model with Keynesian Features', *Quarterly Journal of Economics*, vol. 103, no. 4, pp. 609–45.

_____ (1995a), 'Market Failure with Moral Hazard and Side Trading', *Journal of Public Economics*, no. 58, pp. 159–84.

_____ (1995b), 'Coalition Proof Equilibrium in an Adverse Selection Insurance Economy', *Journal of Economic Theory*, vol. 66, no. 1, pp. 113–38.

Mailath, G.J. and Andrew Postlewaite (1990), 'Asymmetric Information Bargaining Problems with Many Agents', *Review of Economic Studies*, vol. 57. no. 3, pp. 351–67.

Megginson, W.L. and J.M. Netter (2001), 'From State to Market: A Survey of Empirical Studies on Privatization', *Journal of Economic Literature*, vol. 39. no. 2, pp. 321–88.

Mokyr, J. (2001), 'Innovation and its Enemies: The Economic and Political Roots of Technological Inertia', in S. Kahkonen and M. Olson, ed., *A New Institutional Approach to Economic Development* (New Delhi, Vistaar Publications).

Mookherjee, D. (1994), 'Market Failure and Information', in B. Dutta, ed., *Welfare Economics* (New Delhi: Oxford University Press).

_____ (1997), 'Informational Rents and Property Rights in Land', in J. Roemer, ed., *Property Relations, Incentives and Welfare*, Macmillan Press.

Murphy, K., A. Shleifer, and R. Vishny (1989a), 'Industrialization and the Big Push', *Journal of Political Economy*, vol. 97, pp. 1003–26.

_____ (1989b), 'Income Distribution, Market Size and Industrialization', *Quarterly Journal of Economics*, vol. 104.

Neeman, Z. (1998), 'Property Rights and Efficiency of Voluntary Bargaining Under Asymmetric Information', *Review of Economic Studies*, forthcoming.

Olson, M. (1965), *The Logic of Collective Action* (Cambridge: Harvard University Press).

Ostrom, E. (1990), *Governing the Commons: Evolution of Institutions for Collective Action* (Cambridge: University Press).

Prescott, E. and R. Townsend (1984), 'Pareto Optima and Competitive Equilibria with Adverse Selection and Moral Hazard', *Econometrica*, vol. 52, pp. 21–45.

Rob, R. (1989), 'Pollution Claim Settlements under Private Information', *Journal of Economic Theory*, vol. 47, pp. 307–33.

Rothschild, M. and J. Stiglitz (1976), 'Equilibrium in Competitive Insurance Markets: An Essay in the Economics of Imperfect Information', *Quarterly Journal of Economics*, vol. 90, pp. 629–50.

Rosenberg, N. and L. Birdzell (1986), *How the West Grew Rich* (New York: Basic Books).

Rosenstein Rodan, P. (1943), 'Problems of Industrialization of Eastern and South-Eastern Europe', *Economic Journal*, 53, June–Sept., pp. 202–11.

Scitovsky, T. (1954), 'Two Concepts of External Economies', *Journal of Political Economy*, vol. 62, pp. 143–51.

Shapiro, C. and R. Willig (1990), 'Economic Rationales for the Scope of Privatization', in E. Suleiman and J. Waterbury, ed., *Political Economy of Private Sector Reform and Privatization* (Boulder, Col.: Westview Press).

Shapiro, C. and J. Stiglitz (1984), 'Equilibrium Unemployment as a Worker Discipline Device', *American Economic Review*, vol. 74, pp. 433–44.

Shleifer, A. (1986), 'Implementation Cycles', *Journal of Political Economy*, vol. 94, pp. 1163–90.

Wade R. (1990), Governing the Market: Economic Theory and the Role of Government in East Asian Industrialization. Princeton: Princeton University Press.

Weitzman, M. (1982), 'Increasing Returns and the Foundations of Unemployment Theory', *Economic Journal*, vol. 92, pp. 787–804.

8

Reforming Power Sector Markets

Kirit S. Parikh

INTRODUCTION

The power sector in India has been engaged in a time-consuming and gradual process of reforms that began in 1991 when it was opened up for private power producers. Power is a critical infrastructure for rapid economic development. Yet, many states in India have persistent power shortages. Scheduled power cuts, unscheduled outages, and fluctuating voltages have been common in many states. The economic costs of this poor quality power supply are enormous. Voltage stabilizers, inverters for storing electrical energy to tide over power failures, small diesel generator sets that adorn shops, burnt out motors and consequently overdesigned motors, etc., all impose large economic costs. Even in the tenth year of reforms now, the problems persist. Power shortages both in terms of peak capacity as well as electrical energy have been common in most of the states.

I first met Mrinal in 1962 when he joined the Economics Department of MIT as a graduate student. I was then a research associate at the Centre for International Studies working with Sukhamoy Chakravarty, Richard Eckaus, and Luis Lefeber on developing a planning model for India. We became good friends almost instantly and have remained so over the years. Mrinal and I became colleagues at the Indian Statistical Institute in Delhi which I joined in 1967. He has been also a member of the governing board of IGIDR for many years. Over all these years, the two things I have admired most about Mrinal are his commitment to the development of academic institutions of excellence in the country and his intellectual integrity. Of course, every one knows about his sense of humour and his delightful stories. As one of his friends and admirers, I am happy to write this paper, which deals with a theme that Mrinal has been interested in.

The power shortage reflects an inadequate investment in building generating capacity and transmission network. To understand why this has been the case, we need to study the working of the power sector in India. Till 1991, the power sector was mainly in the public sector. Electricity distribution and supply, with a few historical exceptions, was the prerogative of the State Electricity Boards (SEBs) of the state governments. The SEBs also set up and operated generating plants. There were also central government agencies that set up and operated large generating plants that served more than one state.

The National Thermal Power Corporation (NTPC), the National Hydel Power Corporation (NHPC), and the Nuclear Power Corporation (NPC) today have significant generating capacities. The output of each central sector station is allocated to selected states. Their entitlement shares are fixed. The central sector plants can sell electricity only to the SEBs. By 31 March 1998, the central sector had generating capacity of 27,379 MW, SEBs had 55,467 MW, and private firms 6256 MW, totalling 89,102 MW.

Resources were provided by the government for the expansion of generating capacity as per the approved five years plans of the states and Centre. The SEBs were expected to earn a 3 per cent rate of return on invested capital. The capital cost did not include interest during construction. Thus, delays and cost overruns in building plants were common. Delays were often justified on the ground that needed funds were not released in time and that the domestic supplier, often a public sector corporation, did not supply equipment in time. Cost overruns were explained by delays and inflation. Also, the initial estimates were at constant prices and did not account for anticipated inflation. There was also a tendency to underestimate costs so as to get approval and a tendency to start as many projects as possible.

The SEBs set tariffs for the final consumers under the recommendation of periodically set up *ad hoc* tariff commissions and guidance of the state governments, and there was no compulsion to set tariff in a commercial manner. The SEBs did not retain profits, and the state government appropriated the profits and bore the losses. Political considerations of the state governments have played increasing roles in the management of SEBs. Over the years, the SEBs became financially sick, and by 1991 most of them were making losses. The central government was also in a financial crisis then and was unable to provide funds for creating new generating capacity.

The sickness of the power sector is directly attributable to the financial sickness of the SEBs, which is a consequence of the political power of various lobbies. One such lobby is the agricultural lobby. Electricity is provided to agricultural users at highly subsidized rates. The agricultural lobby was able to extract this subsidy since, initially, the electricity demand by agriculture was a small part of the total demand: it was 3.9 per cent in 1950–1, 6 per cent in 1960–1, and had grown to 30.75 per cent in 1997–8. Since electricity consumption by agriculture is not measured, a great deal of the consumption ascribed to agriculture is probably theft of power, euphemistically called commercial losses. The burden of the subsidy till the mid-1970s was relatively small and spread out over a large number of other users who did not oppose it. The farm lobby had no difficulty getting electricity (and other agricultural inputs) at concessional rates. Perhaps there was also some social justification for such subsidy as it accelerated the diffusion of new technology. Although the farm lobby is not organized as such, its political power is substantial. The rural rich, and relatively large farmers, exercise considerable influence over the smaller farmers and agricultural labourers. They constitute vote banks which are still (though somewhat less now) controlled by the rural rich. Those political parties that obtained their support had to concede their demands for various agricultural subsidies.

Apart from agricultural subsidies, overstaffing and large transmission and distribution (T&D) losses contribute to the financial sickness of SEBs. These are also the outcomes of political compulsions. The SEBs, with their geographically widespread distribution system, provides an ideal opportunity to give jobs to party workers spread all over the state, thus letting elected representatives belonging to the ruling party from all over the state dispense favours to their supporters. The SEBs have nearly a million employees and are grossly overstaffed; also, the overstaffing varies across states. Thus, in 1990–1 Gujarat had 9 employees per million units of electricity sold, Bihar had 30, Orissa had 44, Uttar Pradesh had 24, and West Bengal had 27. Overstaffing creates a vested interested in the clandestine sale of electricity. It is common knowledge that a substantial part of T&D losses are in fact theft of power carried out with the connivance of the SEB staff.

Over the years, the situation has changed and new political pressures are developing for reforms. Power consumption by agriculture is not metered and hides quite a bit of pilferage. What is called 'agricultural power consumption' is now nearly 30 per cent of the total, and the burden of cross-subsidy is biting other users who are beginning to resist. At the same time, these subsidies have so crippled the SEBs that their ability to meet the demand is severely limited. The farmers too have began to feel the loss due to unreliable and frequently interrupted power supply, and some of them would be willing to pay more for better quality power. Thus, reforms in the power sector can be politically popular.

The macroeconomic and structural reforms initiated in June 1991 have unwittingly created an infrastructure bottleneck in the country. The primary aim of the reforms was and is to make the Indian economy efficient and fast growing. For efficiency, competition is essential. Domestic deregulation, carried out in June–July 1991 itself, was to provide domestic competition, and trade liberalization, carried out gradually over the years, was to provide international competition. Along with these, a reduced emphasis on the public sector was considered to be necessary. Because of the political interference to which it is subject to, as also the difficulty of imposing effectively a hard budget constraint, the probability of inefficiency in the public sector is high. Thus, public sector reforms and privatization were part of the reform strategy. A lowering of public sector investment was also called for, by the need to reduce the fiscal deficit. Control of inflation and price stabilization were and are needed to stimulate investment and protect the real incomes of the poor. Thus, the reforms led to a significant reduction in public investment in infrastructure.

The government had recognized the problem that reduced investment in infrastructure could lead to. It had hoped, however, that private investment would come forth to take the place of the public investment. Thus, shortly after the initiation of the reforms process in June 1991, the Government of India, in October 1991 (Ministry of Power 1991), opened up the power sector for foreign private plants—100 per cent ownership was permitted and the requirement to balance dividend by export earnings was waived.

The attempt to attract private investors has, however, resulted in little success, despite the massive interest shown by private investors. One reason for this is that the private generators were required to sell only to the SEBs. When one's only customer is financially sick, one would think twice before getting into the business. The difficulties that the Maharashtra SEB is facing in meeting Enron's bills would make private producers think even more before they invest. In fact, unless the financial sickness of the SEBs is taken care of, private power generators are even less likely to come now.

Once the reluctance of the private generators was perceived, the government thought of mega projects. These are to be large projects, which would supply power relatively cheaply. To reduce the price of power, the government offered concessions such as no customs duty and longer tax holiday. Thus, the government provides the subsidy up front. But here too, the unreliability of the SEBs as customers who may not honour bills is a problem. To get around this, a new public corporation called power trading corporation (PTC) is envisaged. This will buy all the power from a mega project, pay the bill, and in turn sell the power to different SEBs. How would the PTC collect its bills from the SEBs? If it cannot, presumably the central government will foot the bill. The sick SEBs would have an even greater incentive to default on payment to a public corporation than to a private generator. This is evident as today the various SEBs together owe public sector corporations such as the NTPC, Coal India, NHPC, etc. a sum of Rs 27,000 crores (Rs 270 billion).

Pricing and pilferage reforms are essential. If we delay these reforms, even good firms like the NTPC would be dragged down by the sick SEBs. State Chief Ministers agree in New Delhi to raise the power tariff for agricultural consumers, but as soon as they return to their state capitals, they get cold feet. Only a handful of Chief Ministers have made some progress here. To force state governments to raise the price of power, the idea of setting up state electricity regulatory commissions (SERCs) was mooted. SERCs are to be independent statutory bodies and are to prescribe power tariffs. If a state government wants to subsidize any particular set of consumers, it has to give direct budgetary support to the SEB. This roundabout way to raise tariffs has not yet produced substantial result and progress is understandably slow, as the SERCs are appointed by the state governments. Only three SERCs had issued tariff orders by the end of June 2000, though by July 2001 this number increased to nine.

The poor success of the reform measures undertaken is due to the inadequate consideration given to markets, to demand and supply, and to the economic incentives of various agents. A solution that respects these is likely to succeed. Such a solution would involve privatization of various elements of the sector. The question, however, is how to go about it, that is, what to privatize and how? These are the questions that I address here.

THE MARKETS IN A POWER SYSTEM

A power system consists of a number of actors: the power producers who generate electricity, the transmission system operators who transmit it over long distances at usually high voltages, the distributors who supply it to consumers, and the consumers of different types who consume electricity. Thus, there are three different markets where exchange takes place. Of the many ways in which these markets can be organized, one way is shown in Figure 8.1. These three markets are interconnected and have different structures. Their broad characteristics are as follows.

The Bulk Supply Market has usually one buyer, namely the transmission company, call it TRANSCO. The sellers are a number of producers. The number of producers however, is not large, and some of them may be of large size, having some market power. Moreover, electricity supplied at different times of the day and year can have different prices. This is not a competitive market.

The TRANSCO is a monopsonist. It is also a monopolist when comes to selling power to the distribution companies, DISTCOs. Each DISTCO has a number of final consumers who are usually numerous, some of whom may be large consumers. Most of the consumers have no market power, since consumers are usually required to buy electricity from one particular DISTCO. The DISTCO thus has monopoly power. Large consumers, or a cluster of them, can set up their own captive power plant, if the law permits it, in which case the cost of electricity from a captive plant constrains the market power of the DISTCOs.

The system can be organized in many different ways. For example, consumers can be free to buy electricity from any DISTCO that they prefer. The DISTCOs may be free to buy electricity directly from any producer they want. All kinds of vertical integration are possible. For example, in the existing system in India, an SEB owns generating plants, is the sole owner of transmission network, and is also the sole distributor. This is shown in Figure 8.2.

Here the SEB owns many generating plants and also buys electricity from some central sector plants. There is some conflict about how much power should the SEB buy from the central sector plants. Sometimes, a SEB uses its own more expensive plant instead of buying electricity from a central sector plant because the marginal cost of generating from its own plant is smaller than the (average) purchase price of electricity from a central sector plant. However, since for much of the period there

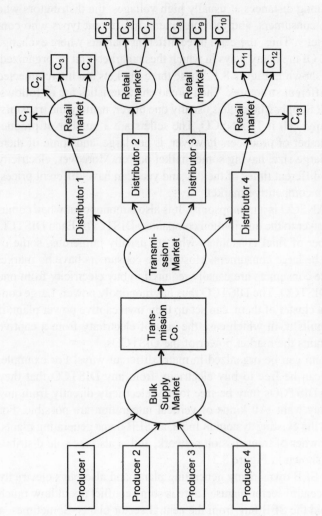

Fig. 8.1: Interconnected Markets in a Power System

Note: C—Consumer

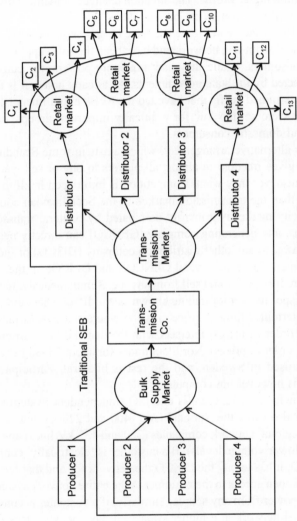

Fig. 8.2: Jurisdiction of State Electricity Boards

has been a situation of supply shortage, this conflict has not been important. Also, since all the SEBs are public sector enterprises, the conflicts have been resolved amicably, as neither side has been too concerned about maximizing its profits. The situation changes fundamentally when some electricity generators are private plants.

The SEBs, as shown in Figure 8.2, have by and large owned the transmission and distribution network and have been the sole supplier in their state to consumers. While they had monopoly powers, the consumers were protected by the state governments. As already noted, it is the politically determined tariffs that have led the SEBs into a financial mess. The tariffs were set too low for politically important groups, such as farmers and domestic consumers.

A polar alternative arrangement, which exists in some Scandinavian countries, gives freedom to almost all players to buy or sell electricity from whomsoever they want. Competition is introduced in all the markets other than the transmission market. In the Scandinavian countries, the electricity market is primarily dominated by bilateral transactions. That means, any generating company (GENCO) can directly negotiate and sell power to any other distribution company (DISCO) or independent customer. There are several GENCOS and DISCOS in the market and they are free to buy and sell from anyone. Simultaneously, there is a day-ahead spot-market for trading known as NordPool where the market price is determined through price-crossing where sell bids (arranged in increasing order of prices) intersect with the demand bids (arranged in decreasing order of prices). NordPool trades for about 25–30 per cent of all energy used in Sweden, and the rest is bilateral. Participation in NordPool is however not compulsory.

On the network side, there is one ISO (Independent System Operator) which also owns the National Grid (400 and 220 kV lines). There are some regional network companies (220 and 132 kV lines) and many DISCOS (lower voltage levels). If a customer is 'electrically' connected to a DISCO, it has to pay the DISCO the network fee and that fee itself, gives a full open access to the customer to the entire network system and it can buy power from any source. Similarly, if a customer is connected to a regional network at a higher voltage, it pays network fees to that company and gets full access to the system. The same situation prevails when connecting to the national grid directly.

There are many distributors in the whole system including some small municipal companies. However, note that, there is only one distributor in one region. Consumers are, however, free to buy power from any GENCO. But based on its location, it has to seek a network connection from the network company serving that location. This provides choice to consumers as to which DISCO they want to buy from, but does not duplicate the distribution network.

Domestic consumer prices are in two separate parts. One is the 'network charge' that is generally fixed for one year and regulated by the Swedish Energy Administration. The 'energy charge' is based on which DISCO one is buying the energy from. The consumers have various options to choose—'fixed-rate' options and 'market-rate' based variable tariff options. The DISCOs use standard load-curves for customer types, to charge on an hour-to-hour basis. For bulk customers, the network fee is as mentioned above; the energy fee depends on how they are buying— either bilateral or NordPool, etc. Most of the time the DISCOs buy from the GENCOs. Some DISCOS also have their own generating facilities.

Bulk prices are either determined in the spot-market 'NordPool' or through bilateral negotiations. Note that NordPool also operates a 'Futures' market up to three years in advance. These market prices often influence, and are sometimes influenced by, the spot-market prices.

The national transmission market in the Scandinavian countries is not competitive at all. In fact, there is a major difference between the European and the US way of operating the transmission system. In Europe, the transmission operation is virtually nationalized and the transmission system operators are also the Independent System Operators (ISOs). They are responsible for system stability, security, etc. and hence have to remain out of the market. They manage the ancillary services markets, that is markets for voltage control services, frequency control services, etc., which are separated from the energy markets.

There is, however, one problem. When everything is free, how does one ensure that adequate investments in capacity building and transmission takes place? Even in Scandinavia, that is a major problem. In Sweden, during the past 5 years, about 15 per cent of the costly GENCOS have shut down. This is because NordPool prices had been falling and many GENCOS were operating at very low plant load factors (PLFs). No further investments are forthcoming. Moreover, because of the government's policy of shutting down nuclear units, there is the danger of a further crisis looming. In the winter of 2001, the Swedish system was virtually close to collapse on two separate days and NordPool prices went up 10 times, during the peak hours!

Transmission investments are also very rare. Though the transmission system is a public sector corporation, the protests from some environmental groups have delayed construction. However, there are some international projects coming up—SWE-POL link, etc.—which will probably bail out the system through exports and imports. These are funded and owned by individual power companies from both sides.

Though the futures market does give some guidance to investors, the problem of sustainability over time is not fully solved. Even in such a free competitive market set-up, there is a role for regulation. For example, the transmission network usually involves large economies of scale and constitutes a natural monopoly. The regulator determines transmission charges for taking electricity from one place to another. Once such wheeling charges are determined, the generators, distributors, and consumers can be in a competitive set-up. Apart from transmission, there are economies of scale in generation as well. In a large system, this does not provide any substantial monopoly power. For example, if the optimal generator size is 500 MW and the total system size is 10,000 MW, there will be at least 20 generating units in the system.

With this background, we can examine why the experience with power sector reform in India so far has not been happy, and suggest ways in which reforms should be carried out.

THE POWER SECTOR REFORMS EXPERIENCE

The power sector reforms were initiated in 1991. In 1992, the power sector was opened up to independent (domestic and foreign) power producers (IPPs), in order to expand the generating capacity. This posed the problem: at what price should an SEB buy power from an IPP? As many final consumers were subsidized and much pilferage was going on, it was recognized that tariff reforms were needed if the SEBs are to pay a reasonable price to an IPP. This led to the second step in reforms: The establishment of regulatory commissions to rationalize tariffs.

The Central Electricity Regulatory Commission (CERC) was set up in late 1998. The states were also urged to set up State ERCs (SERCs). These have been set up in most of the states, and a number of the SERCs have issued tariff orders by now. Tariff orders, however, have not been sufficient to solve the problems of high T&D losses, inefficient functioning of the SEBs, deteriorating transmission and distribution networks, large receivables, and poor quality of supply. At the same time, the state governments are not willing to raise tariffs for the farmers while their capability to provide budgetary support to the SEBs is declining. Thus, it is now generally accepted that privatization and restructuring of the SEBs are essential, if reliable power is to be supplied at competitive prices, which is critical for economic development.

Restructuring reforms have been attempted so far in four states,— Andhra Pradesh, Orissa, Haryana, and Uttar Pradesh. The reforms in these states have some common features.

(i) They unbundled the vertically integrated SEBs along functional lines into (a) a single state owned transmission company which was the sole purchaser of power from generating companies, and (b) a number of distribution companies, each of which had a mix of subsidized and subsidizing consumers.

(ii) Tariffs were determined annually by the SERCs.

(iii) Past liabilities of the SEBs were retained by the state. However, some of the employee-related liabilities were transferred to the distribution companies.

Orissa started the reform process in 1996 by unbundling the SEB into state-owned companies. The state-owned Grid Corporation of Orissa (GRIDCO) performed both transmission and distribution activities from April 1996 to November 1998. The Orissa Power Generation Corporation (OPGC) was vested with the entire hydro capacity. Subsequently, 49 per cent of the equity in OPGC was divested to a private firm. It was only in 1999 that the distribution part of GRIDCO was privatized into four companies covering the central, north, west, and south zones of the state.

The reform experience in Orissa so far has been disappointing, to say the least. The private distribution companies are in financial stress and their operations are not viable. Even after three years of privatization, T&D losses for the private distribution companies remain at 42.7 per cent whereas they were told at the time of privatization that T&D losses were only 35 per cent. Consumer tariffs fixed by the Orissa ERC (OERC) have not fully accounted for these losses. The consumers, thus, see no improvement in the quality of supply or a reduction in tariff, though privatization was expected to bring greater efficiency and lower costs. The lesson one learns is that by itself the privatization of distribution does not create a competitive market nor does it provide incentives for efficiency. An appropriate regulatory framework is needed, to which we will turn later.

The private distribution companies, unable to reduce T&D losses, do not pay the transmission company, GRIDCO, in time for the power it supplies. The private companies are able to get away with it as GRIDCO is a state-owned company and the government, as majority shareholder, is unwilling to force a slowdown and disruption in power supply. Thus, GRIDCO is also in financial distress and unable to meet its working expenses, let alone service past liabilities. GRIDCO, in turn, does not pay to the generating companies, the NTPC, OPGC, and Orissa Hydro Power Corporation (OHPC). Failure in one market of the power system cascades into failures in other markets. Orissa's restructuring has not led to competitive markets, commercial operation, or efficiency improvement.

The Orissa GRIDCO combines the function of bulk purchase from power generators and sale to distributors with that of transmission of power from producers to distributors. The two functions are separate and can be separated. With a pure transmission company collecting a pre-specified wheeling charge, the distributing companies can by permitted to buy power directly from the generating companies. One can even permit larger consumers to buy directly from distributors. This can introduce more competition in the system.

In Andhra Pradesh, the Andhra Pradesh State Electricity Board (APSEB) was unbundled through segregation of its transmission and distribution assets into the Andhra Pradesh Transmission Company (APTRANSCO), while its hydro and thermal generation assets were combined (unlike Orissa) under the Andhra Pradesh Generating Company (APGENCO) as the Government of Andhra Pradesh did not wish to divest its generation assets. These entities continue to be owned by the government. Following unbundling, APTRANSCO was vested with the responsibility of buying power from APGENCO and other power producers—IPPs, joint ventures, central sector utilities, and other SEBs—and distributing it to end consumers.

While the OERC has consistently disallowed expenditure on power purchase associated with loss levels greater than a benchmark level of 35 per cent, regardless of the actual extent of the loss, the Andhra Pradesh ERC (APERC) has been more flexible. There are limits to the rapid increase of tariffs. In June 2000, the APERC issued its first tariff order, recommending a 20 per cent increase in the tariff, which instantly triggered intense and widespread opposition to reform. The original order was predicated upon a subsidy support of about Rs 1345 crore from the government. The APERC moderated its order somewhat when the government expressed its willingness to provide more subsidies in order to reduce the impact of tariff shocks on the final consumers. Yet the APERC has had difficulty in ensuring performance improvement as it does not get the needed information from APTRANSCO. Thus, in Andhra Pradesh also, the restructuring has not led to efficiency gains.

The experience of unbundling and privatization in other countries has also been mixed (see Besant Jones and Tenenbaum 2001; Reddy 2001; and Parikh J. and Parikh K. 2002). The experience of restructuring in India raise some questions: How should the power system be restructured to provide incentives to improve efficiency? How can the move to such a system from the present state of power systems in India be made?

RESTRUCTURING INDIAN POWER SYSTEMS

The goal of restructuring should be to have distributors who supply power to consumers at competitive prices. If reforms are done properly, consumers who are not subsidized at present should benefit from the reforms. Reforms should improve the efficiency of the system, reduce costs, and hence the price for such consumers. This would imply that they minimize T&D losses and purchase power from producers at least cost. The following framework can deliver these goals.

- The generation, transmission, and distribution are unbundled.
- A number of private distribution companies supply power to consumers.
- A regulatory commission sets the prices for consumers for several years at a time. The price may be set as a formulae which permits pass through of certain costs beyond the control of the distributors.
- The regulator also sets transmission (wheeling) charges.
- The distributors are free to purchase electricity at a mutually agreed price from the generators. They are also free to set up their own generating plants.

How should reforms, that have the desired effects be carried out? Privatization of distribution is the necessary first step. However, it should be done in a way that does not turn the consumers away from the reforms. For this, a process which ensures that consumers are not required to pay any more for the inefficiency of the system should be set up. This requires the following: First, the minimum cost at which an efficiently working power system, without pilferage, would supply power to different consumers should be worked out. Consumers should be informed about it and made to accept that they have to pay such a price. Next, the SERC should not permit the distributor to charge a price higher than the optimal price or the present price, whichever is higher. If the present price is higher, it should be brought down to the optimal level in a time bound schedule over three years. The private distribution company should be asked to give a plan for eliminating pilferage over a period of three years as per an agreed schedule. The state should compensate the private distributor for pilfered power only as per the agreed schedule. If the private firm eliminates pilferage at a faster pace, it would make extra profit. If it delays it, it loses money. That is its incentive. Such a scheme makes privatization of distribution acceptable to consumers who should see better, cheaper power with higher efficiency. This requires that there is an agreement on the extent of pilferage at the time of privatization. We have seen that this has not been done always. To do so before privatization, the SEB accounts should be clear and transparent, and transformers be installed at all sub-station and critical junctions in the network. With these steps, a clear assessment of T&D loss can be made.

Another requirement is that if any power subsidy is to be given to farmers, it should be through a direct budgetary transfer from the state government. It should be, however, possible to persuade farmers to pay for power. So far, the farm lobby has resisted any increase in the power tariff. The farmers themselves would be better off if they were to pay a higher price and get an assured supply of power. They would be, therefore, willing to pay a higher price if only they are convinced that this will result in better quality of power. At present, they do not trust that this would indeed happen. There is, thus, a chicken or egg problem. Power supply quality cannot be improved without raising power prices for farmers, and farmers will not pay more unless power quality is improved.

How to get around this 'which came first, chicken or egg', problem? One way of doing so is by linking power tariff to the actual quality of power supplied. Farmers pay the higher price only if they get good quality power supply, otherwise, they pay what they pay now. Thus, for example, suppose in a state the farmers today pay 50 paise per unit and the supply is so bad that they get power only at night for eight hours. We tell the farmers that they will have to pay Rs 2.00 per unit but only if the power is supplied round the clock at the right voltage and with a given confidence level, say for example, 99.5 per cent of the time. If the supply is not of this quality, they pay only 50 paise. This can be implemented by installing a meter at the sub-station level, which will record round the clock the power supplied and the voltage at which it is supplied. The meter can be under the joint control of the SEB and the framers' co-operative and should be tamper proof. Thus, the quality of power supplied can be indisputably established. A meter that traces a graph round the clock will be difficult to falsify. Even then, to guard against collusion between SEB meter readers and farmers, a cellular phone transmitter that sends the reading once a day to the central computer can be employed. Such a transmitter can be put in a sealed steel box, if need be. The cell phone network is today widespread and the technology is readily available and inexpensive. This system can be introduced *taluka* by *taluka*. The electricity boards will get money only if they improve the supply. They would also have to be responsible. The small amount of resources needed to improve the supply in a *taluka* and initiate the process may be provided to the SEBs.

The farmers should be willing to accept this. If a farmer were to get power on demand instead of for only eight hours a day, he can run his pump round the clock and either irrigate more land or sell surplus water to his neighbour. In either case, he will make much more money than he would pay for the power, even at Rs 2.00 per unit. The cost of irrigation would increase to a range of Rs 500 to Rs 700 per hectare. Farmers who buy water from their neighbour today pay Rs 800 to Rs 1200 per hectare.

If T&D losses were to be curtailed and if farmers were to pay a proper price for power, power shortage could easily be dealt with. Without it, nothing else is likely to work. Today, the SEBs lose more than Rs 15,000 crore (Rs 150 billion) a year on T&D losses and agricultural subsidy. This is the main cause (apart from stealing) of the financial sickness of SEBs. If they had this money, they could borrow an additional Rs 30,000 crores (Rs 300 billion) from the market as they can offer good interest rates on loans. With this, they can install 10,000 MW of additional capacity every year. Unfortunately, the SEBs are unable to do this. Hence, If the discipline of the market is to be used to obtain quality power at competitive prices, restructuring and privatization are inevitable.

REFERENCES

Besant-Jones, John E. and Bernard W. Tenenbaum (2001), 'California Power Crisis: Lessons for Developing Countries', An ESMAP Report, The World Bank, Washington DC.

Government of India (1991), 'Resolution No. 7/8/88 Thermal', *The Gazette of India*, No. 237, 22 October, Ministry of Power, New Delhi.

Parikh, Jyoti and Kirit Parikh (2002), 'Reforms in the Power Sector', in Kirit Parikh and R. Radhakrishna, eds., *India Development Report 2002*, Oxford University Press, New Delhi.

Reddy, A.K.N. (2001), 'California Energy Crisis and Its Lessons for Power Sector Reform in India', *Economic and Political Weekly*, 5 May 2001, p. 1533–40, Mumbai.

9

The Interaction between Child Labour and Child Schooling: Comparative Evidence on Cross-country Data

Ranjan Ray

INTRODUCTION

Child labour is a good example of a subject matter that does not lie exclusively in the sphere of either markets or of government. Given the costs of child labour for the child's development, the market, left to itself, is unlikely to arrive at an optimal solution that maximizes the child's welfare. However, while there is scope for intervention by the State and child welfare agencies to avoid the excesses of child labour, economists agree that the problem cannot be eradicated overnight simply by legislative measures by the government. The prominence accorded to the subject of child labour at the World Trade Organization meeting in Seattle is a reflection of its pivotal importance in the international policy arena. Basu (1999b) provides a lucid exposition of the policy implications of child labour for the setting of international labour standards in an era of rapid globalization. Fallon and Tzannatos (1998) discuss ways in which the World Bank can assist member nations in reducing child labour.

I am very pleased to contribute this essay to the collection of papers that is being published to honour Mrinal Datta-Chaudhuri. As a teacher and, later, a colleague of mine at the Delhi School of Economics, Mrinal has been an important influence in my life and that of many others who were associated with that great institution. I have appreciated his intellectual guidance and his friendship over the years. I am grateful to Geoffrey Lancaster for his research assistance for this paper. This research was supported by a grant from the Australian Research Council.

There has been, in recent years, a rapidly expanding literature on child labour that provides empirical evidence on its nature and determinants (for surveys, see Grootaert and Kanbur 1995, Basu 1999a, and Jafarey and Lahiri 2000). Within the empirical literature on child labour, there has been a shift in emphasis from mere quantification to an econometric analysis of its determinants. The present study is in the latter tradition. It pays particular attention to the interaction between child labour and child schooling, recognizing the simultaneity of the decisions on employment and education. Since child employment adversely affects the child by reducing the time available for her/his education, which is essential for the child's long term development,[1] the quantification of the impact of child labour on child schooling and *vice versa* is of considerable importance in assessing the nature and magnitude of the problem. That is one of the chief motivations of the present study.

The following features distinguish it from most previous investigations. First, the present study extends the studies of Jensen and Nielsen (1997), Psacharopoulos (1997), Ray (2000a), and others who assume that a child either attends school or is in employment. The present exercise recognizes other possibilities such as a child combining schooling with employment or a child who does neither. While the former is a feature in many Latin American countries, the latter phenomenon, referred to as that of 'nowhere children', is widespread in South Asian countries (see Weiner 1991). Second, the child labour and child schooling variables are jointly estimated using a three stage least squares (3SLS) estimation procedure that takes note of the simultaneity of these variables. In this exercise, we also endogenize household poverty which is identified as one of the main causes of child labour in the analytical literature (see Basu and Van 1998). We, therefore, pay particular attention to the interaction between a child's labour hours, her/his schooling experience, and the economic circumstances of the child. Third, in keeping with the international nature of the child labour problem, the present study provides comparative evidence based on data from countries in three continents, namely, Peru, Ghana, Pakistan, and Nepal. As Table 9.1, reproduced from Basu (1999a), shows, South Asia contains the largest concentration of child labour in the world. Nearly one in three child labourers is from South Asia. However, the child labour participa-

---

[1] See Dréze and Sen (1995) for a discussion of the importance of literacy and education in the economic development of the country.

tion rate in South Asia lags behind that in Africa. Even in Latin America and the Caribbean, the child labour participation rate in 1990 was estimated to be over 8 per cent. One of the principal results of our exercise is the wide cross-country variation in the nature and magnitude of the interaction between child labour and child schooling.

Table 9.1: Child Labour: Aggregate and Distribution[a]

	Number of Children (below 15 years) Working (in thousands)		
	1980	1985	1990
World	87,867	80,611	78,516
	(19.91)	(n.a.)	(11.32)
Africa	14,950	14,536	16,763
	(30.97)	(n.a.)	(24.92)
Latin America and the Caribbean	4122	4536	4723
	(12.64)	(n.a.)	(8.21)
Asia:	68,324	61,210	56,784
	(23.42)	(n.a.)	(10.18)
East Asia	39,725	33,463	22,448
	(n.a.)	(n.a.)	(n.a.)
South East Asia	6518	6079	5587
	(n.a.)	(n.a.)	(n.a.)
South Asia	20,192	19,834	27,639
	(n.a.)	(n.a.)	(n.a.)

n.a.: not available
[a] Figures in bracket denotes the child labour participation rate.
Source: Basu (1999a), table 1.

The rest of this paper is organized as follows. The second section discusses the methodology, describes the data sets, and focuses on some of its summary features. The empirical results are presented and discussed in the third section. The fourth section concludes by spelling out the policy implications.

METHODOLOGY AND DATA

The empirical exercise estimates both child labour participation/school enrolment rates and child labour hours/years of schooling. With respect to the former, the exercise uses a multinomial logit estimation procedure[2] that analyses the participation and non-participation of children in schooling and in employment and, in particular, allows the possibility that a child combines schooling with employment or does neither. We also use an ordered logit estimation procedure based on a ranking of the various child schooling/employment/non-schooling/non-employment outcomes. The multinomial logit estimation procedure estimates a reduced form equation, involving the four alternative states that a child could find herself in, using maximum likelihood procedure based on a multinomial logistic distribution of the errors, $\in$. These 4 states correspond to: (i) child does not work, attends school; (ii) child works and attends school; (iii) child neither works nor attends school; and (iv) child works and does not attend school. Since the probabilities of being in the 4 states (i)–(iv) must add to unity for each child, the multinomial logit strategy involves estimating three equations. In this study, we have normalized category (ii), that is, adopted the state of child working and attending school as the baseline case in the multinomial logit regressions. The ordered logit estimation is based on the following ordering of the four states, arranged in decreasing order from the viewpoint of child welfare: (a) only school, (b) school and work, (c) neither school nor work, (d) only work.

The empirical exercise is based on the simultaneous equations estimation, using 3SLS, of a set of three equations, namely, the annual labour hours of the child, the years of schooling experience of that child and the poverty status (1 = poor, 0 = non poor) of the household that the child belongs to. The poverty line was set at half the sample median of per adult equivalent household expenditures. The 3SLS estimation procedure not only takes note of the joint endogeneity of these three variables but, also, recognizes the mutual interaction between the equations through allowing a non-diagonal covariance matrix of the errors of the estimated system.[3] A key feature of this exercise is that we examine the impact of a child's current school attendance on her/his labour hours. This last aspect of our empirical exercise is of considerable policy significance since many have argued (for example, Weiner 1991) that compulsory

[2] The results are reported and discussed in greater detail in Maitra and Ray (2002).

[3] The 3SLS procedure adopted here extends the single equation based approach of Ray (2000b) which ignored the simultaneity of the child labour and child schooling equations.

schooling or, alternatively, encouraging schooling via an enrolment subsidy is a useful vehicle for reducing child labour.[4]

The data on child labour comes from the 1994 Peru Living Standards Measurement Survey (PLSS), the 1991 Pakistan Integrated Household Survey (PIHS), the 1988–89 Ghana Living Standards Measurement Survey (GLSS), and the 1995 Nepal Living Standards Survey (NLSS). We restrict ourselves to the labour hours and schooling of Ghanian children aged 5–15 years engaged in full-time, paid work, consistent with the definition used by the International Labour Organisation (ILO).

Evidence on the difference between countries in the nature of child labour is contained in Table 9.2, which presents the share of household income contributed by child labour earnings in 3 of the 4 countries considered here. The following features are worth noting. First, the Peruvian household is much less dependent on child labour earnings than its counterpart in Pakistan or Ghana. Second, as we move from children who only work to those who combine schooling with employment, the share of child labour earnings in household income drops in all cases. Note, however, that the drop is the least in the case of Peruvian girls, suggesting that schooling has relatively little impact on their ability to contribute to the household income through their labour earnings. Third, the sizeable proportion of household income that comes from child labour, especially in Pakistan and Ghana, points to the high vulnerability of several households to poverty, if their access to child labour earnings is reduced or removed through legislation without corresponding improvement in credit availability or the employment opportunity of their adults.

Table 9.2: Percentage Share of Income from Child Labour

	All	Boys	Girls
Peru			
Only Work	9.77	14.11	4.77
Both Work and School	3.58	3.79	3.26
Pakistan			
Only Work	23.37	30.33	16.05
Both Work and School	10.18	8.56	10.57
Ghana			
Only Work	30.14	30.33	31.22
Both Work and School	19.87	25.77	13.96

Source: Maitra and Ray (2002), table 3.

[4] See Ravallion and Wodon (2000) for evidence on Bangladesh.

RESULTS

MULTINOMIAL AND ORDERED LOGIT ESTIMATION RESULTS

The multinomial logit estimation based analysis of child labour and child schooling participation rates was performed for Ghana, Peru, and Pakistan. The multinomial logit regression estimates for each country have been reported in Maitra and Ray (2002). Table 9.3 presents the marginal probabilities implied by the multinomial logit estimates of the four choice outcomes (i)–(iv), as described in the previous section, for a selection of comparable variables between the three countries. The marginal probabilities show the marginal changes in the probabilities of the four outcomes when the corresponding child, family, or community characteristic changes by one unit. The estimates allow ready comparison between the three countries. In all these countries, older children are more likely to combine schooling with employment and less likely to be doing neither, with the child age effect proving strongest in Ghana. Again, in all these countries, girls are more likely than boys to be neither in schooling nor in employment, and less likely to combine schooling with employment. In Pakistan and Ghana, girls are much less likely than boys to be exclusively in schooling with no outside work involvement, while the exact reverse, though not as strongly, is indicated for Peru. In all the three countries, household poverty tends to have a detrimental effect on exclusively school going children, though in varying degrees, the strongest being in Ghana, the weakest in Peru. These countries, also, agree that household poverty encourages children to migrate to the 'work only' category. However, differences exist between countries with respect to the 'poverty effect' on the other choice categories. There is wide agreement between countries on the impact of urbanization on the child's choice of categories—the urban child is more likely than the rural to be in the 'school only' category, though the urbanization effect is not as strong in Ghana. The base probabilities confirm the high priority that Peruvian parents attach to their children's education, since a much larger percentage of children in Peru are purely school going or combine schooling with employment than in Pakistan or Ghana.

Table 9.4 presents the corresponding marginal probabilities implied by the ordered logit estimates. The outcomes, it may be recalled, are arranged in a decreasing order from the viewpoint of child welfare. The base probabilities in Peru show that the probability based ordering of

Table 9.3: Multinomial Logit Marginal Probabilities for a Selection of Variables

Variable	Peru				Pakistan				Ghana			
	School only	Both school and work	Neither school nor work	Work only	School only	Both school and work	Neither school nor work	Work only	School only	Both school and work	Neither school nor work	Work only
Age	0.0212	0.0735	-0.0887	-0.0060	0.0275	0.0412	-0.1173	0.0486	0.0518	0.1137	-0.2168	0.0513
Girl	0.0797	-0.1029	0.0321	-0.0089	-0.2363	-0.0754	0.2858	0.0259	-0.1159	-0.0449	0.1344	0.0264
Urban	0.2733	-0.2587	-0.0028	-0.0118	0.2029	-0.0412	-0.1055	-0.0562	0.0493	-0.0026	-0.0102	-0.0364
Nchild	-0.0100	0.0060	0.0040	0.0000	-0.0061	0.0002	0.0035	0.0024	-0.0033	0.0037	-0.0003	-0.0001
Nadult	0.0105	-0.0148	0.0041	0.0002	0.0246	-0.0019	-0.0036	-0.0190	-0.0178	-0.0065	0.0206	0.0037
FHH	-0.0007	-0.0050	-0.0055	0.0112	-0.0468	0.0207	0.0154	0.0107	0.0652	-0.0206	-0.0071	-0.0375
Headage	-0.0010	-0.0001	0.0009	0.0002	-0.0012	-0.0001	0.0007	0.0006	-0.0002	0.0006	-0.0006	0.0001
Maxfemed	0.0064	-0.0045	-0.0002	-0.0017	0.0283	-0.0009	-0.0104	-0.0169	0.0373	0.0062	-0.0333	-0.0103
POV	-0.0385	-0.0006	0.0364	0.0027	-0.1144	-0.0225	0.0890	0.0479	-0.1494	0.0224	0.0790	0.0481
Base Probability	0.7539	0.1596	0.0691	0.0174	0.5309	0.0554	0.2399	0.1738	0.5370	0.0990	0.2922	0.0717

Note: Age = Age of child; Girl = 1, if girl, and 0, if boy; Urban = 1, if child resides in urban area, and 0, if child resides in rural; Nchild = no. of children in the household; Nadult = no. of adults in the household, FHH = 1 if child belongs to a female headed household, 0, otherwise; Headage = Age of household head; Maxfemed = years of education of the most educated female in the household of the child; Pov. = 1 if the child resides in a poor household, 0, otherwise.

Table 9.4: Ordered Logit Marginal Probabilities for a Selection of Variables

Variable	Peru				Pakistan				Ghana			
	School only	Both school and work	Neither school nor work	Work only	School only	Both school and work	Neither school nor work	Work only	School only	Both school and work	Neither school nor work	Work only
Age	-0.0810	-0.0535	-0.0179	-0.0095	0.0018	0.0000	-0.0008	-0.0009	0.0899	-0.0042	-0.0550	-0.0307
Girl	0.0489	-0.0323	-0.0109	-0.0058	-0.1927	0.0034	0.0853	0.1040	-0.1108	0.0049	0.0676	0.0384
Urban	0.2256	-0.1424	-0.0536	-0.0296	0.0942	-0.0018	-0.0425	-0.0498	0.0665	-0.0048	-0.0406	-0.0210
Nchild	-0.0084	0.0056	0.0019	0.0010	-0.0062	0.0001	0.0028	0.0032	-0.0009	0.0000	0.0006	0.0003
Nadult	0.0013	-0.0009	-0.0003	-0.0002	0.0208	-0.0004	-0.0095	-0.0109	-0.0183	0.0009	0.0112	0.0063
FHH	-0.0235	0.0154	0.0053	0.0028	-0.0352	0.0003	0.0155	0.0194	0.0860	-0.0056	-0.0526	-0.0278
Headage	-0.0012	0.0008	0.0003	0.0001	-0.0011	0.0000	0.0005	0.0006	-0.0002	0.0000	0.0001	0.0001
Maxfemed	0.0085	-0.0056	-0.0019	-0.0010	0.0292	-0.0006	-0.0133	-0.0153	0.0385	-0.0018	-0.0236	-0.0131
POV	-0.0461	0.0300	0.0105	0.0056	-0.1189	-0.0018	0.0480	0.0727	-0.1316	-0.0022	0.0787	0.0551
Base Probability	0.7112	0.2135	0.0506	0.0248	0.4832	0.0914	0.2706	0.1549	0.4612	0.1537	0.2917	0.0935

Note: Age = Age of child; Girl = 1, if girl, and 0, if boy; Urban = 1, if child resides in urban area, and 0, if child resides in rural; Nchild = no. of children in the household; Nadult = no. of adults in the household; FHH = 1 if child belongs to a female headed household, 0, otherwise; Headage = Age of household head; Maxfemed = years of education of the most educated female in the household of the child; Pov. = 1 if, the child resides in a 'poor' household, 0, otherwise.

the four outcomes coincide with that based on child welfare—for example, the Peruvian child is most likely to choose the best outcome, the least likely to choose the worst outcome. The ordering of the intermediate outcomes in Pakistan and Ghana are inconsistent with their child welfare ordering. The second highest base probability attached to the third outcome reflects the high percentage of children in Pakistan and Ghana who are neither in school nor in employment. With respect to the sign and magnitude of the marginal probabilities, Pakistan and Ghana are closer to one another than to Peru. The gender effect is particularly strong in Pakistan, placing the girl child there in a position of disadvantage *vis-à-vis* Pakistani boys in trying to attain the most desirable outcome.

SIMULTANEOUS EQUATIONS ESTIMATES OF CHILD LABOUR HOURS AND CHILD SCHOOLING YEARS

The 3SLS estimates of the child's labour hours and her/his schooling experience are presented in Tables 9.5–9.7 for Nepal, Pakistan, and Ghana, respectively. While the numbers in these tables are worth examining individually and provide considerable insights into child labour and child schooling in each country, a comparison between them helps to keep these results in perspective.

The following features are worth noting from these tables. First, in all the three countries, the current school attendance by a child significantly and sharply reduces her/his labour hours. Again, in all these countries, a *ceteris paribus* increase in the child's labour market activity has a significantly adverse impact on the child's schooling experience. The tradeoff between child employment and child schooling is clearly established from these tables. The policy implication is clear—compulsory schooling or measures such as free school meals that encourage the child's school attendance provide effective means of reducing child labour hours.

Second, in all the three countries, boys work significantly longer hours in market activities than girls, though the gender disparity is much more in Pakistan than in the other two countries. Similarly, while girls experience significantly less schooling than boys in all these countries, the gender effect in schooling is weaker in significance in Ghana than in Nepal or Pakistan.

Third, an interesting result, with considerable policy significance, is that while rising levels of adult education significantly and positively impact on child schooling, it's anticipated negative impact on child labour is considerably weaker in absolute magnitude to the point of statistical insignificance in several cases. This result stems from the joint endogeneity of child employment and child schooling. It suggests that the previously observed negative impact of rising adult education on child labour (Ray 2000a, 2000b) worked through the positive impact of adult education on child schooling and the subsequent tradeoff between child schooling and child labour. Once the latter has been incorporated in the estimation, as in this study, the residual impact of adult education on the child's labour market activity is quite limited. This points, once again, to the enhancement of child schooling as the core strategy for making a serious dent on the problem of child labour.

Fourth, household poverty, though a significant determinant of child labour and child schooling in Nepal and Pakistan, does not always impact on these dependent variables in the manner expected. However, it does explain longer child hours in case of Nepal and less child schooling in case of Pakistan. In contrast, the poverty status of the household does not have a statistically significant impact on the child's labour hours or schooling experience in Ghana. In both Nepal and Pakistan, for which the relevant estimates are available, the presence of one or more employed adults in the household adds to the schooling experience of its children.

REDUCED FORM HECKMAN ESTIMATES OF CHILD LABOUR HOURS

The above discussion raises the issue of robustness of the magnitude of some of the coefficients between the structural equation estimates presented in Tables 9.5–9.7, and the reduced form equation for child labour hours which are specified as functions of exogenous determinants (that is, do not involve child schooling years or the household poverty status as regressors). To provide evidence on this, we estimated the child labour equation, in reduced form, using the Heckman (1979) two step procedure. The results for Pakistan, Nepal, and Ghana are presented in Table 9.8 in a form that allows ready comparison between the estimates for the three countries.

The following features are worth noting. First, the estimates reveal some significant differences between the country estimates. For example,

Table 9.5: 3SLS Estimates[a] of Child Labour Hours and Child Schooling Years in Nepal

	Labour hours		Schooling years	
Variable	Coefficient estimate	Variable		Coefficient estimate
Child characteristics		*Child characteristics*		
Currently attending school	−389.66[d]	Annual child labour hours		−0.01[d]
(0 = no, 1 = yes)	(25.75)			(0.00)
Age of child	5.31	Age of child		0.52
	(94.41)			(0.81)
(Age of child)[2]	0.63	(Age of child)[2]		0.01
	(3.78)			(0.03)
Child gender	−60.84[d]	Child gender		−0.93[d]
(0 = boy, 1 = girl)	(21.21)	(0 = boy, 1 = girl)		(0.18)
Child wage	13.43[d]	Child wage		0.11[d]
	(.46)			(0.01)
Family characteristics		*Family characteristics*		
Household poverty[b]	705.60[d]	Household poverty		4.09[c]
	(207.46)			(1.78)
Region of Residence	21.77	Region of residence		−0.15
(1 = urban, 2 = rural)	(64.32)	(1 = urban, 2 = rural)		(0.55)
No. of children	−15.75[d]	No. of children		−0.16[d]
	(5.49)			(0.05)

(Contd.)

Table 9.5: (Contd.)

	Labour hours		Schooling years
Variable	Coefficient estimate	Variable	Coefficient estimate
No. of adults	9.34 (6.04)	No. of adults	-0.01 (0.05)
Gender of household head (0 = male, 1 = female)	-54.49 (36.84)	Gender of household head (0 = male, 1 = female)	-0.30 (0.32)
Age of household head	-1.33 (0.87)	Age of household head	-0.01 (0.01)
Years of education of most educated male member	-3.38 (3.20)	Years of education of most educated male member	0.12[d] (0.03)
Years of education of most educated female member	-5.28 (3.50)	Years of education of most educated female member	0.11[d] (0.03)
At least one adult works (0 = no, 1 = yes)	154.60 (85.14)	At least one adult works (0 = no, 1 = yes)	2.01[d] (0.74)
Maximum wage earned by the male members	-0.24 (0.46)	Maximum wage earned by the male members	-0.00 (0.00)
(Maximum wage earned by the male members)^2	0.00 (0.00)	(maximum wage earned by the male members)^2	0.00 (0.00)
Maximum wage earned by the female members	-0.68[c] (0.31)	Maximum wage earned by the female members	-0.00 (0.00)
Credit received by the household	-0.00 (0.00)	Credit received by the household	-0.00 (0.00)

(Contd.)

Table 9.5: (Contd.)

Cluster/Community characteristics		Cluster/Community characteristics	
Atkinson inequality	−602.52	Atkinson inequality	1.90
	(1061.24)		(9.13)
(Atkinson inequality)^2	946.75	(Atkinson inequality)^2	−4.18
	(1730.57)		(14.88)
Cluster poverty	34.70	Cluster poverty	0.78
	(129.35)		(1.11)
Cluster credit availability	0.00	Cluster credit availability	0.00
	(0.00)		(0.00)
Water supply	6.01	Water supply	0.04
(1 = yes, 0 = no)	(24.91)	(1 = yes, 0 = no)	(0.21)
Electricity supply	−48.74	Electricity supply	−0.39
(1 = yes, 0 = no)	(34.59)	(1 = yes, 0 = no)	(0.03)

[a] Standard errors in brackets;

[b] Poverty status = 1 if the child comes from a 'poor' household, 0, otherwise;

[c] Significant at 5 per cent level;

[d] Significant at 1 per cent level.

Table 9.6: 3SLS Estimates[a] of Child Labour Hours and Child Schooling Years in Pakistan

	Labour hours		Schooling years
Variable	Coefficient estimate	Variable	Coefficient estimate
Child characteristics		*Child characteristics*	
Currently attending school (0 = no, 1 = yes)	−506.53[d] (26.50)	Annual child labour hours	−0.01[d] (0.00)
Age of child	−89.91 (108.54)	Age of child	0.02 (0.96)
(Age of child)^2	5.05 (4.36)	(Age of child)^2	0.04 (0.04)
Child gender (0 = boy, 1 = girl)	−225.73[d] (23.51)	Child gender (0 = boy, 1 = girl)	−2.26[d] (0.20)
Child wage	22.39[d] (2.33)	Child wage	0.18[d] (0.02)
Family characteristics		*Family characteristics*	
Household poverty[b]	477.11[c] (206.56)	Household poverty	−5.92[d] (1.82)
Region of residence (1 = urban, 2 = rural)	52.50 (27.06)	Region of residence (1 = urban, 2 = rural)	0.59[c] (0.24)
No. of children	−0.55 (4.41)	No. of children	−0.00 (0.04)

(Contd.)

Table 9.6: *(Contd.)*

No. of adults	-19.65^d	-0.25^d
	(6.23)	(0.06)
Gender of household head	86.22	0.90
(0 = male, 1 = female)	(84.06)	(0.74)
Age of household head	2.19^c	0.02
	(1.01)	(0.01)
Years of education of most	-1.04	0.07^d
educated male member	(2.67)	(0.02)
Years of education of most	8.71^c	0.16^d
educated female member	(3.44)	(0.03)
At least one adult works	170.68^d	1.44^d
(0 = no, 1 = yes)	(39.30)	(0.36)
Maximum wage earned by	-3.88	-0.03
the male members	(2.24)	(0.02)
(Maximum wage earned by	0.03	0.00
the male members)^2	(0.03)	(0.00)
Maximum wage earned by	-5.78^d	-0.05^d
the female members	(1.59)	(0.01)
Credit received by the	-0.001	0.00
household	(0.001)	(0.00)
Cluster/Community characteristics		*Cluster/Community characteristics*
Atkinson inequality	-786.91^d	Atkinson inequality -6.48^d
	(258.11)	(2.31)

(Contd.)

Table 9.6: (Contd.)

	Labour hours		Schooling years	
Variable	Coefficient estimate	Variable		Coefficient estimate
(Atkinson inequality)^2	1027.71[d]	(Atkinson inequality)^2		8.63[d]
	(319.87)			(2.86)
Cluster poverty	145.11	Cluster poverty		1.56
	(90.03)			(0.80)
Cluster credit availability	–0.00	Cluster credit availability		0.00
	(0.00)			(0.00)
Water supply	–5.55	Water supply		–0.07
(1 = yes, 0 = no)	(6.52)	(1 = yes, 0 = no)		(0.06)
Electricity supply	15.77	Electricity supply		0.55
(1 = yes, 0 = no)	(54.58)	(1 = yes, 0 = no)		(0.48)

[a] Standard errors in brackets
[b] Poverty status = 1 if the child comes from a 'poor' household, 0, otherwise
[c] Significant at 5 per cent level
[d] Significant at 1 per cent level

Table 9.7: 3SLS Estimates[a] of Child Labour Hours and Child Schooling Years in Ghana

	Child labour hours		Child schooling years	
Variable	Coefficient estimate	Variable		Coefficient estimate
Child characteristics		*Child characteristics*		
Child gender	−2.17[c]	Child gender		−0.59[c]
(0 = boy, 1 = girl)	(0.71)	(0 = boy, 1 = girl)		(0.13)
Age of child	1.07	Age of child		−0.12
	(0.57)			(0.15)
(Age of child)²	0.02	(Age of child)²		0.05[c]
	(0.03)			(0.01)
School attendance	−6.42[c]	Child labour hours		−0.26[c]
(1 = currently attending, 0 = otherwise)	(0.84)			(0.03)
Family characteristics:		*Family characteristics:*		
Household poverty status	−21.84	Household poverty status		−1.15
(1 = poor, 0 = otherwise)	(15.65)	(1 = poor, 0 = otherwise)		(3.11)
Region of residence:		*Region of residence:*		
Rural	3.80[c]	Rural		0.88[c]
	(1.09)			(0.24)
Semi urban	0.29	Semi urban		0.34[c]
	(1.02)			(0.23)
No. of children	0.79	No. of children		0.05
	(0.51)			(0.10)

(Contd.)

Table 9.7: (Contd.)

Child labour hours		Child schooling years	
Variable	Coefficient estimate	Variable	Coefficient estimate
No. of adults	0.49	No. of adults	-0.05
	(0.33)		(0.07)
Gender of household head	-0.93	Gender of household head	-0.53
(0 = male, 1 = female)	(1.27)	(0 = male, 1 = female)	(0.30)
Age of household head	0.01	Age of household head	0.01
	(0.03)		(0.01)
Most educated adult male's education	-0.14	Most educated adult male's education	0.02
	(0.09)		(0.02)
Most educated adult female's education	-0.11	Most educated adult female's education	0.05[c]
	(0.07)		(0.02)
Male wage	-0.00	Male wage	-0.00
	(.00)		(0.00)
(Male wage)^2	0.00	(Male wage)^2	0.00
	(0.00)		(0.00)
Female wage	-0.00	Female wage	-0.00
	(0.00)		(0.00)
(Female wage)^2	0.00	(Female wage)^2	0.00
	(0.00)		(0.00)

(Contd.)

Table 9.7: *(Contd.)*

Community characteristics:		*Community characteristics:*	
Schooling costs per household in cluster	-0.00[c]	Schooling costs per household in cluster	-0.00
	(0.00)		(0.00)
Percentage of households with electricity	0.96	Percentage of households with electricity	0.51
	(1.29)		(0.30)
Cluster inequality[b]	4.50	Cluster inequality[b]	-0.43
	(5.43)		(1.15)
(Cluster inequality)^2	7.53	(Cluster inequality)^2	0.62
	(4.74)		(1.04)

[a] Standard errors in brackets;
[b] The Atkinson inequality measure (with e = 0.5) was used;
[c] Significant at 5 per cent level.

Table 9.8: Heckman Estimates[a] of Child Labour Hours (Weekly) Equation in Reduced Form

Variable	Coefficient estimate				
	Pakistan[b]	Nepal		Ghana	
		Rural	Urban	Rural	Urban
Child characteristics:					
Child gender	−14.67[d]	2.98[d]	2.01	−6.44[d]	0.35
(0 = boy, 1 = girl)	(1.64)	(1.41)	(3.14)	(1.61)	(2.76)
Age of child	−1.44[d]	−0.03	11.50	−1.28[d]	0.04
	(0.05)	(1.96)	(14.07)	(0.02)	(3.44)
(Age of child)^2	0.06[d]	0.00	−0.54	0.06[d]	0.02
	(0.00)	(0.07)	(0.56)	(0.00)	(0.14)
Child wage dummy[c]	2.31[d]	0.04	7.24[d]	1.26[d]	1.14
	(0.01)	(0.69)	(3.57)	(0.01)	(2.69)
Family characteristics:					
No. of children	0.11[d]	0.24[d]	−1.10	0.08[d]	−0.75
	(0.00)	(0.09)	(0.94)	(0.00)	(0.73)
No. of adults	−1.15[d]	1.82[d]	−0.12	−0.06	3.01[d]
	(0.43)	(0.37)	(1.03)	(0.43)	(0.93)
Gender of household	−1.30	−4.90	1.50	0.86	−3.39
(0 = male, 1 = female)	(5.38)	(2.58)	(7.13)	(3.00)	(8.42)
Age of household head	0.27[d]	−0.02	0.67[d]	0.23[d]	−0.20
	(0.07)	(0.06)	(0.17)	(0.06)	(0.15)

(Contd.)

Table 9.8: (Contd.)

Most educated adult male's education	-1.51[d] (0.19)	-1.00[d] (0.21)	-0.65 (0.50)	0.08 (0.19)	-0.59 (0.36)
Most educated adult female's education	-1.41[d] (0.27)	-3.30[d] (0.25)	-1.03 (0.59)	-0.52[d] (0.22)	-0.52 (0.37)
Male wage	-7.72[d] (3.17)	-1.09 (0.88)	5.75 (3.44)	0.00 (0.00)	-0.00 (0.00)
$(\text{Male wage})^2$	2.31[d] (0.03)	0.23[d] (0.05)	-0.39 (0.37)	-0.00[d] (0.00)	0.00 (0.00)
Female wage	24.47[d] (5.16)	23.60[d] (2.27)	-36.73[d] (7.97)	0.00[d] (0.00)	-0.00 (0.00)
$(\text{Female wage})^2$	0.50[d] (0.01)	-3.07[d] (0.45)	0.00 (0.00)	-0.00[d] (0.00)	0.00 (0.00)
Community characteristics					
Head count poverty rate of cluster	1.45[d] (0.03)	2.59[d] (6.85)	-67.12[d] (25.37)	4.75[d] (0.03)	-1.31 (15.78)

[a] Standard errors in brackets
[b] Because of convergence problems, we were unable to obtain separate estimates for rural and urban Pakistan
[c] 1 if the child wage is observed, 0, otherwise
[d] Significant at 5 per cent level

the girl child works, *ceteris paribus*, significantly lesser market hours than boys in Pakistan and Ghana (rural), but significantly more hours in rural Nepal. Second, the headcount poverty rate of the cluster of residence of the child has a sharp positive impact on child labour hours in Pakistan, Nepal (rural), and Ghana (rural), but the exact reverse is indicated in urban Nepal. The Nepalese and Ghanaian estimates suggest that the nature of the impact of the child's economic environment, as measured by the cluster's poverty rate, on the child's labour hours differs between the rural and the urban areas. This is a result that needs further investigation. Third, at low adult wages in the rural areas, an increase in female wages tends to increase child labour hours, thus, suggesting a complementary relation between child and adult female labour markets (see also, Ray 2000b). However, the significance of the negative quadratic female wage co-efficient in Nepal (rural) and Ghana (rural) suggests that this complementary relationship weakens and gives way to substitutability at higher wage levels. Fourth, consistent with the structural equation estimates, improvements in the adult education levels tend to discourage child labour, that is, reduce child labour hours.

CONCLUSIONS

There has not been much empirical attempt, until recently, to examine systematically the causes of child labour with a view to identifying factors that could lead to its reduction and eventual elimination. That is now changing with a proliferation of empirical studies on child labour. The present study, which belongs to this recent tradition, compares the results of countries which account for a significant proportion of child labour in the world.

The study analyses both child labour participation rates and child labour hours. The results of multinomial logit estimation used to analyse child labour force participation rates suggest that while the overall goal of child welfare enhancing policies must be to move the child from 'work only' to 'school only' status, such a strategy can only be a long term one. In the short run, any policy that moves a child from a 'work only' or 'neither in work nor in school' status to one where she/he combines schooling with employment must be considered to be a success. The multinomial logit estimation results, reported in greater detail in Maitra and Ray (2002), identified the key variables that could prove effective in this regard.

Another important finding of this study, arising out of the joint estimation of the child labour hours and child schooling experience equations, is the significant role that a child's current school attendance plays in sharply diminishing her/his labour hours. Improvements in the schooling infrastructure, by making them more relevant to the child's needs as viewed by the parent, and locating them near places of child employment will be conducive to shorter working hours and encourage the combination of child labour with child schooling to a greater extent than has happened in countries such as Pakistan in relation to Latin American countries such as Peru (see Ray 2000a). Moreover, government assisted programmes such as the District Primary Education Projects and the Integrated Children Development Schemes (ICDS) in India (see Fallon and Tzannatos 1998, p. 15) can play a useful role in promoting schooling and reducing child labour.

REFERENCES

Basu, K. (1999a), 'Child Labour: Cause, Consequence and Cure with Remarks on International Labour Standards', *Journal of Economic Literature*, vol. 37, no. 3, pp. 1083–19.

_____ (1999b), 'International Labour Standards, Globalisation and Marginalisation, with Special Reference to Child Labour, Mimeo, Cornell University, Background Paper prepared for the WDR, 2000.

Basu, K. and P.H. Van (1998), 'The Economics of Child Labour', *American Economic Review*, vol. 88, no. 3, pp. 412–27.

Dreze, J. and A. Sen (1995), *India: Economic Development and Social Opportunity* (Oxford: Clarendon Press).

Fallon, P. and Z. Tzannatos (1998), *Child Labour: Issues and Directions for the World Bank*, Human Development Network (Washington, DC: World Bank).

Grootaert, C. and R. Kanbur (1995), 'Child Labour: An Economic Perspective', *International Labour Review*, vol. 134, no. 2, pp. 187–203.

Heckman, J. (1979), 'Sample Selection Bias as a Specification Error', *Econometrica*, vol. 47, no. 1, pp. 153–61.

Jafarey, S. and S. Lahiri (2000), 'Child Labour: Theory, Policy and Evidence', Discussion Paper No 2000–09, University of Wales, Swansea.

Jensen, P. and H.S. Nielson (1977), 'Child Labour or School Attendance? Evidence from Zambia', *Journal of Population Economics*, vol. 10, no. 4, pp. 407–24.

Maitra, P. and R. Ray (2002), 'The Joint Estimation of Child Participation in Schooling and Employment: Comparative Evidence from Three Continents', *Oxford Development Studies*, vol. 30, no. 1, pp. 41–62.

Psacharopoulos, G. (1997), 'Child Labour Versus Educational Attainment', *Journal of Population Economics*, vol. 10, no. 4, pp. 377–86.

Ravallion, M. and Q. Wodon (2000), 'Does Child Labour Displace Schooling? Evidence on Behavioural Responses to an Enrolment Subsidy', *The Economic Journal*, vol. 110, no. 162, pp. C158–75.

Ray, R. (2000a), 'Analysis of Child Labour in Peru and Pakistan: A Comparative Study', *Journal of Population Economics*, vol. 13, no. 1, pp. 3–19.

————— (2000b), 'Child Labour, Child Schooling, and Their Interaction with Adult Labour: Empirical Evidence for Peru and Pakistan', *The World Bank Economic Review*, vol. 14, no. 2, pp. 347–67.

Weiner, M. (1991), *The Child and the State in India* (Princeton, NJ: Princeton University Press).

10

Privatization and Its Benefits: Theory, Evidence, and Challenges

Eytan Sheshinski and Luis Felipe López-Calva

INTRODUCTION

For more than a decade now, both developed and developing countries have engaged in ambitious privatization programmes. The number of privatization transactions has been growing over the years. During 1996–8 itself, some financial turmoil notwithstanding, the sale of state-owned assets reached US$ 65 billion in Europe, more than US$ 27 billion in Canada, Latin America, and the United States, and nearly US$ 12 billion in Asia. As an illustration of the relevance of this policy, Table 10.1 shows the change in state-owned enterprises' share in gross domestic product (GDP) between 1980 and 1998 for all the economies in the world, grouped by income level according to the World Bank classification. Even though the change is not all due to privatization strategies, the two are strongly linked, as explained below.[1] The change reflects a major revision of the role of the public sector as owner of the productive assets in the economy.

This paper was first prepared as part of the *Consulting Assistance on Economic Reform II* (CAER II) programme at the Harvard Institute for International Development, Harvard University. We thank Antonio Estache, Michael Klein, and Florencio López-De-Silanes for useful conversations and suggestions. We also wish to thank Juan Belt and Orest Koropecky of USAID for their encouragement, guidance, and comments on the course of the study. Mabel Andalón provided excellent research assistance. All remaining errors are our own.

[1] In principle, it would be enough to have the private sector growing faster than the public sector to get the same trend.

Table 10.1: Change in SOEs' Activity as a Percentage of GDP

(in per cent)

Countries (by income group)	1980	1997	Change
Low income countries	15	3	−12
Lower middle income countries	11	5	−6
Upper middle income countries	10.5	5	−5.5
High income countries	6	5	−1

Source: Estimations based on the *World Development Indicators*, The World Bank.

In terms of the proceeds obtained from privatization, most countries have been successful. Between 1990 and 1998, for example, Brazil, Argentina, and Mexico obtained US$ 53.5, US$ 28.4, and US$ 30.4 billion, respectively, as a result of privatization sales. Smaller countries like Peru, Indonesia, and Colombia obtained US$ 11.2, US$ 6.0, and US$ 8.0 billion, respectively, during the same period.[2] Table 10.2 shows the proceeds from privatization for a selected group of countries from 1990 to 1998.

Table 10.2: Cumulative Proceeds from Privatization, 1990–8

Country	Amount (million dollars)
Argentina	28,431.4
Brazil	53,566.10
Bulgaria	1528
Chile	1288.70
China	20,142.90
Colombia	8006.30
Cote d'Ivoire	354.8
Czech Republic	942.1
Ghana	1457.20
India	8315.30
Indonesia	6008.80

(*Contd.*)

[2] These figures are taken from the *World Development Indicators*, The World Bank.

Table 10.2: (*Contd.*)

Kazakhstan	7205.40
Kenya	387.8
Mexico	30,424.20
Pakistan	3367.60
Peru	11,272.60
South Africa	2742.10
Thailand	2117.70
Venezuela	8002.80

Source: World Development Indicators.

It would be a mistake to assess the relevance of the privatization programme of a country by looking at the revenue generated for the government, even though the latter is important from a macroeconomic perspective, as discussed below. The set of objectives that the privatization programme are meant to achieve is much broader and involves, as a fundamental component, the improvement of microeconomic efficiency. In general, there are four explicit objectives in these programmes:

(i)   to achieve higher *allocative* and productive efficiency;
(ii) to strengthen the role of the private sector in the economy;
(iii) to improve the public sector's financial health; and
(iv) to free resources for allocation in other important areas of government activity (usually related to social policy).

The first two objectives have a normative rationale and relate to the microeconomic perspective. The first objective consists of increasing their aggregate surplus by increasing output and lowering prices (*allocative* efficiency), as well as through a more efficient use of resources within the firm (productive efficiency). The second has to do with the creation of well-functioning markets and an investor-friendly environment in the economy. The last two objectives, aimed at improving public sector finance, are the reduction of borrowing requirements and the potential reallocation of expenditure towards social policy areas. Thus, privatization programmes ought to be assessed by looking at the extent to which the stated objectives have been achieved. This paper reviews the theoretical arguments behind the belief that privatization can achieve these objectives and provides a survey of the empirical literature which tests whether the effects have been observed in countries that have undertaken privatization policies. Further, macroeconomic figures are presented to support the hypothesis that privatization has improved the public sector's financial health in those countries. We also discuss those aspects that have been especially problematic for privatization to be successful, namely, the creation of appropriate regulatory policies and the establishment of the legal basis for a renewal in corporate governance structures.

From a theoretical perspective, it is known that incentive and contracting problems create inefficiencies due to public ownership. This is so because managers of state-owned enterprises pursue objectives that differ from those of private firms (*political view*) and face less monitoring (*management view*). Not only are the managers' objectives distorted, but the budget constraints they face are also softened. The soft budget constraint emerges from the fact that bankruptcy is not a credible threat to public managers, for it is in the central government's own interest to bail them out in case of financial distress.

Empirically, the microeconomic empirical research has faced a severe data availability constraint. In this area, the literature is still small, yet growing. There are three groups of empirical studies: those based on firm-specific data in different countries with very small samples (*case studies*),[3] studies with a large sample of firms in different sectors for a specific country (*within-country studies*),[4] and cross-section analyses for privatized firms that are publicly traded (*cross-section studies*).[5] Those papers have shown important efficiency gains and productivity improvements in privatized firms—for well-defined measures—and allow us to evaluate the privatization experience from a microeconomic, partial equilibrium perspective.[6]

The macroeconomic effects of privatization programmes are more difficult to evaluate. It is possible, however, to look at aggregate measures—like public sector financial health and the capitalization of the stock market—and their evolution during the reform period. Given the

---

[3] These include Galal et al. (1994) and Eckel et al. (1997).

[4] See, for example, LaPorta and López-De-Silanes (1998).

[5] Megginson et al. (1994), D'Souza and Megginson (1998), and Bourbakri and Cosset (1998), for example.

[6] Chisari et al. (1999), a within-country study, is the only one with a general equilibrium setting. An excellent review of the empirical studies, including an analysis of the impact of privatization on financial markets, is Megginson and Netter (2000).

level of aggregation, it is difficult to isolate the effect of privatization on variables like gross domestic product (GDP) growth, employment level, and fiscal deficit, because of the diversity of events taking place at the same time.[7] This paper, however, shows the evolution of selected aggregate measures and relates that evolution with privatization, invoking established theoretical principles.

The scope for the evaluation of privatization programmes includes, as mentioned above, not only efficiency, but also equity issues. This paper argues that the distributive effect of privatization policies is an area on which more research effort should be focused, especially at the empirical level.[8]

The paper has five more sections. The second section is devoted to reviewing the theoretical arguments at the microeconomic and macroeconomic levels that support the idea that private ownership is preferred to public ownership. Specific testable implications are proposed as guidelines to the empirical survey. The third section then shows a survey of the micro evidence and presents aggregate data to link the reform process with a healthier macro environment. Privatization of infrastructure, the sector in which most of the privatization activity is taking place, is discussed in the fourth section, as it represents one of the main challenges of privatization in developing countries. The fifth section continues the discussion of the challenges, moving towards corporate governance issues. The last section presents the conclusions.

THEORY

The idea that private ownership has advantages over public ownership in terms of being inherently more efficient, as well as inducing a better public sector financial health is not new. In 1776, Adam Smith wrote:

In every great monarchy in Europe the sale of the crown lands would produce a very large sum of money which, if applied to the payments of the public debts, would deliver from mortgage a much greater revenue than any which those lands

---

[7] This problem is easier to deal with at the micro level when we have accounting data for the firms over time.

[8] An interesting analysis of distributive implications of privatization of utilities is in Chisari et al. (1997), applied to the case of Argentina. For the conceptual analysis and the review of some existing evidence, see Estache et al. (2001). The most consistent cross-country analysis is summarized in McKenzie and Mookherjee (2003).

have ever afforded to the crown...When the crown lands had become private property, they would, in the course of a few years, become well improved and well cultivated. (Smith 1776, p. 824).

The mechanisms through which those improvements in efficiency would take place, however, and the reason why the government's financial health would necessarily improve were not clear for a long period of time. The theoretical arguments supporting such views are summarized in the next section.

PRIVATIZATION AND MICROECONOMIC EFFICIENCY: THE ORIGINAL DEBATE

There exists a vast literature in microeconomics that addresses the question of why ownership matters.[9] This question can be restated by asking whether and in which ways the decision process of the firm is distorted when the government intervenes. This can be analysed by looking at the components of the optimization problem: the objective and the constraints, and at how these are affected under different types of ownership structures. Within the microeconomic literature, it has been theoretically established that, under conditions of perfect competition, absence of information problems, and complete contracts, ownership does not matter, i.e, you would observe the same performance of the firms regardless their ownership structure.

The original arguments in favour of public ownership were justified as a solution to the failure of the first of those three conditions: the *market failure* argument. Under non-competitive conditions—characterized by decreasing average costs in the relevant range of demand within the specific market—the existence of more than one firm is not justified on efficiency grounds. The possibility of exploitation of monopoly power by a private owner created the need for public ownership in those 'natural monopoly' sectors. This argument in favour of public ownership was used by important scholars for a long time, as shown by the opinions expressed by Nobel Laureates such as Lewis, Meade, and Allais early in their careers—during the 1940s—in favour of the nationalization of

---

[9] See, for example, Kay and Thompson (1986); Vickers and Yarrow (1989); Stiglitz (1991); Yarrow (1992); Laffont and Tirole (1993, ch. 17); Willig (1993); Galal et al. (1994); Tirole (1994); World Bank (1995); McLindon (1996); Shleifer and Vishny (1996); Schmidt (1990, 1996); Perotti and Guney (1993); Hart, et al. (1997); Shleifer (1998); and Nellis (1997).

industries with such characteristics (Shleifer 1998). The market failure argument, and the perspective that the government takes into consideration social marginal costs, has been called the social view.

The formal analysis of information problems and contract incompleteness, and thus the role of incentives in promoting efficiency within the firm, has shown that efficiency losses involved in public ownership are non-negligible.[10] In many cases, they are higher than the gains that can be obtained by solving a market failure problem. This is especially so as the scope of competition becomes larger when the size of the market increases, the economy is opened to international trade, and technology develops. Thus, the weakening of the market failure argument and the evidence in favour of the relevance of the other two conditions—asymmetries in information and market incompleteness—led to a re-thinking of the original views in favour of public ownership.

In relatively competitive markets, the advantages of public ownership were put in doubt. In non-competitive sectors, however, the natural monopoly argument cannot be abandoned as a justification of public ownership without solving one important policy question relating to how to deal with the possibility of exploitation of market power by private owners. In this regard, the evolution in the theoretical work on regulatory mechanisms and their properties to function as a second-best solution to the above problems showed that there was an alternative to public ownership. Thus, the question was translated into how to efficiently impose a regulatory constraint on the decision-making process of the private firms without deterring innovation and cost-reducing effort.[11]

INCENTIVE AND CONTRACTING PROBLEMS

One of the views in favour of privatization can be characterized by moving away from the natural monopoly argument—appealing to the

[10] The problem of contract incompleteness refers to the impossibility of a contract containing all possible contingencies that may arise. A contract, as detailed and comprehensive as it may be, shall always be subject to *ex-post* conflicts if an unforeseen event occurs.

[11] A new question immediately follows: why are inefficient public managers assumed to be efficient regulators? The answer, discussed below, has to do with the cost of inefficiencies or political intervention under regulation as compared to public ownership. Both financial and political costs are higher under the former (see Willig 1993).

regulation literature—and considering contracting and incentive problems within the firm as the relevant issues to foster efficiency at the microeconomic level. This perspective is termed the *agency view*.[12]

Within the *agency view*, there are two perspectives on the causes of the existence of poor incentives for efficiency. The first one, termed the *managerial* perspective, tells us that monitoring is poorer in publicly owned firms and, therefore, the incentives for efficiency are low-powered (Vickers and Yarrow 1989). The second, the *political* perspective, claims that political interference is what distorts the objectives and the constraints faced by public managers (Shapiro and Willig 1990); Shleifer and Vishny 1994). Within the managerial view, the impossibility of complete contracts plays a fundamental role in explaining why ownership indeed matters (Williamson 1985); Sappington and Stiglitz 1987). According to Williamson (1985), the impossibility of writing complete contracts with the private owners would make state-owned enterprises (SOEs) to function at least as well as privately owned firms (under the same conditions), whereas 'selective intervention' by the government when unforeseen contingencies arise could actually result in a socially preferred outcome. The latter argument relies heavily on the 'benevolence' of the government, in the sense that it always has the right social welfare function as an objective to be maximized.

The Political Perspective

The *political perspective* argues that distortions in both the objective function that managers seek to maximize (Shapiro and Willig 1990) and the constraints they face, through the so-called soft budget constraint problem (Kornai 1980, 1986), result in lower efficiency under public ownership. Public managers, who tend to report to a politician and pursue political careers themselves, incorporate to the objective function aspects related to the maximization of employment—at the cost of efficiency—and political prestige (the empire building hypothesis).[13] The reason why managers are able to do that without facing the threat of bankruptcy relates to the second distortion, the soft budget constraint. In any situation in which the firms have engaged in unwise investments, it will be in the interest of the central government to bail the firm out using

---

[12] A summary of these social and agency views is in LaPorta and López-De-Silanes (1998).

[13] The 'empire building' hypothesis tells us that managers maximize the size of the firm, for that gives them prestige.

the public budget. The rationale for this relies on the fact that the bankruptcy of the firm would have a high political cost, whose burden would be distributed within a well-defined political group, like unions. On the other hand, the cost of the bailout can be spread over the taxpayers, a less organized, larger group in society, with diversified interests and preferences. The threat of bankruptcy is non-credible under public ownership.

Under a very simple assumption, we can obtain the soft budget constraint result as the equilibrium in a game between the public manager and the central government (or 'ministry of finance'). This assumption is that the political loss involved in closing a publicly owned company is larger than the political cost of using taxpayer money to bail it out (or public debt, that is, future tax collection).[14]

Let us analyse a simple version of such strategic interaction. Consider the decision that the public manager has to make as to whether to invest or not in a new project. Let us denote this investment by I (see Figure 10.1). The alternative decision is not to invest (NI). If the decision is not to invest, the central government gets a payoff of zero, and so

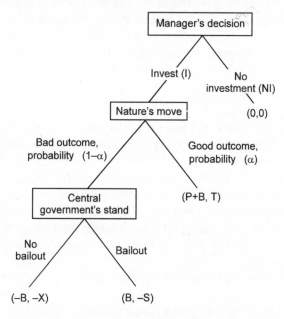

Fig. 10.1: The Soft Budget Constraint

[14] The appropriate equilibrium concept is that of *subgame perfection*.

does the public manager. If the investment takes place, it would be profitable with probability α and non-profitable with probability $(1 - \alpha)$. Regardless of whether the investment turns out to be profitable or not, the manager gets a personal benefit from the expansion of the firm's activities (B), following the 'empire-building' hypothesis. Positive profits give an extra-payoff to the manager (P) and give a positive transfer to the central government via tax revenue. In the case in which the project fails, the central government faces a decision between two possible actions: to bail the firm out or let it go bankrupt. In the former case, the central government has a negative payoff $(S$, the subsidy) though the manager still gets the benefit of managing a larger firm. If there is no bailout the manager loses the job and has a negative payoff $(-B$, loses prestige), whereas the central government faces a political cost of closing the firm (facing union problems, explaining to public opinion why the firm failed, and so on). The political cost is denoted by X in Figure 10.1.

It is simple to see now that, as long as $X > S$ (the political cost incurred by the central government by closing the firm is higher than the cost of giving a subsidy and bailing it out), the manager will always make the investment, regardless of the probability of failure. This is a simple case to illustrate the idea behind the concept of the soft budget constraint.[15]

The Managerial Perspective
According to the *managerial* perspective, imperfect monitoring is the first cause of low-powered incentive. The reason why the managers of state-owned enterprises are poorly monitored has to do with the fact the firms are not traded in the market, unlike the case of a private firm. This fact eliminates the threat of takeover when the firm performs poorly. Additionally, shareholders cannot observe and influence the performance of the enterprises (Yarrow 1992; Vickers and Yarrow 1989). Debt markets cannot play the role of disciplining the managers, because SOEs' debt is actually public debt that is perceived and traded under different conditions.

Some have argued that partial privatization can solve this problem without having to pursue full divestiture. Shleifer and Vishny (1996) and others have argued against partial privatization using the *political*

---

[15] Assuming $X > S$, the manager will invest if $\alpha P + B > 0$, which always holds, even for a probability of failure equal to one.

perspective as an explanation. Even partial ownership allows the politicians to have an influence on the performance of the firm and give covered subsidies to achieve political goals. The cost of intervention increases as the share of public ownership decreases, full divestiture being an important commitment device to signal no political intervention.[16] According to the model, partial privatization could solve the monitoring problem by making public information that was previously not available. That policy, however, would not be enough to solve the problem of political intervention through 'side-payments'.

The relevance of the existence of 'side-payments' through which the government can achieve political objectives at the cost of efficiency is related to another argument in favour of the irrelevance of ownership. Sappington and Stiglitz (1987) provide a result termed the 'Fundamental Privatization Theorem' that states that, through mechanism design, an optimal contract can be implemented so that whatever is feasible through private ownership can be achieved through public ownership and vice versa.[17]

Williamson's original claim is that 'selective intervention' makes incomplete contracting a favourable argument for public ownership. However, when the distortions in the objective function of public managers are introduced, the argument severely weakens. More sophisticated incomplete-contracting models have shown that there are costs and benefits attached to privatization under unforeseen contingencies that cannot be specified *ex ante*. Laffont and Tirole (1991) based their analysis on the existence of *ex-post* renegotiation possibilities that led to profitable investments being foregone by public managers. The costs were associated to the need for regulation under informational asymmetries. Shapiro and Willig (1990) used the distortions in the objectives of the public managers (a 'malevolent' government) to show the benefits of private ownership under incomplete contracting. Finally, Schmidt (1990) eliminates the assumption of a 'malevolent' government and shows the costs and benefits involved in privatization. The fact that bankruptcy is a non-credible threat under public ownership (soft budget constraint, discussed above) makes the managers increase the scale of production,

---

[16] In the review of the empirical evidence, we show below that fully privatized firms did perform better than partially privatized companies, under the same competitive conditions (Bourbakri and Cosset 1998).

[17] This result is also Proposition 1 in Shapiro and Willig (1990). For a summary of this debate, see Schmidt (1996).

whereas a private manager would face a real threat of failure that induces productive efficiency. The implication is that, under competitive conditions, privatization must result in a net gain.

Taking the argument above to the limit, it has been argued that competition is what matters, putting ownership at a lower level in the hierarchy of policy prescriptions (Stiglitz 1993; Vernon-Wortzel and Wortzel 1989). Though it is true that important efficiency gains can be achieved through the introduction of competition and the maximization of market contestability via deregulation policies, there are two caveats to this argument. First, the existence of a publicly-owned firm as the incumbent—in most cases, subsidized—may deter other firms from entering that market, even when it becomes legal to do so. Real competition would be difficult to introduce under those conditions. Competition implies not only free entry in the market, but also freedom to fail, that is, the existence of free exit. Maintaining public firms in the market, given the arguments discussed above, would make free exit a non-credible commitment for such firms. The argument, however, makes economic sense. Introducing competition, if possible, could be an alternative to privatization whenever the latter is not feasible.

An incomplete-contracting model that shows conditions under which public ownership is superior to private ownership is Hart et al. (1997).[18] The incompleteness of contracts discussed in their model has to do with non-contractible quality, and is applied to the case of prisons. When the scope of competition is limited in terms of consumer choice and the incentives for cost-reduction may lead to a reduction of non-contractible quality, there is a case for public ownership. This is termed 'the proper scope of government'. Table 10.3 summarizes the different perspectives for and against public ownership.

Summarizing the discussion from the microeconomic perspective, the following testable implications can be stated (see Galal et al., 1994):

Implication 1: Publicly owned enterprises in competitive environments do not perform better than privately owned companies in the same circumstances in terms of profitability and efficiency, and could perform worse.

Implication 2: One should expect important efficiency gains from the change in ownership structure in competitive sectors.

---

[18] Also discussed in Shleifer (1998).

Table 10.3: Public Ownership: For and Against

	For	Against
	X	
Market Failure/ Natural Monopoly	*Social View* The government takes into consideration social marginal costs	
	X	
Contracting Perspective	*Selective intervention* SOEs can do at least as well as private firms and the government would consider social costs in unforeseen contingencies	
		X
Incentive Problems		*Agency view*
		X
A. Managerial Perspective		Inherent poor monitoring and lack of high-powered incentives under public ownership
		X
B. Political Perspective		Political interference distorts the objectives and the constraints of the problem the manager faces

Implication 3: Increases in profitability are not equivalent to increases in efficiency in general. This will only be true in a competitive environment.

Implication 4: Fully privatized firms should perform better than firms that have been partially privatized, under the same conditions.

The evidence presented in the third section addresses the empirical validity of these implications.

MACROECONOMIC EFFECTS OF PRIVATIZATION

The discussion of the macroeconomic effects of privatization is not as rich from the theoretical perspective as that of the microeconomic effects. There are few theoretical models that link the reform at the microeconomic level—such as privatization—with macroeconomic performance.[19] There are, however, country studies that show data on the interaction between privatization transactions and macroeconomic variables.[20] The most important reason why this work has not been done extensively is the difficulty to isolate the effect of privatization from other events that have an influence on aggregate measures. We would expect to observe certain trends, but the causality is weak. Similar evidence for which this caveat applies shall be shown below.

The first interaction between privatization and macroeconomics comes from the fact that macro instability, especially large budget deficits, tend to accelerate privatization. The effect of poor public sector financial health on the willingness to reform and on the political acceptability of such reform results in a clear relation between higher public deficits and faster public sector restructuring. The evidence has been shown in Serven et al. (1994) and López-De-Silanes et al. (1997), among others.

It is obvious then that an examination of interaction between privatization and public sector financial health is required. It should be expected that more aggressive privatization programmes would lead to lower budget deficits, *ceteris paribus*.[21] Privatization allows the government to raise funds in the short term and eliminates the need of permanent subsidies to previously publicly owned enterprises. That privatization entails necessarily a fiscal gain is incorrect, though under the assumption that firms will perform better and net subsidies will be eliminated—supported by the micro evidence—that is a plausible scenario. If firms go from deficit to surplus in their operation, the government will not only eliminate subsidies, but actually start collecting taxes from them. The actual change in the financial position of the

---

[19] An important work in that area is Blanchard (1997), analysing transition economies.

[20] World Bank (1995) shows macro data for several countries. Mansoor (1992), Marcel (1989), Larraín and Vergara (1993), Luders and Hachette (1993), Leffort and Solimano (1993), and López-De-Silanes (1993) are country-specific studies.

[21] In the analysis of all these effects, the available evidence is, of course, *mutatis mutandis*.

government is determined by the difference between foregone dividends and taxes collected from the company. Future higher dividends of the firms under private ownership should also be reflected in the proceeds the government obtains during the sale, corrected for underpricing in the case of public offerings.[22]

The use of the proceeds from privatization determines to a large extent the impact of privatization on public sector's cash flows. If the revenue from the sales is used to reduce public debt, as has been the case in most countries, we would observe lower interest payments and consequently a stronger cash-flow position of the public sector. The common policy advice has been to use the proceeds for once-and-for-all disbursements, especially if those eliminate future negative cash flows, in lieu of using them for permanent expenditure.[23] The effect of privatization on public sector borrowing requirements should be reflected in lower interest rates, which foster investment, growth, and lower inflation.

Another important macroeconomic effect of privatization, especially when carried out through public offerings and mixed sales, is the increase in the level of stock market capitalization and, in general, the development of the financial sector. As shown, for example, in World Bank (1995), SOEs tend to crowd out private investors in the credit market—given that they represent a less risky investment for the banks. Privatization mobilizes resources in the financial sector, reallocating credit to more productive uses.[24] Finally, from a theoretical perspective, the sale of public sector enterprises would reduce the aggregate level of employment in the short-run, because of the elimination of redundant labour. Unemployment, however, may decrease in the medium and long-run as the rate of growth of the economy increases as a result of the efficiency gains at the micro level and the increasing stability at the macro level. However, this has not been tested empirically in a robust manner.

Privatization has typically been one policy among a set of structural reform policy measures. These measures include trade liberalization,

---

[22] For a discussion of the determinants of underpricing in privatization public offerings, see Perotti and Guney (1993), Menyah et al. (1996), and López-Calva (1998).

[23] This is due to the fact of the once-and-for-all nature of the revenue from privatization sales. See, for example, Rogozinski (1998).

[24] Megginson and Netter (2000) reviews the impact of privatization on the capital market.

deregulation, financial sector restructuring, and opening to foreign direct investment. Though the effect of privatization as such cannot be isolated, the implications that should guide the analysis of the aggregate data are the following: *ceteris paribus*, privatization:

Implication 5: improves the public sector's financial health (lower deficits, lower debt).

Implication 6: reduces the net transfer to SOEs in the aggegate. These transfers become positive if the government actually starts collecting taxes from privatized firms.

Implication 7: has a positive impact on the development of the financial sector.

Implication 8: has a negative effect on employment in the short-run, a positive effect in the medium and long-run.

Variables that specifically capture the effects discussed above shall be shown below.

EVIDENCE

The empirical evidence that tests the theoretical implications can be grouped into macroeconomic and microeconomic evidence. From the microeconomic perspective, more concrete conclusions can be drawn. The different types of studies can be grouped as follows:

 (i) Case studies that deal with specific firms and their evolution before and after privatization;
 (ii) Country-specific, cross-industry evidence that looks into performance changes for firms in different sectors within the same country, before and after privatization;
(iii) Cross-country evidence that uses data from firms that are publicly traded in different countries to evaluate changes in their financial status, before and after privatization.

MICROECONOMIC EVIDENCE

At the microeconomic level, the empirical evidence strongly supports the view that privatization has positive effects on profitability and efficiency. It also shows that capital expenditures tend to increase after privatization. The evidence on firm-level employment is mixed—though for large firms employment seems to rise after divestiture. When the effect is measured in terms of estimated total surplus in a counterfactual basis, welfare increases in almost all the cases under analysis. We analyse the results in detail below.

Case Studies

The first piece of evidence consists of case studies, among which Galal et al. (1994) shows comprehensive evidence. The authors show results for twelve privatized firms in four different countries.[25] The methodology is counterfactual and makes projections of the performance of the firms under the privatized scenario and a hypothetical 'public ownership scenario'.[26] The change in welfare can be measured by a comparison between these two situations. Welfare is measured through changes in total surplus, decomposed into several components. From the so-called 'basic divestiture equation'—the decision to sell the firm from a cost–benefit perspective—the changes in welfare are decomposed originally as

$$\Delta W = \Delta S + \Delta \pi + \Delta L + \Delta C$$

Where ΔW represents the change in total welfare, ΔS the change in consumer surplus, $\Delta \pi$ the change in welfare of buyers, government, and any other shareholders,[27] ΔL the change in welfare of labour, and ΔC is the change in welfare of competitors. Starting from this basic equation, a complication is added by introducing the distinction between domestic and foreign welfare effects.

The results are summarized in Table 10.4. In all the cases except one, the net effect of privatization on welfare is positive. Surprisingly, workers gained in all cases through an increase in their welfare.[28] Consumer welfare increases in four cases, decreases in five of them, and remains unchanged in the rest. According to the implications stated in the theoretical part, the effect on consumer welfare is sensitive to market structure. The government has a net gain in nine cases, and the buyers of the firms gained in all of them. These firm studies show a clearly positive

[25] These countries are United Kingdom, Chile, Mexico, and Malaysia.

[26] A detailed description of the methodology can be found in Jones et al. (1990) and Galal et al. (1994), chapter 2.

[27] If Z is the payment received by the government during the sale of the firm, and Z_p is the willingness to pay of the buyers, the net gain for buyers is $(Z_p - Z)$, and the government's share is $\Delta \pi - (Z_p - Z)$, therefore the sum of the government's and the buyers' share is only $\Delta \pi$.

[28] These includes workers that remained in the company, and the effect is both as wage earners and as shareholders.

Table 10.4: Case Studies in Four Countries

Country and enterprise	Domestic sector						Foreign sector			
	Government	Buyers	Consumer	Workers	Others	Net welfare change	Buyers	Consumer	Others	World net welfare change
United Kingdom										
British Telecom	2.7	3.1	4.9	0.2	-0.1	10.8	1.2	0.0	0.0	12.0
British Airways	0.9	1.4	-0.9	0.3	0.0	1.7	0.4	-0.5	0.0	1.6
National Freight	-0.2	0.8	0.0	3.7	0.0	4.3	0.0	0.0	0.0	4.3
Chile										
Chilgener	-1.4	2.0	0.0	0.1	0.0	0.7	1.4	0.0	0.0	2.1
Enersis	-1.6	7.6	2.2	3.9	-7.4	4.6	0.6	0.0	0.0	5.2
CTC	8.0	1.0	131.0	1.0	4.0	145.0	10.0	0.0	0.0	155.0
Malaysia										
Malaysian Airline Systems	5.2	2.0	-2.9	0.4	0.0	4.6	0.8	0.8	15.8	22.1
Kelang Container Terminal	37.6	11.5	6.2	7.0	-11.9	50.4	2.9	3.1	-3.0	53.4
Sports Toto	13.6	10.7	0.0	0.0	-13.0	10.9	0.0	0.0	0.0	10.9

(Contd.)

Table 10.4: (Contd.)

Mexico										
Teléfonos de México	13.3	11.4	-62.0	15.6	28.3	6.6	25.1	0.0	17.9	49.5
Aeroméxico	62.3	3.9	-14.6	2.4	-2.3	52.9	1.8	-6.2	0.0	48.5
Mexicana de Aviación	3.5	-1.4	-7.7	0.0	3.2	-2.4	-1.3	-3.3	0.0	-7.0

Note: Figures are in percentages. All figures are the annual component of the perpetuity equivalent to the welfare change, expressed as a percentage of annual sales in the last pre-divestiture year.

Source: Galal et al. (1994), Table 23–1.

effect of privatization on total welfare without negative distributive consequences, though this result is driven by the partial equilibrium nature of the analysis. A model that incorporates the distributive effects in a general equilibrium framework, applied to privatization of utilities in Argentina, shall be discussed below.

Country Specific Cross-industry Evidence

The second type of studies focuses on one specific country and analyses evidence across industries. Among these, the most consistent evidence is that for Mexico (LaPorta and López-De-Silanes 1998) and Slovenia (Smith et al. 1996).[29] An earlier work by Barberis et al. (1996) provided evidence of the effectiveness of privatization of retail shops and small businesses in Russia, following Earle et al. (1994) that shows similar evidence for small businesses in Central Europe.

In the case of Mexico, LaPorta and López-De-Silanes (1998) analyse the performance of 218 enterprises in 26 different sectors, privatized between 1983 and 1991. One of the most important features of this work is that the authors decompose the changes in profitability into price increases, labour reduction, and productivity gains. Changes in taxes paid by the firms are also measured. The analysis addresses two criticisms usually made about privatization: (i) that profitability of the firms increases at the expense of society through price increases, and (ii) that profitability comes at the expense of workers, whose labour contracts are less generous, involving important layoffs.

The results show that profitability, measured by the ratio of operating income to sales, increased by 24 percentage points. These gains can be decomposed into the following components: (i) 10 per cent is due to increase in prices;[30] (ii) 33 per cent comes from laid-off

---

[29] Chisari, Estache, and Romero (1999) analyse utilities' privatization in Argentina, but focus on the distributive effects, as discussed below. Jin and Qian (1998) analyse the relative performance of privately owned firms in rural China, focusing on the efficiency of township-village enterprises and the influence of the central government in their activities.

[30] Changes in product prices are calculated through a *Paasche* index. The price contribution to increases in profitability are calculated through the following formula:

$$\text{Price contribution} = \frac{\text{Sales}(1993) - \text{Cost}(1993)}{\text{Sales}(1993)} - \frac{\dfrac{\text{Sales}(1993)}{1+\pi} - \text{Cost}(1993)}{\dfrac{\text{Sales}(1993)}{1+\pi}}$$

Where sales are defined as net sales, cost is defined as operating costs, and π is the increase in real prices.

Table 10.5: Performance Changes in Privatized Firms in Mexico

	Changes in industry-adjusted performance					Competitive vs. non-competitive industries (according to prospectus)			Competitive vs. non-competitive (according to market share)		
	N	Mean change	s.s. (%)	Median change	s.s. (%)	N c/nc	Mean change (difference)	s.s. (%)	N c/nc	Mean change (difference)	s.s. (%)
Profitability (Operating income/sales)	168	0.3532	1	0.153	1	134 32	0.0612		104 62	0.1087	
(Net income/sales)	168	0.4127	1	0.2108	1	134 32	-0.1462	10	103 62	-0.0261	10
Operating Efficiency cost per Unit	168	-0.1837	1	-0.1527	1	134 32	0.1066	1	104 62	-0.0492	
Log (Sales/ Employees)	166	0.9359	1	0.8966	1	134 32	0.1505		107 62	0.3301	5
Labour Log (Number of Employees)	169	-19.05	10	-24.47	1	136 33	-0.2728	5	107 62	-0.0694	

(Contd.)

Table 10.5: (Contd.)

	Changes in industry-adjusted performance					Competitive vs. non-competitive industries (according to prospectus)			Competitive vs. non-competitive (according to market share)		
	N	Mean change	s.s. (%)	Median change	s.s. (%)	N c/nc	Mean change (difference)	s.s. (%)	N c/nc	Mean change (difference)	s.s. (%)
Assets and Investment (Investment/Sales)	168	−0.0477	1	0.0665	1	134 32	−0.0054	1	104 62	−0.0048	
Output Log (sales)	170	0.4891	1	0.4239	1	136 33	−0.2154		105 61	0.2060	
Net Taxes	168	26,441	5	2161	1	135 33	−7024	1	106 61	1013.6	

Notes:
1. s.s. (%) = statistical significance to a % level., c/nc = competitive, non-competitive.
2. The columns that compare competitive vs. non-competitive show the difference in mean change (ΔCompetitive − ΔNon-competitive).
3. There are two definitions of competitive: 1. According to privatization prospectus and 2. According to market share (>10 per cent is considered non-competitive).
   For details on the data and methodology, see part 3 in text.
Source: LaPorta and López-De-Silanes (1998), tables 5, 6-A, and 6-C.

workers;[31] (iii) 57 per cent was induced by productivity gains.

It is also shown that deregulated markets induce a faster convergence of the performance indicators of the privatized firms towards the industry-matched control groups—consistent with the implications stated in the theoretical section.[32] When competitive and non-competitive sectors are compared, not only have the former higher increases in profitability as compared to the latter, but those changes are related to higher gains in efficiency and lower price increases. The privatized firms went from receiving a positive subsidy from the government to a net tax payment after the sale. Table 10.5 shows the change in selected indicators of privatized firms. The data shown in the table are corrected by the authors for macro and industry-specific effects to control for the increase in profitability associated with changes in the macro environment.

LaPorta and López-De-Silanes (1998) also carry out a regression analysis. The aim of such regressions is to identify the role of market power and deregulation in determining privatization outcomes, measured by the performance indicators mentioned above. They use three deregulation indicators: (i) the existence of state-imposed price and quantity controls, (ii) barriers to foreign trade, and (iii) restrictions to foreign ownership. In order to analyse the role of market structure, the authors use a dummy variable that takes the value of 1 if the 'privatization prospectus' described the firm as monopolistic or oligopolistic, and zero otherwise. According to the regression results, less regulated markets facilitate the 'catch-up' of privatized firms' performance indicators with respect to the market benchmark. The data does not support the view that more concentrated markets induce the firms to increase profitability by increasing prices and lowering quantities. The market power dummy

---

[31] The contribution of layoffs is calculated in a counterfactual basis. It is assumed that the firms maintained the redundant labour and the difference between the profits between the observed scenario and the hypothetical-redundant labour one gives the savings. Concretely, the contribution is

$$\text{Contribution of layoffs} = \text{Wage}_{pre} * \frac{L_{pre} - L_{1993}}{\text{Sales}_{1993}}$$

where $Wage_{pre}$ represents the average wages in the four years before privatization, L_{pre} is the average level of employment in the four years before privatization, L_{1993} is the level of employment in the year of comparison post-privatization (1993), and $Sales_{1993}$ is net sales after privatization.

[32] Firms in the same industry that are privately owned.

turns out to be non-significant to explain the change in performance indicators.

Smith et al (1996) show evidence for Slovenia, using a country-wide database with privatized firms for 1989–92. The objective of the paper is to analyse the effect of different types of ownership on performance. The exercise is different to the one discussed above because the authors do not have data for the pre-privatization stage. The results, however, show a clearly positive effect of private ownership on performance. When distinguishing the effects of different types of ownership, foreign ownership has a significant positive effect on performance. Employee owned firms perform well when they are small, but the effect of this type of ownership diminishes with size. Employee-owned firms do better when foreign ownership is also present in the same firm.

Cross-country Evidence

Starting with a pioneering work by Megginson et al. (1994), researchers have used the data available for publicly traded companies that have been privatized to analyse different performance indicators on a cross-country basis. Evidence shall be shown here from Megginson et al. (1994), D'Souza and Megginson (1998), Bourbakri and Cosset (1998), and, for the case of Central and Eastern European Countries, Frydman et al. (1997, 1998), and Claessens and Djankov (1998).

Megginson et al. (1994) analyse data for 61 companies and 32 industries from 18 countries that were privatized between 1961 and 1990, through public offerings. D'Souza and Megginson (1998) compare pre- and post-privatization performance of 78 companies from 25 countries—including 10 LDCs—that faced privatization between 1990 and 1994, also through public offering. Their sample included 14 firms from the banking industry, 21 utilities and 10 from telecommunications. Bourbakri and Cosset (1998) use data of 79 companies from 21 developing countries. These firms were privatized between 1980 and 1992 through public offerings. The largest data set is that used in Claessens and Djankov (1998) which consists of 6300 manufacturing firms in seven Central and Eastern European countries (Bulgaria, Czech Republic, Hungary, Poland, Romania, Slovak Republic, and Slovenia).

The performance indicators that are analysed in those papers are related to mean and median levels of profitability, sales, operating efficiency, leverage, capital expenditures, and employment. In most cases, there are controls for whether the markets are competitive or not and

Table 10.6: Performance Change in Privatized Firms, 1961–90

Variables	N	Mean change (after – before privatization)	Median change (after – before privatization)	Significance of median change (%)	Competitive (c) vs. non-competitive (nc) industries
Profitability					
Return on sales	55	0.0249	0.041	1	$\Delta c > \Delta nc$
Efficiency					
Sales efficiency	35	0.1064	0.1157	1	$\Delta c > \Delta nc$
Investment					
Capital expenditures/ Sales	43	0.0521	0.016	5	$\Delta c > \Delta nc$
Output					
Real sales	57	0.241	0.190	1	$\Delta c > \Delta nc$
Employment					
Total employment	39	2346	276	10	$\Delta c > \Delta nc$
Leverage					
Debt to assets	53	−0.0243	−0.0234	5	$\Delta c > \Delta nc$
Dividends					
Dividends to sales	39	0.0172	0.0121	1	$\Delta c < \Delta nc$

Note: $\Delta c/nc$ = mean performance change of firms in competitive/non-competitive industry (after privatization – before privatization). Median changes are consistent in that column except for employment (in that case $\Delta c < \Delta nc$). For details on the data and methodology, see the third section of the chapter.

Source: Megginson et al. (1994), tables III and IV.

Table 10.7: Performance Change in Privatized Firms during the 1990s

Variables and type of firm	n	Change in mean (after – before privatization)	Change in median (after – before)	Significance of change in median (%)
Return on sales				
Competitive	48	0.01	0.02	
Non-competitive	30	0.06	0.04	1
Control	34	0.01	0.04	1
No control	37	0.03	0.02	5
Real sales				
Competitive	46	1.33	0.98	1
Non-competitive	28	2.32	2.11	1
Control	35	1.95	2.29	1
No control	35	1.59	0.87	1
Employment				
Competitive	35	–480	–685	
Non-competitive	26	94	–194	
Control	27	–290	–471	
No control	31	16	–810	
Sales efficiency				
Competitive	34	1.23	0.80	1
Non-competitive	27	2.32	2.22	1

(*Contd.*)

Table 10.7: (Contd.)

Control	28	1.78	2.57	1
No control	30	1.79	0.85	1
Capital expenditure/sales				
Competitive	34	0.01	0.00	
Non-competitive	31	−0.02	0.02	
Control	33	−0.04	0.03	
No control	29	0.03	0.01	
Debt/assets				
Competitive	40	−0.03	−0.06	
Non-competitive	30	−0.11	−0.09	1
Control	31	−0.06	−0.08	
No control	34	−0.08	−0.13	5

Note: 'Control' refers to firms that have been privatized by more than 50 per cent. For details on the data and methodology, see the third section in the chapter.

Source: D'Souza and Megginson (1998), tables IV and VI.

Table 10.8: Performance Change of Privatized Companies in Developing Countries

Variables and type of firm	n	Change in mean (after − before privatization)	Change in median (after − before)	Significance of change in median (%)
Return on sales				
Competitive	41	0.0585	0.0193	5
Non-competitive	37	0.0627	0.0181	5
Full	30	0.0637	0.0145	10
Partial	42	0.0636	0.0191	1
Real sales				
Competitive	42	0.2417	0.1930	1
Non-competitive	36	0.2662	0.1835	1
Full	30	0.2105	0.1625	1
Partial	42	0.2995	0.2343	1
Employment				
Competitive	26	−80.92	117	
Non-competitive	31	323.4	94	10
Full	23	82.6521	88	
Partial	30	303.36	325.5	5
Sales efficiency				
Competitive	26	0.2834	0.2875	1
Non-competitive	30	0.2171	0.2041	1

(*Contd.*)

Table 10.8: (Contd.)

Full	23	0.1731	0.2290	1
Partial	29	0.3057	0.2456	1
Capital expenditure/sales				
Competitive	22	0.2138	0.0181	5
Non-competitive	26	0.0632	0.0078	
Full	19	0.0957	0.0166	1
Partial	25	0.1818	0.0192	
Debt/assets				
Competitive	42	−0.0379	−0.0117	10
Non-competitive	23	−0.0745	−0.0205	1
Full	20	0.0153	0.0062	
Partial	39	−0.0793	−0.0882	1

Note: Full/partial tell us whether the firms were privatized fully or there was just a partial sale of shares.

Source: Bourbakri and Cosset (1998), tables 6 and 7.

regulated or unregulated, and for partial vs. full privatization. The main results are shown in Tables 10.6–10.8.

The evidence is robust in the direction of a clearly better performance of the firms after privatization. Profitability increases significantly for different specifications, different periods of time and groups of countries. An interesting result is that, in both Bourbakri and Cosset (1998) and D'Souza and Megginson (1998), profitability increases more in regulated (or non-competitive) industries, whereas operating efficiency increases less in those cases. It is clear then that higher profitability does not necessarily imply higher efficiency and the link between the two comes from the market structure. The evidence supports the idea that there is a certain degree of market power being exploited by those firms. Capital expenditure (investment) systematically increases in all cases, reflecting both growth and the restructuring that takes place after the sale.[33] Employment increases in all the cases, including developing countries. This evidence on employment seems to be inconsistent with that in, for example, LaPorta and López-De-Silanes (1998). There are two explanations for that inconsistency. First, the fact that the cross-country studies analysed here use only data for firms that were sold via public offerings generates a non-negligible selection bias. One would expect those firms to be the ones with higher potential for profitability. Second, the country-specific study includes data from three years before privatization for all the firms, which could be capturing the elimination of labour redundancy before the sale. In all the cases, fully privatized firms perform better than partially privatized ones.

There is one important caveat to these results. For reasons of data availability and homogeneity, these samples include firms that were privatized through public offerings and are publicly traded in the stock market. This may induce a selection problem that biases the result in a favourable direction. Larger and more profitable firms tend to be privatized through public offerings far more than through other privatization methods.[34] That bias, however, does not eliminate the robustness of the results for firms with those characteristics.

For the case of transition economies, Frydman et al. (1997) reported an improvement in corporate performance consistent with the results

---

[33] The 'adjusted' results in Bourbakri and Cosset (1998) are precisely controlling for those macro and sector-specific factors.

[34] See the discussion in López-Calva (1998) and the evidence in Megginson, Nash, Netter, Poulson (1998).

shown above. Frydman et al. (1998) and Claessens and Djankov (1998) report robust positive performance changes in a large sample of firms in Central and Eastern Europe. In the case of Claessens and Djankov (1998), the sample includes 6300 firms with a wide range of characteristics. In these cases, the caution in terms of the selection bias does not apply. Both Claessens and Djankov (1998) and Frydman et al. (1998) look into the forces that are driving those changes. Concretely, they are interested in a test of the *political view*, that is, whether the withdrawal of political intervention explains the positive results. Claessens and Djankov (1998) find significant improvements in total factor productivity and reductions in excess employment in firms without state intervention, controlling for institutional differences and endogeneity of privatization choices. Frydman (1998), with data for Central Europe, finds evidence that entrepreneurial behaviour drives the efficiency gains when state intervention is removed. They confirm the hypothesis that the performance results in privatized companies are a function of greater willigness to accept risks and their freedom to make decisions without state intervention.

MACROECONOMIC EVIDENCE

As mentioned above, there is no strong evidence of the effects of privatization at the macroeconomic level. It is possible, however, to give an overview of the trends observed in key aggregate variables and relate those to the privatization programmes that have been implemented. Along with privatization, other structural reform measures were also put in place in most countries to a certain extent. These policy measures include trade liberalization, fiscal adjustment and tax reform, and weakening of controls to capital inflows, among others. Because of this, it is not possible to attribute the observed patterns to one isolated policy, though we can argue—based on theoretical arguments—that they are related, given the implications stated in theoretical section.[35]

Figures 10.2a and 10.2b show the decrease in the share of SOE activity as a proportion of GDP. The highest proportion is observed in

[35] For the discussion of different macroeconomic aspects of privatization and its effects, see Hachette and Luders (1993), Larraín (1991), McLindon (1996), Rogozinski (1998), Serven et al. (1994), Demirgue–Kurt and Levine (1994), and World Bank (1993). A model that integrates privatization into a macroeconomic model to analyse the effects of the transition to a market economy—designed for transition economies—is Blanchard (1997).

low-income countries, but also the biggest decline is in that group, with a clear acceleration of the changes during the last four years. We call these 'late reformers'. Middle-income countries show a level around 6 per cent, about the same as high-income ones, after a period of aggressive reform in which that proportion fell from 12 per cent (especially for lower middle income).

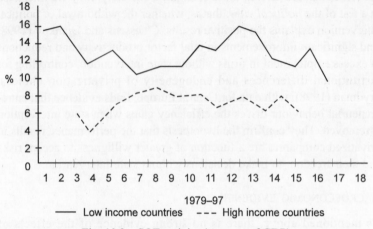

1979–97

—— Low income countries   – – – High income countries

Fig. 10.2a: SOE activity (per cent of GDP)

Source: Authors' calculations based on data from *World Development Indicators*, various issues.

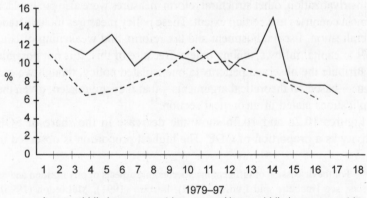

1979–97

—— Lower middle income countries   – – – Upper middle income countries

Fig. 10.2b: SOE activity (per cent of GDP)

Source: Authors' calculations based on data from *World Development Indicators*, various issues.

The data on SOE activity (see Figures 10.3a and 10.3b) is consistent with the share of SOE employment to GDP. In low-income countries, that share fell from around 20 per cent to 10 per cent, in middle-income economies it is currently below 1 per cent, after having reached more than 14 per cent.

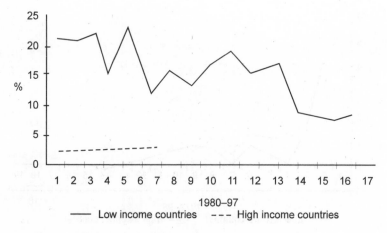

1980–97

—— Low income countries - - - High income countries

Fig. 10.3a: SOE Employment (per cent of total)

Source: Authors' calculations based on data from *World Development Indicators,* various issues.

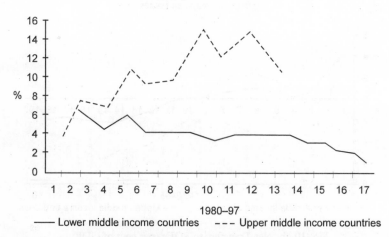

1980–97

—— Lower middle income countries - - - Upper middle income countries

Fig. 10.3b: SOE Employment (per cent of total)

Source: Authors' calculations based on data from *World Development Indicators,* various issues.

The evidence supporting the claim that privatization reduces the burden on public financing is shown in Figures 10.4a, 10.4b, 10.5a, and 10.5b. After reform, both low and middle-income countries have succeeded in eliminating net subsidies to public enterprises on average. In the case of middle income countries, SOEs show a surplus in their

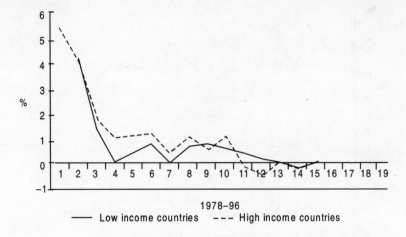

Fig. 10.4a: Net Transfers to SOEs (per cent of GDP)

Source: Authors' calculations based on data from *World Development Indicators*, various issues.

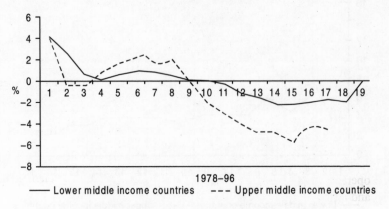

Fig. 10.4b: Net Transfers to SOEs (per cent of GDP)

Source: Authors' calculations based on data from *World Development Indicators*, various issues.

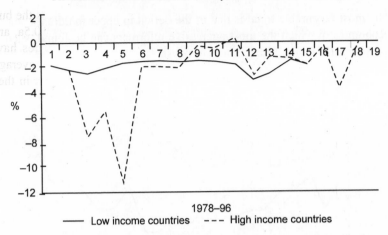

Fig. 10.5a: Overall SOE Balance before Transfers (per cent of GDP)

Source: Authors' calculations based on data from *World Development Indicators*, various issues.

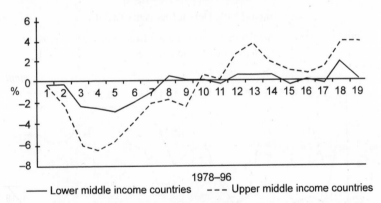

Fig. 10.5b: Overall SOE Balance before Transfers (per cent of GDP)

Source: Authors' calculations based on data from *World Development Indicators*, various issues.

operation, which can be the result not only of reforms of management and introduction of competition, but also of the fact that the 'best' firms are those that have remained in the hands of the government. Examples of those are oil companies and natural monopolies, like electric utilities.

As shown in Figures 10.6a and 10.6b, the trend in fiscal deficit is favourable, though still negative, and largely so for the late reformers.

The most favourable trend is that of the deficit in upper middle income economies in which the most aggressive reformers can be found, such as Argentina, Chile, Mexico, and Malaysia.

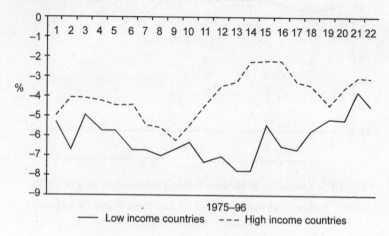

— Low income countries   – – – High income countries

Fig. 10.6a: Fiscal Deficit (per cent of GDP)

Source: Authors' calculations based on data from *World Development Indicators*, various issues.

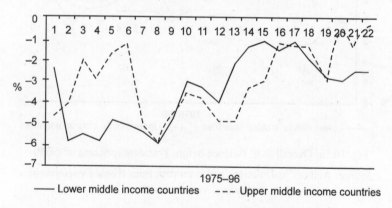

—— Lower middle income countries   – – – Upper middle income countries

Fig. 10.6b: Fiscal Deficit (per cent of GDP)

Source: Authors' calculations based on data from *World Development Indicators*, various issues.

One important effect observed in all income groups is that on the financial sector development (see Demirguc and Levine 1994); McLindon

1996). Whereas in high-income countries, the capitalization of the stock market remains basically stable, for both low and middle-income economies the reforms have had an impact on that indicator of capital market development (see Figures 10.7a and 10.7b). The trend is positive in all of

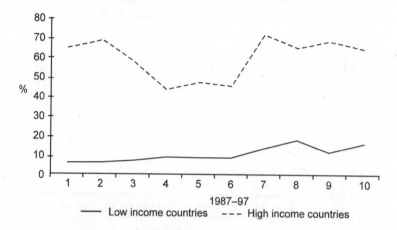

Fig. 10.7a: Stock Market Capitalization (per cent of GDP)

Source: Authors' calculations based on data from *World Development Indicators*, various issues.

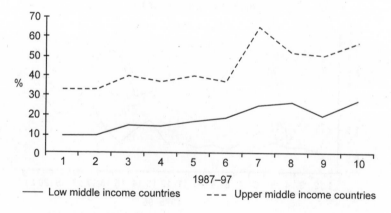

Fig. 10.7b: Stock Market Capitalization (per cent of GDP)

Source: Authors' calculations based on data from *World Development Indicators*, various issues.

them. Upper middle-income countries have reached levels of capitalization similar to those in high-income economies (around 55 per cent of GDP). Lower middle-income economies are around 25 per cent, and the low-income group is about 16 per cent. This mobilization of resources and the consistency of the reforms in many cases have attracted more foreign direct investment. In Figures 10.8a and 10.8b, middle income

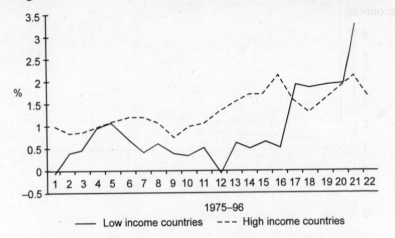

1975–96

—— Low income countries - - - High income countries

Fig. 10.8a: Foreign Direct Investment Net Inflow (per cent of GDP)
Source: Authors' calculations based on data from *World Development Indicators*, various issues.

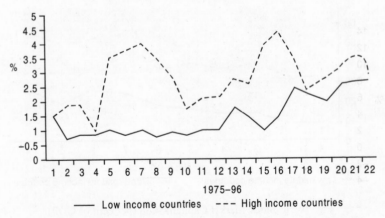

1975–96

—— Low income countries - - - High income countries

Fig. 10.8b: Foreign Direct Investment Net Inflow (per cent of GDP)/
Source: Authors' calculations based on data from *World Development Indicators*, various issues.

countries show a positive trend in this respect, whereas the low-income group shows an important increase during the later years, those in which the reforms and privatization have been more aggressive.

Finally, in terms of GDP growth, the pattern is rather stable across income groups—with no clear trend (see Figures 10.9a and 10.9b). The variability is, however, larger in low-income and lower middle-income economies.

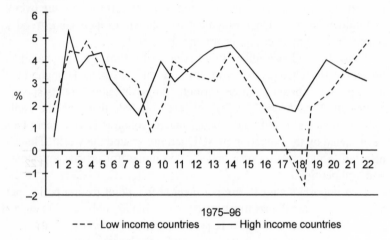

1975–96

- - - Low income countries ——— High income countries

Fig. 10.9a: GDP Growth (per cent)

Source: Authors' calculations based on data from *World Development Indicators*, various issues.

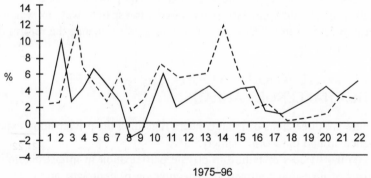

1975–96

- - - Lower middle income countries ——— Upper middle income countries

Fig. 10.9b: GDP Growth (per cent)

Source: Authors' calculations based on data from *World Development Indicators*, various issues.

Unemployment, however, shows a very erratic pattern across countries. Aggressive reformers show an increase in the unemployment rate, but so do late and less aggressive reformers. Examples of the former are Argentina and Poland, where the unemployment rate increased by 9 and 8 percentage points, respectively, between 1990 and 1996. Among the latter, we have France and Hungary, where unemployment grew by 3.5 per cent and 3 per cent, respectively, during the same period. It is not possible to draw any conclusion in terms of privatization on the overall unemployment rate. Unemployment has shown an increasing trend in recent years in most countries around the world.

Thus, the evidence tells us that structural reform has in general induced positive changes in key macroeconomic variables. Though not all these positive changes can be attributed to privatization nor its specific contribution has been identified, we can conclude that both the public sector's financial health and a better macroeconomic environment have been fueled by the reduction of SOE activity around the world. This has also led to the creation of a better environment for private investment and competition.

Two important caveats are pertinent at this point from a policy perspective. In general, privatization proceeds should not be used in current expenditure or subsidies that require a permanent disbursement. Given that they are a once-and-for-all income for the government, they should be applied to disbursements of equal nature (Rogozinski 1998).[36] Reduction of public debt, or investment in certain types of infrastructure, are recommended as reasonable alternatives. The proceeds could also be linked to specific budgetary purposes in a transparent way, as was the case in Bolivia in which the income was used to finance the reform of the pension funds.[37]

IS PRIVATIZATION ENOUGH?
THE CHALLENGES AHEAD

There are three areas of great concern regarding the privatization experience around the world, namely:

(i) the success or failure in private participation in infrastructure in terms of investment attraction, renegotiation of contracts, and credible

[36] The relevance of the long-run perspective that ought to be followed when deciding the use of privatization proceeds is also emphasized in Kelegama (1997).

[37] See López-Calva (1998) and Pierce (1998).

regulatory agencies; (ii) the distributive impact of privation, including the impact on poverty; and (iii) corporate governance issues after privatization.

FORMS OF PRIVATE SECTOR PARTICIPATION IN INFRASTRUCTURE

Infrastructure privatization deserves special mention because of the important privatization activity that has taken place during the last decade. Moreover, infrastructure privatization involves issues related to regulation, long-term growth possibilities of the economy, as well as equity considerations. In the evidence shown above, the sectors regarded as non-competitive, as well those under regulation, are in general in the infrastructure sectors.[38]

There are different degrees of involvement of the private sector in infrastructure projects. Figure 10.10 show that these options go from the usual contracting for supply and civil works under public ownership, all the way to full private ownership through the so called 'Build-Own-Operate' schemes (BOO). Among these, the most widely used in practice, and the ones that have proven successful in different countries are the ones termed 'Lease-and-Operate' (also known as affermage contracts), 'Rehabilitate-Operate-Transfer', and 'Build-Operate-Transfer' schemes (BOT) (Guislain and Kerf 1996). Projects under BOT contracts imply the transfer of control without transfer of ownership and are generally used for greenfield concessions. Those concession contracts are usually awarded to private investors for a pre-determined period of time.[39] All these concession-type arrangements involve a public entity (at the level of federal government, state, or municipality) that awards the right and obligation to provide the service to a private investor. The conditions under which the service has to be provided are fully specified in the contract. In the case of BOT schemes, for example, the conditions under which the assets will be transferred either to the public entity or to another private investor once the concessions are over have to be spelled out in the contract. These contracts thus are complex and involve regulatory aspects, distribution of commercial and political risks, public guarantees when needed, investment requirements, and the so

---

[38] The infrastructure sector includes, for example, electricity, telecom, airports, ports, water distribution, natural gas distribution, and toll roads.

[39] For a thorough review of BOT schemes and its advantages and disadvantages, see Klein (1998). The basic contracting issues are discussed in López-Calva (1998).

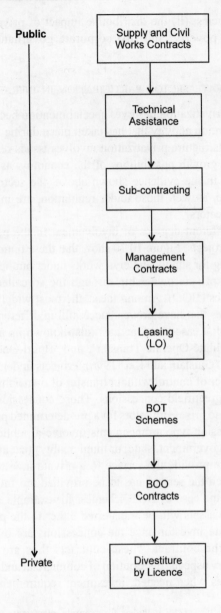

Public

Supply and Civil Works Contracts

↓

Technical Assistance

↓

Sub-contracting

↓

Management Contracts

↓

Leasing (LO)

↓

BOT Schemes

↓

BOO Contracts

↓

Divestiture by Licence

Private

Fig. 10.10: Options of Private Sector Participation in Infrastructure

Source: Guislain and Kerf (1995).

called 'universal service obligations' (USO). These obligations require the private company in charge of providing the service to give access to all groups in the area of the concession, regardless the level of income. In the case of USO, the contract must also specify pricing schemes (possibility of cross-subsidies) and mechanisms for public subsidies when they are necessary.[40]

DETERMINANTS OF SUCCESS: DESIGNING CONCESSION CONTRACTS

From a theoretical perspective, the implications mentioned in the theoretical discussion in terms of the advantages of private ownership hold, provided the appropriate regulatory mechanisms and enforcement are in place. The weaker results in terms of efficiency that the evidence shows in non-competitive (infrastructure) sectors are precisely related to the differences in regulatory mechanisms and regulatory capacity in different situations. Failures in privatization of infrastructure can be explained fundamentally by two types of policy mistakes: first, poor design of concessions—mainly in the area of distribution of risks and public guarantees, and second, inappropriate regulatory structure and/or weak enforcement by regulatory institutions.[41]

Concessions create the so-called 'competition for the market' when 'competition in the market' is not feasible. In that sense, these contracts open the possibility of a market-based mechanism to discipline the companies and assure higher efficiency levels and investment. In concession design, the fundamental question is how to allocate risk. In principle, all commercial risk should be borne by the private investors, whereas only political (non-commercial) risk ought to be shared by the public sector, through guarantees. The most 'popular' failures, like the concessions of toll-roads in Mexico, are explained by the existence of implicit and explicit guarantees that opened the room for *ex-post* renegotiation. The latter, combined with a poor design of the auction of the concessions that involved bidding over concession period, led to short concession

---

[40] Access to the service, in the case of USO, does not necessarily involve access to the network itself, given that there are alternative technologies for the provision of the service (Chisari, Estache, and Laffont 1997).

[41] For an analysis of concession contracts, their design, and review of the 'failures', see Engel, et al. (1997), and Klein (1998). A discussion of the relevance of regulatory capacity and institutions is in Smith (1996).

periods, higher tolls, low demand, and financial trouble.[42]

The design of the regulatory mechanisms and institutions ought to consider the objectives of the government (related to efficiency, investment, and equity issues), as well the restrictions it faces.

These restrictions are informational, institutional, technological, and financial. Cross-country studies show important differences in terms of the post-privatization outcome that are explained by differences in regulatory capacity (Levy and Spiller 1997).[43]

Infrastructure privatization is indeed a topic that deserves special attention. In most cases, it involves a repeated interaction between the investors and the public sector, as opposed to privatization in competitive sectors, where the transactions tend to be a one-shot game.[44] These repeated interaction makes it necessary to design contracts in a way that reduce the room for *ex-post* renegotiation, as well as to choose appropriate regulatory mechanisms with credible enforcement.

A PIECE OF EVIDENCE

The experience shows, by and large, a positive effect of the privatization of the infrastructure sector. Not only have the private investment flows in infrastructure increased, but important efficiency gains have emerged. Some evidence has been shown in the third section where, for example, Chisari, Estache, and Romero (1997) have estimated efficiency gains around 0.9 per cent of GDP that are also consistent with distributive improvements in Argentina. In addition, the evidence by sector in the same country is shown in Tables 10.9–10.11. These tables show selected performance indicators of privatized utilities, before and after privatization.

Finally, Tables 10.12 and 10.13 show selected indicators of performance improvement and investment carried out by the privatized telecommunications company in Mexico. This company, TELMEX, was sold under strict investment and performance improvement goals and was awarded monopoly power in local telephony for a predetermined

[42] This is in addition to the intrinsic difficulty in forecasting the demand in the case of toll roads. The toll roads under concession in Mexico required a major bailout and went back to public hands, with a high fiscal and political cost (See Engel et al. 1997; Ruster 1997).

[43] A discussion of the regulatory mechanisms, with emphasis on informational constraints, is in Laffont and Tirole (1993).

[44] The post-privatization interaction would involve issues of competition policy that are not sector-specific.

period of time. The price of the service in that case, however, increased, and that explains the reduction in consumer surplus after privatization as estimated by Galal et al. (1994).[45]

Table 10.9: Selected Performance Indicators: Infrastructure
Water Concessions in Buenos Aires, Argentina

Indicator	Change (May 1993–December 1995)
Increase in production capacity (%)	26
Water pipes rehabilitated (kilometers)	550
Sewers drained (kilometers)	4800
Decline in clogged drains (%)	97
Meters upgraded and installed	128,500
Staff reduction (%)	47
Residents with new water connections	642,000
Residents with new sewer connections	342,000

Source: Aguas Argentinas, as shown in Crampes and Estache (1996).

Table 10.10: Selected Performance Indicators: Infrastructure
Power Concessions in Argentina

Years	Generation		Distribution	Transmission
	Spot price ($/MWh)	Thermal availability (%)	Losses (%)	Forced outages (hours)
1992	41.85	48.2	21	1000
1993	32.12	59.8	20	900
1994	24.99	61.3	18	650
1995	22.30	69.9	12	300

Note: The generation data in 1992 are unweighted averages for October–December only (privatization took place over the period between mid-1992 and mid-1993). Distribution data are from EDESUR (privatized in September 1992). Transmission data are from Transener (privatized in July 1993). MWh is megawatt-hour.

Source: CAMMESA, ENRE, and company annual reports. Taken from Estache and Rodríguez (1996).

[45] In the case of public phones, for example, the price of a call before privatization in Mexico City was zero pesos (calls in public phones were free). For a description of the sale of TELMEX, see Rogozinski (1998) and López-Calva (1998).

Table 10.11: Selected Performance Indicators: Infrastructure Ports
of Buenos Aires, Argentina

Indicator	1991	1995
Cargo (thousands of tons)	4000	6000
Containers (thousands of 'twenty-feet equivalent units')	300	540
Capacity (thousands of containers per year)	400	1000
Operational area (hectares)	65	95
Productivity (tons per worker per year)	800	3000
Average stay for full containers (days)	2.5	1.5
Cost for container imports (US$ per ton)	450	120
Port tariff for exports (US$ per ton)	6.7	3.0
Port tariff for imports (US$ per ton)	2.1	1.5

Source: Administración Genereal de Puertos. Taken from Estache and Carvajo
(1998a).

Table 10.12: Performance Indicators of the Mexican Telecommunications
Company after Privatization

Indicator	1989	1999
Lines in service (thousands)	4848	10,927
Rural towns with access to telephone	1683	39,691
Number of towns with access to telephone	4219	43,648
Telephone density (per 100 inhabitants)	5.9[a]	11.2
Fiber optics network (kilometers)	72.0	84,253

Note: The privatization took place in 1990 (transfer of control).
[a] These data are for 1990.

Source: Ministry of Communications and Transport, Mexico.

Table 10.13: Telephone Density Lines in Service Per 100 Inhabitants

Year	Telephone density
1990	6.4
1991	7.0
1992	7.8
1993	8.6
1994	9.4
1995	9.6
1996	9.5
1997	9.8
1998	10.3
1999	11.2
2000	11.9

It is thus a fact that the problematic sectors to privatize are those in which there is room for market power. The credibility of the regulatory framework in place is a key determinant of success. Despite all the investment that took place after privatization in the case of the telecoms in Mexico, consumers have not been able to receive a proportional benefit due to the exploitation of market power by the dominant firm. In smaller countries like Nicaragua and Guatemala, the credibility problems could be exacerbated (Larraín and López-Calva, 2001). Recent evidence shows an overwhelming support to the fact that renegotiation of contracts is indeed the rule, rather than the exception (Guasch 2001).

DISTRIBUTIVE IMPACT AND CORPORATE GOVERNANCE

Distributive and poverty-alleviation issues are a matter of concern in competitive sectors, but also in services like electricity, water, transport, and even telecommunications. Theoretically, it is possible to deal with those in the concession design. Exclusion can be dealt with through USO, whereas affordability to poor groups in the population involve the use of subsidies. In general, there will be a trade-off between the existence of a more competitive market with non-uniform pricing, which requires more sophisticated subsidy schemes, and uniform prices that involve cross-subsidies with a higher political cost but a lower financial cost for the public sector (Chisari, Estache, and Laffont 1997). The experience shows that restricting cross-subsidies that take place through uniform pricing, while targeting effectively public subsidies, is a difficult policy to implement, though theoretically preferred. Some countries, however, have put in practice effectively the existence of life-line consumption levels that are subsidized, as well as subsidies to network expansion to less profitable areas.[46] In general, the poor will benefit from access to services they did not have in the past. One important mistake in evaluating privatization prospects in infrastructure sectors is the confusion in terms of *willingness to pay* and *ability to pay* by the poor. The former tends to be high when people do not have access to the services and shows the economic value of such access. The latter has to be dealt with through appropriate subsidy schemes.

From the macroeconomic perspective, privatization has the following effects, *ceteris paribus*: (i) reduction in interest rates; (ii) lower inflation rate; and (iii) it implies higher unemployment, at least in the short run. The first two effects are progressive. Reduction in interest rates goes in favour of net borrowers—typically the poorer sectors, affecting net savers. Lower inflation has also a progressive impact on distribution, according to the evidence in developing countries (Portela 2001). The effect through employment, however, tends to be regressive. Additionally, a positive effect may occur when the government frees resources that can be used for social expenditure.

From the microeconomic perspective, if privatization reduces prices, increases product diversity, and increases efficiency, the expected effect would be progressive. However, the elimination of subsidies increases prices for certain segments of the population. Finally, the wages of people who leave SOEs and are incorporated into the private sector would tend to reflect more closely marginal productivities, increasing wage dispersion. Several projects on the distributive impacts of privatization are being carried out, but the results are ambiguous thus far.[47]

CORPORATE GOVERNANCE

Once the decision-making responsibilities are shifted to the private sector, a proper legal structure for the interaction between shareholders and managers is required. In countries with poor legal protection to

[46] Chile is an example in which the subsidy to the fixed cost in electricity provision, for example, is given through a bidding process where interested companies bid over the 'minimum' subsidy to provide the service to a specific area.

[47] The best piece on this issue is Estache et al. (2000).

shareholders the benefits from private management cannot be realized, while the achievement of positive effects on the financial sector is thwarted. Dyck (2000b) mentions that 'The Czechs invented a word, tunneling, to characterize such behaviour that has left firms with debts, disenchanted workers and investors, and great difficulty in raising capital to fund future investment projects.' Indeed, even though this has been a problem in transition economies especially, many other countries have suffered from poor corporate governance legislations that have prevented the benefits of private management from occurring. Johnson (2000) have shown evidence of such practices even in more developed economies.

Again, the corporate governance issues are related to the institutional design. The independence of the judiciary and an effective and efficient system for dispute resolution is thus a necessary condition for privatization to succeed. More academic research in this area is indeed needed.

CONCLUSIONS

From the theoretical discussion, several empirical implications are proposed. We analyse below how the evidence from different studies supports these implications.

Implication 1: Publicly owned enterprises in competitive environments would not perform better than privately owned companies in the same circumstances in terms of profitability, and could perform worse.

The microeconomic evidence supports this implication. Country-specific data and cross-country data show that privatized firms improve their profitability after the sale, even controlling for macroeconomic and industry specific factors. This result is robust to different definitions of the profitability indicator, and holds for different market structures. Deregulation policies have been shown to speed up the convergence process of firms to industry standards. Partial privatization has a lower effect on profitability when compared with full privatization. The evidence for Central and Eastern European countries is also consistent with the proposition, and the *political view*—that says that political intervention undermines firm performance—seems to be confirmed by the data.

Implication 2: One should expect important efficiency gains from the change in ownership structure in competitive sectors.

The micro evidence also confirms that the introduction of competition enhances productivity gains. Firms in more concentrated and regulated markets, though they also go through an important restructuring after the sale, show lower increases in productivity as compared to those that are under the discipline of the market. Eliminating restrictions to foreign direct investment and trade barriers, and government controls on prices and quantities, fuels the catch-up of firms to competitive standards.

Implication 3: In general, increases in profitability are not equivalent to increases in efficiency. This will only be true in a competitive environment.

Two facts support this proposition in the data. First, it is observed in cross-country studies that profitability increases more and productivity less in regulated or less competitive sectors. This shows that firms are exploiting, at least partially, their market power. Second, in the case studies we observe that consumer surplus is affected by the degree of competition in the sector, even though total welfare changes are positive.[48]

Implication 4: Fully privatized firms should perform better than firms that have been partially privatized, under the same conditions.

Cross-country evidence for developing countries shows that firms that were partially privatized realized lower profitability gains and productivity changes as compared to fully privatized enterprises.

From the macroeconomic perspective, the evidence is much far less strong, and causality cannot be assumed. Important aggregate trends, however, have been identified.

Implication 5: Privatization improves the public sector's financial health (lower deficits, lower debt).

The budget deficit shows a positive trend, i.e., it declines during the reform period. Low-income countries, which are on average less aggressive privatizers during the period analysed, still have a significant deficit on average. Privatization has represented an important policy tool for fiscal reform.

Implication 6: Privatization reduces the net transfer to SOEs in the aggregate. These transfers become positive if the government actually starts collecting taxes from privatized firms.

---

[48] This is the case, for example, in telecommunications privatization in Mexico, where the consumer surplus fell after the sale. The methodology, however, fails to capture dynamic efficiency gains introduced by technological change and new investments as well as changes introduced to the regulatory framework.

The net transfers to SOEs have declined and actually become negative for high-income and middle-income countries. This shows that not only have the subsidies been reduced, but the government has started to collect taxes from previously money-losing firms. This is also supported by the micro evidence. It is only in the case of low-income countries that net subsidies have continued, which is consistent with the fact that the SOEs overall balance in those countries is negative. This shows that there is room to improve the performance of the late reformers.

Implication 7: Privatization has a positive impact on the development of the financial sector.

Stock market capitalization has shown a steady increase in all country groups between 1987 and 1997. In low-income countries, this trend has been accelerated since the early 1990s, when privatization transactions began to occur at a faster pace. This change has also responded to the liberalization of the financial sector and opening to foreign investment, but privatization has played a fundamental role in it.

Implication 8: Privatization has a negative effect on employment in the short-run and a positive effect in the medium and long-run.

The effect on unemployment is ambiguous. Unemployment rates vary widely across countries, regardless of whether they have privatized or not. The macro instability introduced by the Mexican crisis in 1995 and subsequent problems in East Asia can partly explain the different patterns, as well the particular features of stabilization plans in different countries, like the strict management of the exchange rate in Argentina. The microeconomic evidence is also mixed. For country cases, it is shown that employment in privatized firms on average decreased, while cross-country evidence of publicly traded companies shows an increase in average employment.

Finally, it is important to mention the lack of detailed research in the area of the effect of privatization on distribution and poverty. The CGE (Computable General Equilibrium) model discussed above, on the distributive effects of utilities privatization in Argentina, shows a positive result. The case studies carried out by Galal et al. (1994) also allow us to reach positive conclusions from the distributive point of view, though they also highlight the relevance of the market structure for the outcome. In the case of privatization of infrastructure, exclusion *via* either lack of access to the network or pricing is a major concern. Universal service obligations and efficient subsidy schemes are required in that context.

The main challenges for privatization to succeed, as well as the most relevant topics in the agenda for academic research, are in the areas of (i) distributive impact of privatization; (ii) institutional design in privatization of infrastructure; and (iii) corporate governance issues after privatization. Privatization is, indeed, not enough in most cases for the efficiency gains to be achieved.

REFERENCES

Aharoni, Yair (1991), 'On Measuring the Success of Privatization', in R. Ramamurti and R. Vernon, *Privatization and Control of State-owned Enterprises*, EDI Development No. 11863, The World Bank.

Barberis, N., M. Boycko, A. Shleifer, and N. Tsukanova (1996), 'How does Privatization Work?: Evidence from the Russian Shops', *Journal of Political Economy,* vol. 104, no. 4, pp. 764–90.

Bitran, Eduardo and Pablo Serra (1998), 'The Chilean Experience', *World Development*, vol. 26, no. 6.

Blanchard, Oliver (1997), *The Economics of Post-Communist Transition* (New York: Oxford University Press).

Blejer, M. and A. Cheasty, eds, (1992), *How to Measure the Fiscal Deficit*, IMF, Washington, DC.

Bourbakri, Narjess and Jean-Claude Cosset (1998), 'The Financial and Operating Performance of Newly Privatized Firms: Evidence from Developing Countries', mimeo, Universite Laval, Québec, Canada.

Boycko, M., A. Shleifer, and R. Vishny (1995), *Privatizing Russia* (Cambridge, MA: MIT Press).

Chisari, O., A. Estache, and J.J. Laffont (1997), 'The Needs of the Poor in Infrastructure Privatization: The Role of Universal Service Obligations', mimeo, The World Bank, Washington, DC.

Chisari, Omar, Antonio Estache, and Carlos Romero (1999), 'Winners and Losers from Privatization and Regulation of Utilities: Lessons from a General Equilibrium Model of Argentina', *The World Bank Economic Review*, vol. 13, no. 9, pp. 357–78.

Claessens, Stijn and Simeon Djankov (1998), 'Politicians and Firms in Seven Central and Eastern European Countries', mimeo, The World Bank, Washington, DC.

Crampes, Claude and Antonio Estache (1996), 'Regulating Water Concessions: Lessons from the Buenos Aires Concession', *Viewpoint*, Note no. 91, The World Bank Group, September.

Demirguc-Kunt, Asli and Ross Levine (1994), 'The Financial System and Public Enterprise Reform: Concepts and Cases', Policy Research Working Paper no. 1319, The World Bank, Washington, DC.

D'Souza, Juliet and William Megginson (1998), 'The Financial and Operating Performance of Privatized Firms During the 1990's', mimeo, Department of Finance, Terry College of Business, The University of Georgia, Athens, GA.

Dyck, Alexander (2000a), 'Ownership Structure, Legal Protections and Corporate Governance', mimeo, Harvard University, Boston, MA.

_____ (2000b), 'Privatization and Corporate Governance: Principles, Evidence, and Future Challenges', mimeo, Harvard University.

Earle, J., R. Frydman, A. Rapaczynski, and J. Turkewitz (1994), *Small Privatization, The Transformation of Retail Trade and Consumer Services in the Czech Republic, Hungary, and Poland* (Hungary: Budapest-Central European University Press and Oxford University Press).

Eckel, Catherine, Doug Eckel, and Vijay Singhal (1997), 'Privatization and Efficiency: Industry Effects of the Sale of British Airways', *Journal of Financial Economics,* vol. 43, no. 2, pp. 275–98.

Engel, E., R. Fischer, and A. Galetovic (1997), 'Infrastructure Franchising and Government Guarantees', in T. Irwin, M. Klein, G. Perry, and M. Thobani, eds, *Dealing with Public Risk in Private Infrastructure*, (Washington, DC.: The World Bank).

Estache, Antonio and Martín Rodríguez (1996), 'Regulatory Lessons from Argentina's Power Concessions', *Viewpoint*, Note no. 92, September.

Estache, Antonio and José Carvajo (1996a), 'Competing Private Ports: Lessons from Argentina', *Viewpoint*, Note no. 100, December.

_____ (1996b); 'Designing Toll Road Concessions: Lessons from Argentina', *Viewpoint*, Note no. 99, December.

_____ Omar O. Chisari and Catharine Waddams Price (2001), Access by the Poor in Latin America.

Frydman, R., M. Hessel, and A. Rapaczynski (1998), 'Why Ownership Matters?, Politicization and Entrepreneurship in the Restructuring of Enterprises in Central Europe', New York University, mimeo.

Frydman, R., C.W. Gray, M. Hessel, and A. Rapaczynski (1997), 'Private Ownership and Corporate Performance: Evidence from Transition Economies', Research Report 97-28, C.V. Starr Center for Applied Economics, New York University.

Galal, A., L. Jones, P. Tandon, I. Vogelsang (1994), *The Welfare Consequences of Selling Public Sector Enterprises* (New York: Oxford University Press).

Guislain, P. and M. Kerf (1996), 'Concessions: The Way to Privatize Infrastructure Monopolies', *Viewpoint*, Note no. 59, The World Bank, October.

Hachette, Dominique and Rolf Lüders (1993), Privatization in Chile: An Economic Appraisal, International Center for Economic Growth, San Francisco.

Haltiwanger, J. and M. Singh (1996), 'Cross-Country Evidence on Public Sector Retrenchment', *The World Bank Economic Review*, vol. 13, no. 1, pp. 23–66.

Hart, Oliver, Andrei Shleifer and Robert Vishny (1997), 'The Proper Scope of Government: Theory and An Application to Prisons', *Quarterly Journal of Economics*, vol. 112, no. 4, pp. 1127–61.

Irwin, T., M. Klein, G. Perry, and M. Thobani, eds. (1997), *Dealing with Public Risk in Private Infrastructure* (Washington, DC.: The World Bank).

Jin, Hehui, and Yingyi Qian (1998), 'Public vs. Private Ownership of Firms: Evidence from Rural China', *Quarterly Journal of Economics*, forthcoming.

Johnson, Robin (2001), *Privatization is Benefiting Employees, Governments Across the Country*, Reason Public Policy Institute, Los Angeles, CA.

Jones, Leroy, Pankaj Tandon, and Ingo Vogelsang (1990), *Selling Public Sector Enterprises* (Cambridge MA: MIT Press).

Jones, S., W. Megginson, R. Nash, and J. Netter (1998), 'Share Issue Privatizations as Financial Means to Political and Economic Ends', mimeo, Department of Finance, Terry College of Business, The University of Georgia, Athens, GA.

Kay, Anthony and David Thompson (1986), 'Privatization: A Policy in Search of a Rationale', *Economic Journal*, vol. 96, pp. 18–38.

Kelegama, Saman (1997), 'Privatization and The Public Exchequer: Some Observations from the Sri Lankan Experience', *Asia-Pacific Development Journal*, vol. 4, no. 1, June, pp. 129–47.

Kikeri, Sunita (1995), 'Privatization and Labor: What Happens to Workers When Governments Divest', Technical Paper No. 396, *The World Bank*, Washington, D.C.

Kikeri, S., John Nellis, and Mary Shirley (1994), 'Privatization: Lessons from Market Economies', *The World Bank Research Observer*, vol. 9, no. 2, July.

Klein, Michael (1998), 'Bidding for Concessions', *Revista de Análisis Económico*, Forthcoming.

Kornai, Janos (1980), *The Economics of Shortage* (Amsterdam: North Holland).

———— (1986), 'The Soft Budget Constraint', *Kyklos,* vol. 39, no. 1, pp. 3–30.

Laffont, J.J. and Jean Tirole (1991), 'Privatization and Incentives', *Journal of Law, Economics and Organization* vol. 7(s), September, pp. 84–105.

———— (1993), *Theory of Incentives in Procurement and Regulation* (Cambridge MA: MIT Press).

LaPorta, Rafael and F. López-de-Silanes (1999), 'The Benefits of Privatization: Evidence from Mexico', *Quarterly Journal of Economics*, vol. 114, no. 4, p. 1193.

LaPorta, Rafael, Florencio Lopez-de-Sialnes, Andrei Shleifer and Robert W. Vishny (1998), 'Law and Finance', *Journal of Political Economy,* vol. 106, no. 6, pp. 1133–55.

Larraín, Felipe (1991), 'Public Sector Behavior in a Highly Indebted Country: The Contrasting Chilean Experience', in Larraín and Selowsky, eds, *The*

Public Sector and The Latin American Crisis, International Center for Economic Growth, San Francisco, CA: ICS Press.

Larraín, Felipe and Luis F. López-Calva (2001), 'Fostering Economic Growth Through Private Sector Development', in F. Larraín, ed., *Economic Development in Central America* (Cambridge MA: Harvard University Press)

———— and Marcelo Selowsky, eds. (1991), *The Public Sector and The Latin American Crisis*, International Center for Economic Growth, San Francisco.

———— and R. Vergara (1993), 'Macroeconomic Effects of Privatization: Lessons from Chile and Argentina', mimeo, The World Bank, October.

Leffort, Fernando and Andrés Solimano (1993), 'Economic Growth After Market Based Reforms in Latin America: The Cases of Chile and Mexico', mimeo, The World Bank, Washington, DC.

Levy, B. and P. Spiller (1997), *Regulation, Institutions, and Commitment in Telecommunications: A Comparative Study of Five Countries* (Cambridge UK: Cambridge University Press).

Lieberman, Ira W., Stilpon S. Nestor and Raj M. Desai (1995), Mass Privatization in Central and Eastern Europe and the Former Soviet Union: A Comparative Analysis, (Washington, DC.: The World Bank).

López-Calva, Luis F. (1998), 'On Privatization Methods', Harvard Institute for International Development, HIID Development Discussion Paper No. 665, Central America Project Series, Harvard University.

López-De-Silanes, Florencio (1993), 'A Macro Perspective on Privatization: The Mexican Program', John F. Kennedy School of Government, Faculty Research Working Paper Series R96-12, Harvard University.

———— A. Shleifer, and R. Vishny (1997), 'Privatization in the United States', *Rand Journal of Economics*, vol. 28, no. 3, pp. 447–71.

Luders, R. and D. Hachette (1993), *Privatization in Chile: An Economic Appraisal* (California: San Francisco Press).

Mansoor, A. (1992), 'The Budgetary Impact of Privatization', in M. Blejer and A. Cheasty, eds (1992), *How to Measure the Fiscal Deficit: Analytical and Methodological Issues*, IMF Washington, DC.

Marcel, M. (1989), Privatización y Finanzas Públicas: El Caso de Chile 1985–1988', Colección de Estudios *Cieplan*, vol. 26, June, pp. 5–60.

McLindon, Michale P. (1996), Privatization and Capital Market Development (Westport CT: Praeger Publishers).

Megginson, W.L. and J. Netter (2000), 'From State to Market: A Survey of Empirical Studies on Privatization', Forthcoming in the *Journal of Economic Literature*.

Megginson, William L., Robert C. Nash, and Matthias Van Randenborgh (1994), 'The Financial and Operating Performance of Newly Privatized Firms: An International Empirical Analysis', *The Journal of Finance*, vol. 69, no. 2, June, pp. 403–52.

Megginson, W.L., R. Nash, J. Netter, and A. Poulsen (1998), 'The Choice of Privatization Method: An Empirical Analysis', mimeo, Department of Finance, Terry College of Business, The University of Georgia, Athens, GA.

Megginson, W.L., R. Nash, J. Netter, and A. Schwartz (1998), 'The Long-Run Return to Investors in Share Issue Privatizations', mimeo, Department of Banking and Finance, Terry College of Business, The University of Georgia, Athens, GA.

Menyah, Kojo and Krishna Paudyal (1996), 'Share Issue Privatisations: The UK Experience', in M. Levis, ed., *Share Issue Privatisations: The UK Experience in Empirical Issues in Raising Equity Capital*, Elsevier Science, pp. 17–48.

Nellis, John (1997), 'Is Privatization Necessary?', *Public Policy for the Private Sector*, FPD Note no. 7, May, The World Bank.

Pannier, Dominique (1996), 'Corporate Governance of Public Enterprises in Transitional Economies', World Bank Technical Paper no. 323, Washington, DC.

Pierce, Margaret, ed. (1998), *Capitalization: The Bolivian Model of Social and Economic Reform*, Woodrow Wilson International Center for Scholars and The North–South Center, University of Florida.

Perotti, Enrico and Serhat Guney (1993), 'The Structure of Privatization Plans', *Financial Management,* vol. 22, pp. 84–98.

Portela, Andre (2001), 'Inflation and Income Distribution: Evidence from Brazil', mimeo, Department of Economics, Cornell University.

Ramamurti, R. and R. Vernon (1991), *Privatization and Control of State-Owned Enteprises*, EDI Development no. 11863, EDI Development Studies, p. 344.

Raventós, Pedro (1998), 'Telecommunications in Central America', HIID Development Discussion, Paper no. 648.

Roche, David (1996), 'It Depends What You Mean by Privatization', *Euromoney*, no. 2, February.

Rogozinski, Jacques (1998), *High Price for Change: Privatization in Mexico* (Washington, DC: Inter-American Development Bank), distributed by Baltimore, MD: Johns Hopkins Press.

Ruster, Jeff (1997), 'A Retrospective on the Mexican Toll Road Program', *Viewpoint*, Note 125, September, pp. 1–5.

Sappington, D.E. and J. Stiglitz (1987), 'Privatization, Information, and Incentives', *Journal of Policy Analysis and Management,* vol. 6, no. 4, pp. 567–82.

Schmidt, Klaus (1990), 'The Costs and Benefits of Privatization: An Incomplete Contracting Approach', Discussion Paper no. A-287, University of Bonn.

———— (1996), 'Incomplete Contracts and Privatization', *European Economic Review,* vol. 40, pp. 569–79.

Serven, L., A. Solimano, and R. Soto (1994), 'The Macroeconomics of Public Enterprise Reform and Privatization: Theory and Evidence from Developing Countries', Working Paper (unpublished), Macroeconomics and Growth Division, Policy Research Department, The World Bank, Washington, DC.

Shapiro, Carl and Robert Willig (1990), 'Economic Rationales for the Scope of Privatization', in E. Suleiman and J. Waterbury, eds. (1990), *The Political Economy of Public Sector Reform and Privatization* (San Francisco CA: Westview Press), pp. 136–45.

Shirley, Mary (1991), 'Evaluating the Performance of State-Owned Enterprises', in R. Ramamurti and R. Vernon (1991), *Privatization and Control of State-Owned Enteprises*, EDI Development Studies.

Shleifer, Andrei (1998), 'State versus Private Ownership', mimeo, Department of Economics, Harvard University.

_____ and Robert Vishny (1994), 'Politicians and Firms', *The Quarterly Journal of Economics,* vol. 109, no. 9, pp. 995–1025.

_____ (1996), 'A Theory of Privatization', *Economic Journal*, vol. 106, pp. 309–19.

Smith, Adam (1776), *An Inquiry into the Nature and Causes of the Wealth of Nations* (Oxford UK: Edition by Oxford University Press, 1976).

Smith, Stephen, Milan Vodopivek, and Beom-Cheol Cin (1997), 'Privatization Incidence, Ownership Forms, and Firm Performance: Evidence from Slovenia', *Journal of Comparative Economics*, vol. 25, pp. 158–79.

Smith, Warrick (1996), 'Utility Regulators: Creating Agencies in Reforming and Developing Countries', Paper for presentation at the International Forum for Utility Regulation, Expert Group Meeting, Eynsham Hall, U.K., June.

_____ and Ben Shin (1995), 'Regulating Brazil's Infrastructure: Perspectives on Decentralization', Economic Notes Number 6, Country Dept. I, Latin America and the Caribbean Region, The World Bank, Washington, DC., September.

Stiglitz, Joseph (1991), 'Theoretical Aspects of the Privatization: Applications to Eastern Europe', *Institute for Policy Reform*, Working Paper Series.

_____ (1993), 'Measures for Enhancing the Flow of Private Capital to Less Developed Countries, *Development Issues*, no. 1, pp. 201–11.

Suleiman, E.N. and J. Waterbury, eds. (1990), *The Political Economy of Public Sector Reform and Privatization* (Boulder, Colorado: Westview Press).

Tirole, Jean (1994), 'The Internal Organization of Government', *Oxford Economic Papers*, vol. 46, no. 1, pp. 1–29.

United Nations (1993), 'Methods and Practices of Privatization', *Proceedings of the Privatization Workshops held in Kenya and Bangladesh*, November–December, Department for Development, Support, and Management Services.

Vernon-Wortzel, Hiedi and Lawrence H. Wortzel (1989), 'Privatization: Not the Only Answer', *World Development*, vol. 17, no. 5, pp. 633–41.

Vickers, John and George Yarrow (1989), *Privatization: An Economic Analysis* (Cambridge MA: MIT Press).

Vuylsteke, Charles (1988), 'Techniques of Privatization of State-Owned Enterprises', vol. I: Methods and Implementation, and vol. II: Selected Country Case Studies, World Bank Technical Paper no. 88, The World Bank, Washington, DC.

Williamson, Oliver (1985), *The Economic Institutions of Capitalism* (New York and London: Free Press).

Willig, Robert D. (1993), 'Public versus Private Regulated Enterprise', Paper prepared for *The World Bank Conference on Development Economics*, May, Washington, DC, pp. 155–80.

World Bank (1995), *Bureaucrats in Business* (under the direction of Mary Shirley) (New York: Oxford University Press).

Yarrow, George (1992), 'Privatization in Theory and Practice', *Economic Policy*, vol. 2, pp. 324–64.

11

An Examination of Schumpeter's Tax State

Pulin B. Nayak

Among Joseph A. Schumpeter's numerous writings on public finance, his article on 'The Crisis of the Tax State' is possibly the most seminal. The article is an elaboration of a lecture given by him in Vienna in 1917. It appeared in the German in 1918 and the first English translation by Wolfgang Stolper and Richard Musgrave appeared in 1954. Strangely, this article is routinely categorized as a contribution to 'sociology' and the paper seems to have been largely ignored in the public finance literature. This essay was part of Schumpeter's conscious programme to develop a broad economic science or *sozialokonomik*, the main purpose of which was to expand the domain of the economist. Among other issues, in this essay Schumpeter also develops his views on the relative spheres of activity for the state and the market.

Many decades later, Mrinal Datta-Chaudhuri (1990), in his perceptive essay on market failure and government failure, focused on a similar set of concerns. The essay began with the observation: 'For several decades a debate has been raging in development economics on the relative virtues of the free market as opposed to state intervention'. Datta-Chaudhuri is interested in the question as to whether a government may be relied upon to do the 'right' thing and avoid doing the 'wrong' thing. He went on to argue that it is impossible to give a context free answer to this question. Schumpeter too emphasized the importance of the context comprising of the historical and sociological backdrop to any concrete economic problem.

In the opening paragraph Schumpeter sets out the political and economic uncertainties that characterized the post First World War period. He (1991) goes on to say:

Some foresee that 'high capitalism', having culminated in the war, must now collapse; others look forward to more perfect economic freedom than before, while yet others expect an 'administered economy' fashioned by our 'intellectuals'. This is bound to happen because the state—so says the bourgeois smugly— or because the free economy—so says the intellectual enthusiastically—have failed. (p. 99)

Schumpeter lamented the lack of intellectual rigour in the available analyses of the above problems. He observed that 'there remains free competition at least in slogans: the cheapest wins. In no other field of knowledge would such a performance be possible. Only in economic matters does everyone consider himself called upon to speak as an expert; every Tom, Dick and Harry feels entitled ingeniously to recite age-old fallacies and naively to declare his own most subjective economic or ideological interest to be the last word of wisdom'.

Schumpeter's contribution on the 'tax state' was a riposte to Rudolf Goldscheid's (1917) contention that the tax financed capitalist state could not levy sufficient taxes to cover its necessary expenditures and, therefore, would incur increasingly higher debt, which would then lead to a fiscal crisis. This was written in the backdrop of World War I and such a scenario did seem to be quite plausible then. Schumpeter, however, argued that the fiscal consequences of the war could be handled by the 'tax state'. He essentially advocated a two pronged strategy. One strategy comprised of inflation, which would enable the state to gradually confiscate income and property through raising prices, thus reducing demand. The other strategy was the use of a capital levy, to be imposed as a one-time tax on private liquid capital assets. The fact that the major capitalist economies survived the travails of the two World Wars shows that Schumpeter was essentially right in his assessment. Yet this did not prevent him from arguing that as the process of development continued, the capitalist state may be confronted with a deeper fiscal crisis that may have nothing to do with financing wars.

Goldscheid had remarked that 'the budget is the skeleton of the state stripped of all misleading ideologies'. Schumpeter approves of this view and goes on to suggest that the budget is 'a collection of hard, naked facts which yet remain to be drawn into the realm of sociology. The spirit of a people, its cultural level, its social structure, the deeds its policy may prepare—all this and more is written in its fiscal history, stripped of all phrases'. Elaborating on the approaches of fiscal history and fiscal sociology, 'the development of which lies as yet in the lap of the gods, there is one which is of particular interest to us: the view of the state, of its nature, its forms, its fate, as seen from the fiscal side. The word "tax state" is a child of this view'.

According to Schumpeter, a fiscal crisis occurs when the available types of revenue become permanently insufficient to finance the level of expenditure considered necessary. In the 1918 article, Schumpeter describes the transition in Austria and Germany from dues to taxes as the main source of revenue. The expenditure needs of the princes in these countries grew rapidly from the fourteenth to the sixteenth centuries. Courts were enlarged in size to increasingly bring in independent country nobility into its fold. The principal reason was the rising cost of warfare, as mercenary armies became necessary to meet the threat of the larger armies fielded by the invading Turks. Thus, it was the changing structure of the polity and external factors that made an increase in expenditure unavoidable. The existing sources of revenue, arising as dues from the princes' peasant serfs, regalia from mint, market and mining, etc. were insufficient to finance this expenditure. Schumpeter argued that because these changes were both deep rooted and permanent, this was a crisis of the fiscal system as a whole and not a transitory failure due to mismanagement. The crisis was averted when, after a period of indebtedness, taxes were established as a new form of revenue.

In this monograph of Schumpeter's, there is a detailed consideration of how the state finances itself under the capitalist mode of production. Much of traditional mainstream economics abstracts from a government. For example the government is not integral to the Walrasian system of general equilibrium. What Schumpeter was trying to emphasize was that capitalist society needs a government, which in turn needs taxes. The tax state arises as a necessary complement of capitalism because the feudal system could not adequately solve its economic or its public expenditure problem.

Schumpeter goes on to argue that the tax state emerged as an institution to fill the gap left by the decline of the feudal system and its revenue sources. The rise of the tax state precisely met the needs of liberal capitalism as it emerged (Musgrave 1988). The income tax became its most suitable expression. Schumpeter viewed it as a destructive force as it represented for him an intellectual hostility to the capitalist spirit. But he was also reconciled to its inevitability.

Schumpeter then went on to argue, first, that a modern state is born out of its fiscal needs. He observes that 'without financial need the immediate cause for the creation of the modern state would have been absent'. To this one might add that without political need the cause for the creation of the modern finance and tax system would have been absent. Thus, both financial as well as political compulsions contributed to the formation of the modern state and it would be difficult, and possibly even futile, to separate the two effects.

The second major thesis put forward by Schumpeter was that a fiscal crisis is an inevitable as well as an integral part of the decline of the capitalist system. He argued that there exists a definite limit to the fiscal capacity of the state, and that if this limit is transgressed, the state will collapse. For him this was part of a long term perspective, with the implication that the tax state would fall apart due to the inherent internal logic of the development of capitalism. This idea was to be later further developed in his *Capitalism, Socialism and Democracy* (1942).

Specifically there were two implications of the tax state that Schumpeter had emphasized. The first refers to the possible disincentive effects of taxation. He feared that the state may tax entrepreneurial profit in such a manner that the process of economic development would come to a standstill. Individuals' motive to work hard and take risks would be affected by this, and capitalism may grind to a halt. The second implication is that the tax revenues are insufficient to cover the expenses of all the measures that people feel entitled to by the state. Schumpeter (1991) writes:

If the will of the people is to demand higher and higher public expenditures, if more and more means are used for purposes for which private individuals have not produced them, if more and more power stands behind this will, and if finally all parts of the people are gripped by entirely new ideas about private property and the forms of life—then the tax state will have run its course and society will have to depend on other motive forces for its economy than self-interest. This limit can certainly be reached and thereby also the crisis which the state could not survive. Without doubt, the tax state can collapse. (p. 116)

At bottom, the problem is one where a fiscal crisis is brought about because there exists a general tendency for the expenditures of the capitalist state to increase faster than it can raise revenues to finance them. As Swedberg (1991) observes, there thus 'exists a dangerous contradiction between the task of accumulation and the task of legitimation in the capitalist state which leads to the fiscal crisis'.

More than eight decades after Schumpeter envisioned the crisis and collapse of the tax state, the collapse has not occurred, at least not in the major capitalist countries of the world. In a number of poor developing countries of Africa, Asia, and Latin America, the crisis has sometimes seemed imminent but there has really been no fear of collapse. We shall argue here that the crisis of the tax state, or the capitalist state, is part of a broader Schumpeterian vision, which he first developed in his 1917 lecture and then further honed a quarter century later in his *Capitalism Socialism and Democracy* (1942).

Some authors have equated Schumpeter's tax state with the 'capitalist state', (see for example, Richard Swedberg 1991). Robert Loring Allen (1994) has argued that by the tax state, Schumpeter referred to the governmental financial arrangement in a capitalist society. As feudalism gave way to capitalism, a way had to be found to finance the collective activities of the new order; finances were required for defence, law, and order and to provide public goods. Thus the capitalist society, almost by definition, required a government and taxes. Jurgen Backhaus (1994) has, however, argued that while the tax state is related to the modern capitalist system, it is clearly not the same. Instead they may be regarded as complements. The tax state and the capitalist economic system are two systems that exist side by side, mutually supporting and determining each other's mode of production, while these modes of production are completely different. Schumpeter describes the relationship between taxes and the capitalist state thus:

Taxes not only helped to create the state. They helped to form it. The tax system was the organ, the development of which entailed the other organs. Tax bill in hand, the state penetrated the private economies and won increasing domination over them. The tax brings money and calculating spirit into corners in which they do not dwell as yet, and thus becomes a formative factor in the very organism which has developed it. (1991, p. 108)

In Schumpeter's scheme the 'primitive horde' has no state. He argues that its 'social organisation is an entity which also fulfils those functions that later fall to the state, but from which no separate state has as yet developed'. For the same reason a 'socialistically organised people would have no state'. He goes on to say: 'If socialism became a reality through the conquest of the economy by the power of the state, the state would annul itself by its very expansion' (1991, p. 109).

In his early writings, Schumpeter subscribed to a notion of 'methodological individualism', where 'the self governing individual constitutes the ultimate unit of the social sciences, and where all social phenomena resolve themselves into decisions and actions of individuals that cannot be further analysed in terms of super individual factors' (1954). The individual is the key element in his thought, especially in his role as an entrepreneur. It is he who plays a central role in the dynamics of capitalism as one who innovates and creates. Schumpeter seems to have imbibed the notion of creative individuals in the economic process from his teacher Friedrich von Wieser. Schumpeter advocated methodological individualism because he believed that it produced 'usable results' while a 'social' or collectivist methodology offered no intrinsic advantages. It is this view which led him to argue for the maximum role for individual initiative. But interestingly, it is precisely under these conditions that the need for the tax state arises. He argues:

'Only where individual life carries its own centre of gravity within itself, where its meaning lies in the individual and his personal sphere, where the fulfilment of the personality is its own end, only there can the state exist as a real phenomenon. Only there does the state become necessary'. (1954, p. 109)

There is an irony here. The tax state acts as a curb on the free play of the market system. Yet the very rationale of the tax state itself is derived only under conditions where individual potential is given its fullest leash. This obviously leads us to the question of what really ought to be regarded as the optimum extent of the tax state.

In 'The Crisis of the Tax State' Schumpeter delves into the role, scope, and limitation of the state and more specifically of the public sector. Jackson (1994) argues that by the 'tax state' Schumpeter meant the mixed economy. Thus, the questions Schumpeter raised in 1918 are as relevant today as they were then. For example, it is important to ask as to what is the appropriate mix between the public and private sectors, and whether there is a limit to the scope and role of the tax state in modern industrial economies. Schumpeter is careful to emphasize that the tax state, once in place, has a dynamic of its own. He writes:

It goes without saying that there is more to the state than the collection of taxes necessitated by the common need that was their origin. Once the state exists as reality and as a social institution, once it has become the centre of the persons who man the governmental machine and whose interests are focused upon it, finally, once the state is recognised as suitable for many things even by those individuals whom it confronts—once all this has happened, the state develops further and soon turns into something the nature of which can no longer be understood merely from the fiscal standpoint, and for which the finances become a serving tool. If the finances have created and partly formed the modern state, so now the state on its part forms them and enlarges them—deep into the flesh of the private economy (1991, p. 110).

Despite the large encompassing role of the tax state it would be well to remember that there are certain natural limits within which the tax state notion may be expected to be operative. Schumpeter says:

In any case, the state has its definite limits. These are, of course, not conceptually definable limits of its field of social action, but limits to its fiscal potential. These vary considerably in each specific case according to the wealth or poverty of the country, to the concrete details of its national and social structure, and to the nature of its wealth. There is a great difference between new, active, and growing wealth and old wealth, between entrepreneurial and rentier states. The limits of their fiscal potential may also differ according to the extent of military expenses or the debt service, to the power and morality of its bureaucracy, and to the intensity of the 'state-consciousness' of its people. But they are always there and they may be theoretically determined in general terms from the nature of the state (1991, p. 111).

Two points are in order here. First, it should be clear that there cannot be a precise dividing line between what constitutes the optimal mix between market and non-market resource allocation. Much would depend upon the specific historical, sociological, and political bases of the society one is concerned about. Secondly, Schumpeter had no doubt in his mind that the growth of the 'tax state' would mean a limitation of the sphere of the capitalist entrepreneurs and the market mechanism. Even though he recognized that the state has legitimate economic and social roles to play, he was uncomfortable at the prospect of the state becoming too large and powerful. He feared that the tax state may end up destroying the enterprise culture of the capitalist system that it originally seeks to improve and protect. The fear, therefore, is that market failures would be simply replaced by government failures without necessarily bringing about a net increase in welfare.

It would be wrong to conclude from the above that Schumpeter was against state intervention. He was aware of the inherent instability of the capitalist system, as was emphasized in his magnum opus on *Business Cycles* (1939). What Schumpeter did lay emphasis on was in defining clearly the limits of state intervention and being aware of the dangers inherent in transgressing those limits.

★

It is important to note that the reason for the breakdown of the 'tax state' is sociological. Schumpeter emphasizes that while the financial efficiency of the tax state is limited, the popular will is directed towards ever greater public spending. Thus, while the limitation of tax revenue is conditioned by the economic endurance of the taxpayer, the phenomenon of rapidly increasing public expenditure has a sociological basis. His essential thesis was that ultimately the contradiction between these two tendencies would lead to a collapse of the tax state.

The sociological factor was to play a central role in the prognosis of the break-up of the capitalist system which Schumpeter was to develop almost a quarter century later in his *Capitalism, Socialism and Democracy* (1942). In this sweepingly seminal work, Schumpeter had posed the question: 'Can capitalism survive?', and had proceeded to answer in unequivocal terms: 'No, I do not think it can'. The striking thesis of Schumpeter was that it is capitalism's very success that will be its undoing. This is in sharp contrast to the Marxian formulation, which too had predicted the disintegration of capitalism, but owing to reasons that had to do with its own internal contradictions.

There are many paradoxes in Schumpeter's writings. Some of these have their origins in Schumpeter's way of combining economic and sociological tendencies while analysing long run issues. Arthur Smithies (1951) has observed that *Capitalism, Socialism and Democracy* in particular is full of ironic twists that provide cold comfort for anyone who agrees with him. Capitalists, socialists, and intellectuals are all provided with strong emotional grounds for rejecting the argument.'

Schumpeter's essential thesis on the collapse of capitalism is that the capitalist process would attack its own institutional framework. He (1942) writes:

The capitalist process ... eventually decreases the importance of the function by which the capitalist class lives. We have also seen that it tends to wear away protective strata, to break down its own defenses, to disperse the garrisons of its entrenchments. And we have finally seen that capitalism creates a critical frame of mind which, after having destroyed the moral authority of so many other institutions, in the end turns against its own; the burgeois finds to his amazement that the rationalist attitude does not stop at the credentials of kings and popes but goes on to attack private property and the whole scheme of bourgeois values (p. 143).

Schumpeter concedes that even though rational thought precedes the rise of the capitalist order, it is the latter which gives it a new impulse and a particular push to the process. Thus faced with the increasing hostility of the environment the whole stratum that accepts the bourgeois scheme of life will eventually cease to function.

Schumpeter put forward the view that with the decline of capitalism, socialism will be the heir apparent. But it was not the humane socialism that the socialists would like to bring about. He went on to say: 'There is little reason to believe that this socialism will mean the civilization of which orthodox socialists dream. It is much more likely to present fascist features. That would be a strange answer to Marx's prayer (1942, p. 375)'. As regards the institution of democracy Schumpeter believed that socialist democracy may turn out to be more of a sham than capitalist democracy ever was.

Since Schumpeter had so decisively predicted the decay of capitalism it is a matter of some interest to check as to whether he was a socialist. Edgar Salin, in his introduction to the German translation of *Capitalism, Socialism and Democracy* had observed that 'Schumpeter is a socialist', though he also added that 'no socialist, be he a Marxist or Fabian, will detect his socialism in Schumpeter's writings'. Joan Robinson, on the other hand, had remarked after reading the same book that Schumpeter 'has little love for socialism, and none at all for socialists'.

Schumpeter's admiration for Marx for his grand historical vision was well known. Schumpeter also respected Marx for his scholarship. As one who extolled the 'magnificent dynamics' of capitalism and one who accepted the inevilability of socialism only grudgingly, Schumpeter may be categorized as a non-socialist Marxist (see Rothschild 1982). Paul Sweezy was of the view that 'the Schumpeterian system is comparable in its scope to Marxian social science, though not to Marxism as a whole'.

In his own estimation, Schumpeter had no particular predilection for socialism. In his essay entitled 'The March into Socialism' which was delivered before the American Economic Association in New York on 7 December 1949, shortly before his death, he had observed, 'I do not advocate socialism. Nor have I any intention of discussing its desirability or undesirability, whatever this may mean. More important is it, however, to make it quite clear that I do not "prophesy" or predict it.' For him, it was a dispassionate analysis of the evolution of capitalism that unambiguously pointed to the conclusion that capitalism would break down because of its very successes, and that socialism would be the heir apparent.

As regards the exact timing of the transition from capitalism to socialism, Schumpeter, writing in the aftermath of the Great Depression, was willing to concede that 'capitalism may have another successful run'. From the point of view of short run forecasting, he was of the view that 'a century is a short run'. But underneath the surface there may be a process towards another civilization that 'slowly works deep down below'. During this period the capitalist process not only would destroy its own institutional framework but it would create the conditions for another. 'In the end there is not so much difference as one might think between saying that the decay of capitalism is due to its success and saying that it is due to its failure' (p. 162).

Schumpeter was of course fully aware of the fact that in real life no social system is really ever pure. Even in the nineteenth century, in the epoch of unadulterated capitalism, there always was an admixture of public planning. In no socialist economy, even in the heyday of totalitarian regimes, was central planning carried out at full one hundred percent. Schumpeter was aware that there would always be a certain amount of *laissez faire*, with some areas reserved for the market and the price mechanism. What Schumpeter emphasized above everything else was that capitalism would tend to get bureaucratized and that the economic process would tend to socialize itself.

Schumpeter's *Capitalism, Socialism and Democracy* was an instant success with the public. Eduard Marz, one of his students at Harvard in the early 1940s and later his biographer, has observed that some left-wing intellectuals hailed it as a wilful and belated conversion to their own point of view. His conservative friends, on the other hand, were critical of him for writing a book that would contribute to the spread of defeatist feelings, because in it he had postulated the inevitability and higher rationality of socialism. Schumpeter countered such reproaches with the remark that it was better to recognize certain negative sociological tendencies early on, so as to be able to develop adequate counter strategies in time.

Schumpeter was much concerned about the growth of the income tax system, with its attendant adverse effects on incentives and risk bearing as the capitalist system progressed. In his later works he repeatedly emphasized the 'maximum limit' of endurance of the individual tax payer. He (1991) went on to say:

The closer the tax state approaches these limits, the stronger the resistance to it and the losses from friction caused by this state of affairs. The civil service machinery required to administer the tax laws becomes larger and larger, tax collection becomes more insistent and enforcement measures assume ever more unbearable proportions. This absurd waste of energy shows that the purpose of the tax-state organisation is to preserve the autonomy of the private economy and of private life and that it loses its purposes as soon as it can no longer respect the autonomy (p. 139n).

Elsewhere, Schumpeter argued that income taxes can work in the way they are supposed to only if the rates are felt to be moderate, as high rates would be counter productive. Further, if these taxes are to constitute the bulk of government revenues then public expenditure itself ought to be moderate. Schumpeter was, therefore, an energetic votary of a limited state. However, this particular view of the state is contestable, and much can legitimately be said in support of a state that explicitly plays a redistributive role. In the three decades after the Second World War, there was a phenomenal phase of steady growth in the major capitalist countries of the world. The spirit of the Beveridge Report grew to dominate the political economic thinking, leading to a substantial growth of the state sphere. There was a continuous increase in tax and social insurance contributions, and in the case of some countries like Sweden and the Netherlands these contributions exceeded the 'magic' limit of 50 per cent. It is only in the early 1980s during the Reagan–Thatcher era that there was a conscious questioning of the large role of the state.

On a balance of considerations it would perhaps be fair to conclude that the threshold of the individual taxpayer's endurance has proved to be substantially higher than Schumpeter imagined in his 'tax state' article (see Marz 1991). What is certainly true is that most advanced capitalist countries have granted to the modern Leviathan rights of intervention which earlier generations would have objected to as being 'socialist'. This indeed was the mode of analysis that Schumpeter adopted in his last essay, 'The March into Socialism'. In his mind, the justification for state intervention based on the Keynesian recipe for full employment was responsible for the turn towards socialism.

★

Robert Heilbroner (1996) has described Schumpeter's analysis of capitalism as that of an analytical optimist and a visionary pessimist. While Schumpeter celebrated capitalism as the triumph of rationality and progress he was ultimately pessimistic about its final denouement. This was part of a certain vision of capitalism he talked of in his 'tax state' piece in 1917, but this idea was to form the core of his analysis of capitalism in his celebrated *Cgapitalism, Socialism and Democracy*, which he sometimes dismissively used to refer to as a 'potboiler'.

In considering Schumpeter's vision of capitalism, it might be worthwhile to examine what he really meant by 'vision'. For him vision meant a 'pre analytic cognitive act that provides the raw material for analytic effort'. In his *History of Economic Analysis* (1954), Schumpeter had put forward the view that 'before embarking upon analytic work of any kind we must first single out the set of phenomena we wish to investigate, and acquire intuitively a preliminary notion of how they hang together or, in other words, of what appear from our standpoint to be their fundamental properties'. Schumpeter emphasized that analytic work starts only when one has conceived one's vision of the set of phenomena that catches one's interest. 'The first task is to verbalise the vision or to conceptualise it in such a way that its elements take their places, with names attached to them that facilitate recognition and manipulation, in a more or less orderly scheme or picture'. Schumpeter recognized that vision is ideological by definition, and analytic work begins with material provided by our vision of things.

What, then, was Schumpeter's notion of capitalism? In his *Theory of Economic Development* (1912), the differentia specifica of capitalism was described as the 'existence of credit financing of innovations'. Elsewhere (Schumpeter 1928) he had described capitalism as a system in which production and market exchange of commodities function as a result of private decision making, but he always emphasized that the institution of bank credit was the essential ingredient of the functioning of the capitalist system. At the core of the capitalist system is the entrepreneur who engages in the process of innovation, and 'who diverts the factors of production to new uses, or dictates a new direction to production'. Capitalism then is characterized by the process of creative destruction, one that is 'incessantly destroying the old one, incessantly creating a new one'. This is a continuous process, one that Schumpeter so eloquently described as the 'perennial gale of creative destruction'.

As mentioned earlier, having exhaustively studied business cycles in his monumental work by the same name in 1939, Schumpeter was perfectly aware of the instability of capitalism and the serious cyclical problems that the system was prone to. Yet he was sanguine about the basic economic strength of the capitalist system, for he believed fundamentally that the system is defined by the process of 'creative destruction', which imparts the system its essential energy. As regards the propensity of the system to depression, and in particular the Great Depression of the 1930s, Schumpeter believed that 'a depression is for capitalism like a good cold douche' (Heilbroner 1992), implying that it can do wonders for the basic health of the system. Thus, all said, Schumpeter was a great believer in the fundamental economic strength of the capitalist system.

Despite the above dynamism of the capitalist system Schumpeter was pessimistic about its ultimate fate. There is nothing in the strict logic of the capitalist process leading to the conclusion that the system would break down, and that socialism would be the heir apparent. The para-doxical conclusion may rather be better understood as an essential ingredient of Schumpeter's 'vision'. The vision essentially centred on the basic proposition that while capitalism would deliver admirably as an economic system it would be a sociological failure. On the one hand, the tax state may be prone to a collapse owing to 'the revolution of rising expectations', whereas, on the other, capitalism would bring about a system of rationalist thought that would lead the system to question the system itself, leading to its ultimate collapse. This would be a strange fate to befall a successful system. But as Schumpeter had observed, 'history sometimes indulges in jokes of questionable taste'.

The Schumpeterian 'tax state' is full of ironically conflicting features. At the very basic level, the capitalist mode necessarily has to put in place an elaborate system of taxation. Without taxes the capitalist state would grind to a halt. At the same time, Schumpeter was conscious that the state should play a limited interventionist role. It is this which will enable the capitalist system to flourish to the fullest. But then there is a further twist. The very success of the capitalist system will be its undo-ing. Capitalism will decay and socialism will be the heir apparent.

Schumpeter may be thought of as a 'radical' economist who ques-tions the scope of economic theory to be limited to static equilibrium analysis in the quintessential Walrasian formulation (see, for example, Rosenberg 1994). For him, the dynamics of a system is of the essence. Further, he is interested in an analysis of a dynamic process that arises not due to any external factor or force but due to its internal dynamics. Schumpeter was thus concerned with the evolutionary aspects of change in the capitalist mode.

In looking at this change, what we essentially encounter is the follow-ing. Schumpeter is enthusiastic about the unalloyed capitalist process of growth where he thinks of entrepreneurs as being endowed with a certain degree of 'heroism'. But he is also the author of the pessimism which says that this system is doomed to end in a collapse, to be followed by a socialist system. Now, even in the phase where capitalism is supposed to be making rapid progress with a very limited role of the state, there is a rationalist implosion which works towards its demise. If on the other hand, the tax state has expanded its fold and widened its activities, then the process of socialization of capital has been brought about any way. This would also ultimately result in sociologically determined aspirations for public expenditures far outstripping the tax revenues that may be collected. The collapse of the capitalist system is ensured either way.

Schumpeter's tax state is an important analytical device that seeks to broaden the scope of economics by incorporating considerations particularly of sociology and history. Through it, Schumpeter also is able to examine the question of the extent of permissible state activity in a capitalist economy. One may not agree with the limited role that Schumpeter charts out for the government, but this by itself does not diminish the importance of Schumpeter's contribution. The message of the contribution is to carefully examine the economic effects of the tax state. Schumpeter makes a number of specific observations which need to be considered on their merit. For example, he was critical of the reliance on the income tax system and was in favour of a capital levy. Most importantly, the possibility of the collapse of the capitalist system, which was part of the larger Schumpeterian vision and which was first developed in his 'tax state' article, needs to be re-examined with considerable care.

REFERENCES

Allen, Robert Loring (1994), *Opening Doors: The Life and Work of Joseph Schumpeter* (New Brunswick: Transactions Publishers).

Backhaus, Jurgen (1994), 'The Concept of the Tax State in Modern Public Finance Analysis', in Yuichi Shionoya and Mark Perlman, eds., *Schumpeter in the History of Ideas* (Ann Arbor: The University of Michigan Press).

Bottomore, Tom (1992), *Between Marginalism and Marxism: The Economic Sociology of J.A. Schumpeter* (London: Harvester Wheatsheaf).

Datta-Chaudhuri, Mrinal (1990), 'Market Failure and Government Failure', Journal of Economic Perspectives, vol. 4, pp. 25–39.

Goldscheid, Rudolf (1917), *Staatssozialismus oder Staatskapitalismus* (State Socialism or State Capitalism), (Vienna: Anzengruber)

Heilbroner, Robert (1992), 'His Secret Life', *The New York Review of Books*, New York, 14 May.

Heilbroner, Robert (1996), *Twenty First Century Capitalism* (New Delhi: Affiliated East West Press Pvt. Ltd.)

Jackson, Peter M. (1988), 'The Role of Government in Changing Industrial Societies: A Schumpeter Perspective', in Horst Hanusch, ed., *Evolutionary Economics* (Cambridge: Cambridge University Press).

Marz, Eduard (1991), *Joseph Schumpeter: Scholar, Teacher & Politician* (London: Oxford University Press).

Musgrave, Richard A. (1988), 'Discussion', in Horst Hanusch, ed. *Evolutionary Economics* (Cambridge: Cambridge University Press).

Perlman, M. (1994), 'Commentary', in Y. Shionoya and M. Perlman, eds., *Schumpeter in the History of Ideas* (Ann Arbor: The University of Michigan Press).

Rosenberg, Nathan (1994), Joseph Schumpeter: Radical Economist, in Yuichi Shionoya and Mark Perlman, eds., *Schumpeter in the History of Ideas* (Ann Arbor: The University of Michigan Press).

Rothschild, Kurt (1982), 'Schumpeter and Socialism', in Helmut Frisch, ed., *Schumpeterian Economics* (New York: Praeger).

Samuelson, P.A. (1982a), 'Schumpeter as an Economic Theorist', in Helmut Frisch, ed., *Schumpeterian Economics* (New York: Praeger).

Samuelson, Paul A. (1982b), 'Schumpeter's Capitalism, Socialism and Democracy', in Arnold Heertje, ed., *Schumpeter's Vision* (New York: Praeger).

Schumpeter, Joseph (1912, 1934), *Theory of Economic Development, An Inquiry into Profits, Capitalism, Credit, Interest and the Business Cycle* (Cambridge: Harvard University Press).

——— (1918, 1991), 'The Crisis of the Tax State', in Richard Swedberg, ed., *The Economics and Sociology of Capitalism* (Princeton: Princeton University Press).

——— (1927), 'Friedrich von Wieser (1851–1926), *The Economic Journal*, vol. 37, no. 146.

——— (1928), 'The Instability of Capitalism', *Economic Journal*, vol. 38, pp. 361–8.

——— (1939), *Business Cycles: A Theoretical, Historical and Statistical Analysis of the Capitalist Process* (New York and London: McGraw-Hill).

——— (1942), *Capitalism, Socialism and Democracy* (London: Allen and Unwin 5th edn, 1976)

——— (1951), *Ten Great Economists* (New York: Oxford University Press).

——— (1954), *History of Economic Analysis* (New York: Oxford University Press).

Seidl, Christian (1984), 'The Tax State in Crisis: Can Schumpeterian Public Finance Claim Modern Relevance?', in Christian Seidl, ed., *Lectures on Schumpeterian Economics* (Berlin, Springer-Verlag).

Swedberg, Richard (1991), *Joseph A. Schumpeter: His Life and Work* (Cambridge: Polity Press).

Smithies, Arthur (1951), 'Memorial: Joseph Alois Schumpeter 1883–1950', in Seymour E. Harris, ed., *Schumpeter: Social Scientist* (Cambridge, Mass.: Harvard University Press).

Zimmermann, Horst (1988), 'Fiscal Pressure on the "Tax State", in Horst Hanusch, ed., *Evolutionary Economics: Applications of Schumpeter's Ideas* (Cambridge: Cambridge University Press).

Index

Acemoglu, D. 112, 123, 138
actual unemployment, effect of husbands, on employment of women 41
'added worker effect' 39, 41–2, 44–5, 47, 52, 55–6
  unemployment benefit and 50
adult education, impact on child labour and schooling 170, 182
African–Americans, in poverty 25
aggregate employment rate 54
aggregate labour supply curve 56
agriculture (al), de-collectivization of, in China 4
  power consumption and tariff to 146, 148
and subsidized electricity to agriculturists 146–7, 158–9
Akerlof, George 3, 25–6, 111, 124
Allen, F. 127
Allen, Robert Loring 247
Amsden, Alice 115
Andhra Pradesh, power sector in 156–7
reforms in 155–6
Andhra Pradesh State Electricity Board (APSEB) 156
Andhra Pradesh ERC (APERC) 156–7
Andhra Pradesh Generating Company (APGENCO) 156

Andhra Pradesh Transmission Company (APTRANSCO) 156–7
Argentina, infrastructure ports in 230
water and power concessions in 229
Arrow, Kenneth J. 11, 20–1, 98, 123
Arrow–Debreu model 14
Ashenfelter, O. 40, 42, 47
autonomy, importance of, and preferences 19–21
Azariadis, C. 112

Backhaus, Jurgen 247
Banerjee, A. 137
bankruptcy, of firms 192–3, 195
Bardhan, Pranab 4, 40, 60, 63
Barneris, N. 204
Barton, M. 40
Basu, Kaushik 1, 3, 38, 42, 44, 53, 112, 161–2
Belton, M.F. 40
Benabou, R. 135
Bergson, A. 93
Besley, T. 133
'best choice' approach, to one's preference 20–1
Beveridge Report 253
Birdzell, L. 134
Black culture 26
Black middle class, burgeoning of 25